Justice Hugo Black
and the First Amendment

" 'No law' means no law"

Justice Hugo Black

and the First Amendment

edited by
EVERETTE E. DENNIS
DONALD M. GILLMOR
DAVID L. GREY

Iowa State University Press, Ames

About the Editors. At the request of colleagues in the Association for Education in Journalism, the editors undertook the task of assembling a record of the contribution of Supreme Court Justice Hugo LaFayette Black to First Amendment freedom of expression. It was their belief that communication law scholars have a special responsibility to examine and illuminate the workings of this most important judicial mind.

In addition to their contributions to this book, the editors are authors of several other books as well as frequent contributors to the scholarly literature of their fields.

© 1978 The Iowa State University Press
Ames, Iowa 50010. World rights except in the British Commonwealth, but including Canada.

Composed and printed by
The Iowa State University Press

First edition, 1978

Library of Congress Cataloging in Publication Data

Main entry under title:

Justice Hugo Black and the first amendment.

Bibliography: p.
Includes index.
1. Liberty of the press — United States — Addresses, essays, lectures. 2. Liberty of speech — United States — Addresses, essays, lectures. 3. Black, Hugo LaFayette, 1886-1971 — Addresses, essays, lectures. I. Dennis, Everette E. II. Gillmor, Donald M. III. Grey, David L.
KF4774.A75 J8   342′.73 085   78-685
ISBN 8-8138-1905-9

Contents

v

Foreword

Great men deserve great books. This publication is an attempt to carry out that axiom.

Shortly after Associate Justice Hugo LaFayette Black resigned from the Supreme Court of the United States and died, Professor Dwight L. Teeter, Jr., then head of the Professional Freedom and Responsibility Committee of the Association for Education in Journalism (AEJ), discussed with various committee members what could be done as a worthwhile project. Professor J. Edward Gerald of the University of Minnesota, a former head of the same AEJ committee, proposed a book discussing the commitment of Justice Black to the First Amendment freedoms of expression.

As president of the AEJ at that time, I was consulted and gave a highly deserved bureaucratic shove forward. The idea passed through several transmutations and many individuals gave the proposal tender, if not loving, care and guidance. Among them were Professor David L. Grey of San José State University, who joined Teeter almost from the start, and who gave the project much of its early impetus. Teeter, then entangled in administrative duties at the University of Kentucky, withdrew as an editor, leaving the major work of shaping and editing the book in the hands of Grey and Professors Donald M. Gillmor and Everette E. Dennis of the University of Minnesota. To the editors and to all the authors of the chapters the AEJ membership owes congratulations for a job well done.

HILLIER KREIGHBAUM
Visiting Professor
Department of Journalism
Temple University

May 24, 1977

Justice Hugo Black
and the First Amendment

1 Hugo L. Black: *" 'no law' means no law"*

EVERETTE E. DENNIS, DONALD M. GILLMOR

In the years since his death in 1971, biographers and legal commentators have conjured up many images of Justice Hugo LaFayette Black. To some he was essentially a political populist who distrusted power. To others he was an uncompromising absolutist whose pronouncements were rigid and unbending. He could be profoundly sensitive to human rights on the one hand and incredibly petty in his interpersonal relations on the other. And it was said by some that he loved freedom more in the abstract than in its day-to-day applications.

While the legal and historical literature is now welling up with differing interpretations of Justice Black's role on the Supreme Court and in our national life, almost everyone is certain about one thing: Hugo Black was a fierce champion of the First Amendment. To Justice Black the First Amendment was not something to be bargained with or compromised away. He loved the First Amendment and accepted it literally, almost without reservation. He believed that any abridgment of the First Amendment, whether by a

EVERETTE E. DENNIS is associate professor of journalism and mass communication at the University of Minnesota, from which he received the Ph.D. He is the author of *The Media Society, Evidence about Mass Communication in America,* and coauthor of *New Strategies for Public Affairs Reporting* and *Other Voices, the New Journalism in America* as well as editor of *The Magic Writing Machine.* A frequent contributor to law reviews and scholarly journals in mass communication, his interests include mass communication and society, communication law, popular culture and contemporary reporting.

DONALD M. GILLMOR is professor of journalism and mass communication at the University of Minnesota, from which he received the Ph.D. He is the author of *Free Press and Fair Trial* and coauthor (with Jerome A. Barron) of *Mass Communication Law: Cases and Comment.* He has also written numerous articles on communication law, the relationship between legal studies and the behavioral sciences, the economics of the press, popular culture and political theory, and mass communications and society.

balancing of interests or by an appeal to a clear and present danger, was strictly forbidden. As one of his former law clerks, Louis F. Oberdorfer, once wrote:

> Black regarded the First Amendment as the foundation of the American democratic process, the foundation that permitted a man to conceive an idea, express it, and to associate with other men of like persuasion to further their common interests.[1]

Early in his tenure on the Court, Justice Black made clear his view of the vital nature of the First Amendment, writing in *Milk Wagon Drivers Union v. Meadowmoor Dairies* (1941) that "freedom to speak and write about public questions is as important to the life of our government as is the heart to the human body."[2] And in his last opinion in the celebrated *Pentagon Papers* case, Black bitterly attacked the Nixon administration's attempt to abridge press freedom, saying, "The First Amendment was offered to *curtail* and *restrict* the general powers granted to the Executive, Legislative and Judicial branches."[3]

Frequently Black would remind his colleagues and the nation that the command of the First Amendment was unequivocal: when it said, "Congress shall make no law . . ." it meant just that. As he told Professor Edmond Cahn in a public interview:

> I believe when our Founding Fathers, with their wisdom and patriotism, wrote this Amendment, they knew what they were talking about. They knew what history was behind them and they wanted to ordain in this country that Congress, elected by the people, should not tell the people what religion they should have or what they should believe or say or publish, and that is about it. It says "no law," and that is what I believe it means.[4]

It is the purpose of this collection of essays to examine Justice Black's interface with the First Amendment, especially as it applies to freedom of the press. The Justice's view of and impact on First Amendment press freedom is analyzed along several dimensions. All but three of the 11 chapters are original essays by communication law scholars prepared especially for this volume. Together they may represent the most expansive treatment to date of this fundamental aspect of Justice Black's constitutional faith. Two previously published chapters, John Medelman's sensitive portrait of the Justice and Edmond Cahn's public interview, are important links in a full understanding of Justice Black. A more detailed explanation of each of the chapters is offered later in this introductory chapter.

This volume brings to fulfillment the vision of several members of the Professional Freedom and Responsibility Committee of the Association for Education in Journalism who felt that scholarly note should be taken by communications law commentators of Justice Black's First Amendment legacy. Among those most directly concerned were Professors Emeriti J. Edward

Gerald of the University of Minnesota and Hillier Kreighbaum of New York University, Professors J. W. Schwartz of Iowa State University, David Grey of San Jose State University, and Dwight Teeter of the University of Kentucky. Several others who were instrumental both in the planning and execution of this volume are represented in subsequent chapters.

No attempt is made here at legal biography. Although John Medelman's perceptive view of Justice Black, which originally appeared in *Esquire,* is based on personal interviews, it is a journalistic not a historical account. The other essays are analytical examinations using the tools of legal scholarship. This is, we believe, as it should be. Justice Black himself hoped that he would be evaluated on the basis of his legal work and not on personal dimensions. He believed that the Court and its justices should speak once in their formal determinations and then remain silent. As he lay dying, he instructed his son to burn the notes he had taken during Court conferences to avoid second-guessing by historians and journalists which he thought might distort the clarity of his written opinions. Some writers and critics will lament this loss of intelligence on judicial behavior, but it is clearly what Justice Black wished.

Some biographers have said that Justice Black was an egotistical man and perhaps he was, but he scrupulously avoided giving encouragement to flattery and public accolades. In fact, he refused to allow anyone to paint his portrait or sculpt a bust of him. As he used to tell his son Hugo Black, Jr., in his gentle Alabama accent:

> Son . . . this business of paintings and busts and that kind of stuff is a bad business. Fella that yields to it is getting in dangerous territory. He's beginning to believe these nuts are telling him he's some kind of godlike fella.[5]

Much that was written about Hugo Black during his lifetime was unflattering. From the time that he first attracted notice in the public arena, press accounts of Black were mixed. As a young county prosecutor in Alabama his efforts got both praise and scorn. Later, as a United States Senator, his performance in public office received mixed reviews. But never did he feel the sting of the media watchdogs more painfully than in the days after his nomination to the Supreme Court of the United States by President Franklin Delano Roosevelt. Seen at first as a liberal New Deal legislator who had favored the president's program and who would provide a marked contrast to the "nine old men" then serving on the Court, Black became something of a scourge to the man who nominated him. The first justice appointed by Roosevelt after the ill-fated court-packing plan, Black was scrutinized carefully by the press. Shortly after his swearing-in, revelations of his one-time membership in the Ku Klux Klan appeared in the press. Black weathered both this storm and subsequent attacks on his fitness for the high bench.

A man of humble origins, Black appeared in stark contrast to several of his well-bred and well-educated colleagues on the Court. As later accounts have indicated, Black, while a law school graduate, was largely a self-educated man, having embarked on an ambitious reading program when he was in the Senate. Although he later became an intellectual leader on the Court, along with the brilliant Felix Frankfurter, his intellectual capacity was seriously taxed in his early years on the Court. In fact, at the end of his first term on the Court, *Newsweek* strongly hinted that Black's opinions might have been ghostwritten.[6] Later, his conflicts with Justice Robert Jackson and with Frankfurter were the subject of press criticism.

A Southerner, Black may have suffered his most serious drubbing in the press after the 1954 landmark civil rights decision, *Brown v. Board of Education*. Newspapers in his native Alabama vilified the Justice and made the climate so inhospitable in Birmingham that Black's son felt compelled to abandon a promising law practice and political aspirations and leave the state.

Toward the end of his career Black once again was the subject of speculation about his competence. As he seemed to modify his earlier views, newspaper and magazine accounts wondered whether the justice might be sliding toward senility. Of course, much that was written about Justice Black during his 34 years on the high Court was positive. But whatever his personal experiences with the press and whatever the pressure to give in, Justice Black never wavered from his staunch support for press freedom. At times, the Justice was ridiculed for his absolutist view, but he took it with good humor. Black's son in a warm biography quotes his father and comments on his position:

> "Why, right after I really understood that 'no law' means no law and announced it, a certain critic of mine wrote me a letter and said that he had been wanting to express his opinion of me for a long time, but had been afraid of the libel laws. 'Now,' he said, 'I am at last free under your interpretation of the First Amendment to express my precise opinion of you. Mr. Justice, you are a sonofabitch.'" Others paraded examples of extreme libel and obscenity before him, thinking to drive him off his position, but he would reply without the slightest hesitation that the First Amendment is absolute. "It prohibits passing any law to prohibit that stuff, bad as you might think it is. The founders knew that libel and obscenity had been used as excuses to tyrannize free speech."[7]

Justice Black's First Amendment legacy went far beyond the simple rhetoric of his absolutist stance. He was an acknowledged leader in the battle to incorporate the Bill of Rights into the Fourteenth Amendment. "This achievement alone," wrote political scientist Sylvia Snowiss, "would be sufficient to earn a secure place for Justice Black among the most influential Supreme Court Justices and identify him as the commanding figure of the Warren Court."[8] These dual aspects of Justice Black's contribution must be seen as interrelated, Snowiss suggests:

> Before the process of gradual incorporation began in earnest in the middle 1960s, Justice Black's most significant work had been his absolutist

interpretation of the First Amendment. And although incorporation is likely to be his most enduring achievement, First Amendment analysis remains basic for understanding Justice Black. At every stage of his judicial career he reaffirmed his belief in the centrality of First Amendment guarantees.[9]

In one of the first law review articles written about Black in 1940, Vincent M. Barnett, Jr. stood against critics of the Justice, offering this prediction:

> Far more important than particular cases decided individually is the sum of those cases constituting the approach of the judge and the court to legislative and administrative action in general. It is in this realm of judicial attitude that Mr. Justice Black's constitutional opinions are playing and will continue to play their most significant role.[10]

More than 30 years later, a commentator in the *Supreme Court Review* would write, "Justice Hugo LaFayette Black seems not merely to be a part of the climate of our age but to be largely responsible for bringing it into existence."[11]

To Justice Black the First Amendment was a "people's charter of edification and postulates the kind of national community whose practices would do daily honor to the First Amendment."[12] Summing up a career in which Black served with five of the Court's 15 chief justices and more than a third of all justices, Chief Justice Warren Burger wrote:

> In time, I believe, one thing will stand out above all in his work and in his thinking. Throughout his entire life he never wavered in his unbounded faith in the people and in the political processes of a free people under the American Constitution. He loved this court as an institution, and contributed mightily to its work, to its strength and to its future. He revered the Constitution; he had enormous respect for the presidency and the Congress but above all else, he believed in the people.[13]

It was that unbounded faith in the people, a trust in their ability to govern themselves, that explains Black's view of the First Amendment.

This book aims at a better understanding of Justice Black's concept of the First Amendment. In Chapter 2, Sylvia Snowiss provides a framework for understanding Black and his work. In "The Legacy of Justice Black," Dr. Snowiss painstakingly examines Justice Black's premises about limited government and absolute rights and traces them through the whole of his career. This chapter is particularly important for establishing a context in which to view the Justice not simply as a commentator on the First Amendment but in the fuller dimensions of his many constitutional concerns.

Dwight Teeter and Maryann Yodelis Smith in Chapter 3 contend that Black, while undoubtedly a great jurist, was a better libertarian than historian. His sources were frequently outdated, his historical theses simplistic and heavily laden with a "heroic" Federalist bias. For example, he blamed "English-controlled" courts for suppressing speech when he might have found a greater threat from colonial legislatures. He appeared to have discovered the history of freedom of expression, and he revered it as if it were divinely preordained. Black used his sources selectively and rewrote history to fit his optimistically liberal notion of what the past should have been — what John P. Roche has called "retrospective symmetry." In spite of their high regard for Justice Black's achievements, Teeter and Yodelis Smith express concern about the consequences of misusing history.

Chapter 4 is Professor Cahn's interview with Justice Black on the occasion of his 25th year on the Supreme Court in April 1962. It is a lucid commentary on the First Amendment as Black saw it, with incisive questions from Professor Cahn.

Chapter 5 is the already-mentioned article by magazine journalist John Medelman which traces Black's career from his early days in Alabama to the late 1960s. The emphasis here is on the personal, "feeling tone" of the man.

The subsequent chapters elaborate and focus on specific areas of First Amendment applications.

In Chapter 6, David L. Grey reminds us of Black's declaration (shocking to many) that libel laws, because they would proscribe the printed word, were manifestly unconstitutional. Grey is convinced that Black's perspective on libel, and on speech itself, has been oversimplified. Time, manner, and place of speech were important to Black: the newspaper — any kind of newspaper — was a proper forum and permitted no restraints on any kind of speech. Sedition laws were a constitutional abomination: "no law" means no law.

Grey argues that Black was less adamant where other forms of communication were involved; for example, the broadcast media. Grey illustrates Black's vigor in pressing his often dissenting views in the long series of civil libel cases beginning with *New York Times v. Sullivan* (1964) and his accuracy in predicting that libel would slip into the same quagmire as obscenity if the Court continued to deny the simple demands of the First Amendment. Black, in Grey's view, contributed mightily to the crucial public debate that freedom of speech and press deserves, although in doing so he may have depreciated individual values which on close inspection seem to many to be no less precious than freedom of expression.

Discussing rights unaccompanied by any clear constitutional language is Donald M. Gillmor's study of "Black and the Problem of Privacy" in Chapter 7. Gillmor demonstrates that Black was at best ambivalent about the searches and seizures provisions of the Fourth Amendment and the individual rights of privacy they have been presumed to protect, and he detects confusion in Black's references to the right. Black the literalist can find no right of privacy in the Constitution (and he will not fall back on vague natural law concepts to put it there), although he admits that the Fourth Amendment's prohibition of unreasonable searches and seizures does protect privacy to some extent. Black's failure to define privacy may explain his vacillation in cases where the right to privacy seemed to be at issue; what other justices were calling privacy,

Black frequently considered extensions of First Amendment freedoms. For example, Black did vote to protect what could be defined as associational privacy, political privacy, the privacy of anonymous publication, and the privacy of one's thoughts. Nevertheless, Black chastised his liberal colleagues for "roam[ing] at large in the broad expanses of policy and morals . . .," a journey Black would embark upon only when he believed he had a constitutional mandate to do so. Although he could honor no "law" of privacy, the great liberal justice was unable to repudiate the broader "right" of privacy.

Kenneth Devol in Chapter 8 discusses Black's simple literalism in finding in the Constitution no mandate to censor any form of speech or press, even though it may be obscene or pornographic by current notions of taste. Black was unwilling to balance social values where he believed the balancing had already been achieved by the framers. They had opted for free speech — absolutely. It is unfortunate, Devol believes, that Black could never persuade his colleagues to adopt his point of view.

Michael J. Petrick in Chapter 9 argues that Justice Black saw the contempt power of the courts as a pernicious means of restricting freedom of expression, and he sought to confine it by challenging its historical bases. Black's greatest challenge to its "immemorial" justification may have been his opinion for the Court in *Bridges v. California* (1941), although Black in that case used a "clear and present danger" test that he was soon to abandon as an unconstitutional qualification of freedom of speech and press. In 1945, he authored an 8 to 0 decision limiting the power of federal judges to cite for direct or in-court contempt. In 1955, again in an opinion for the Court, Black extended the limitation to state courts. Petrick illustrates how Black considered the power of judges to cite for contempt summarily a denial of due process, but again he was unable to convince a majority of his brethren. Nevertheless, Petrick concludes, Black's efforts to limit this traditional power of the courts were in the service of a broader and more secure freedom of expression.

Antitrust law as a route to newspaper access is Paul Jess's concern in Chapter 10. Jess argues that one can find in Justice Black's opinions "suggestions," at least, of a way better than law professor Jerome A. Barron's for citizens to gain access to the press. Using antitrust law to foster "a multitude of voices," to use Judge Learned Hand's term, would have been more acceptable to Black, Jess speculates, than any court-mandated right of citizen access to newspapers. "The long and short of this problem," said Black, "is that while the First Amendment does guarantee freedom to speak and write, it does not at the same time provide for a speaker or writer to use other people's property to do so." But he also said that "freedom to publish means freedom for all and not for some. . . . Freedom of the press from governmental interference under the First Amendment does not sanction repression of that freedom by private interests." Jess then builds a case-law foundation for an antitrust solution that he says would have comported with Black's constitutional standard.

Chapter 11 is another speculative essay, David Gordon's, "Had Black

Ruled in *Branzburg*. . . ." Gordon believes that had Black taken part in the landmark journalist's privilege ruling, the Court would have decided 5 to 4 in favor of journalists' right to protect the identity of sources and the confidentiality of notes, tapes, and other products of their work. Gordon finds analogues in numerous other cases to support his contention and to suggest Black's strong influence on dissenting opinions in *Branzburg*. Gordon's essay is as much a detailed explication of the complex privilege issue as it is an analysis of Black's thought on the subject. Gordon agrees with Black that liberty of the press must be permitted "the broadest scope that could be countenanced in an orderly society," and part of that liberty is the right of journalists—for the sake of unfettered discussion—to protect the identity and output of sources.

Whether Justice Black vacillated on basic issues of speech and press and in doing so deserted his liberal cohorts in the later years of his tenure is the question considered by Everette E. Dennis, Neil A. Lavick, and J. Edward Gerald in Chapter 12. This chapter examines expression and conduct distinctions in Black's opinions, especially in his final years on the Court. The authors uncover evidence to suggest that Black was not the rock-ribbed absolutist he is purported to have been, that indeed he would examine pragmatically the facts of a case to determine first whether he was dealing with a matter of conduct or a matter of speech. And unlike his close colleague William O. Douglas, Black preferred definitions of speech narrow enough to exclude various forms of speech-plus and symbolic speech (picketing and the wearing of armbands, for example).

Dennis, Lavick, and Gerald find in Black's opinions what Thomas Emerson would call a two-level theory of expression: pure speech deserves absolute protection; any lesser form, for example, that involving conduct as well as speech, could be limited. They also find a consistency in Black's application of his theory to a wide variety of fact situations. This consistency in protecting what he thought to be pristine forms of speech and press, rather than any doctrinaire liberalism, is the legacy of Justice Black.

The essays treat a wide range of First Amendment concerns, including libel, obscenity, contempt, access to the press, journalist's privilege, privacy, symbolic speech and speech plus. Together these essays sketch a portrait of a great jurist and his 34-year defense of the First Amendment as a member of the United States Supreme Court.

2 The legacy of Justice Black

SYLVIA SNOWISS

Professor Paul Freund, speaking on the desired characteristics of Supreme Court appointees, called for individuals who "are sensitive to the climate of the age, not the weather of the day or the weather of the year." He then characterized the climate of this age as one of "increasing sensitivity toward human rights" and "large conceptions of equality under law."[1]

At first glance Justice Hugo Lafayette Black seems not merely to be part of the climate of our age but to be largely responsible for bringing it into existence. He was the acknowledged leader in the battle for incorporation of the Bill of Rights in the Fourteenth Amendment, probably the most significant development in recent constitutional law, and in the development of the judiciary's "increasing sensitivity toward human rights." This achievement alone would be sufficient to earn a secure place for Justice Black among the most influential Supreme Court Justices and to identify him as the commanding figure of the Warren Court. There is more. The Court has either adopted or moved close to his original dissenting positions in freedom of speech and freedom of association cases.[2] The law of libel and obscenity reflects the standards he strongly and consistently enunciated.[3]

Reprinted (in edited version) by permission from 1973 SUPREME COURT REVIEW 187.

AUTHOR'S NOTE: I am grateful to Professor Herbert J. Storing, who read and criticized the entire manuscript. My original research on Justice Black was supported by an American Association of University Women fellowship (1964–65).

SYLVIA SNOWISS is associate professor of political science at California State University (Northridge), where she has been a member of the faculty since 1968. She holds the Ph.D. in political science from the University of Chicago. Dr. Snowiss's scholarly interests include public law and American political thought.

11

Justice Black's efforts to broaden Fifth Amendment protection are not so well known as is his First Amendment absolutism, yet current Fifth Amendment controversy and much Fifth Amendment law was first charted in his dissents. He always viewed police interrogations without counsel as secret inquisitions in violation of the Fifth Amendment's ban on self-incrimination, and he spoke out in dissent foreshadowing *Miranda*[4] as early as 1951.[5] His dissenting position in *United States v. Kahriger,*[6] in opposition to the federal gambling registration statute, was adopted by the Court fifteen years later in *Marchetti v. United States.*[7] *Murphy v. Waterfront Commission*[8] accepted his dissent in *Feldman v. United States*[9] and extended the protection available to those giving testimony under immunity statutes. Although Justice Black's opposition to the use of what the Court calls noncommunicative testimony remains a dissenting position, his dissents are major statements in a still open debate.[10]

Still other areas of Bill of Rights and Fourteenth Amendment adjudication reflect Justice Black's leadership. *Griffin v. Illinois*[11] began a major effort to lessen the disabilities faced by indigent defendants in criminal cases. *Gideon v. Wainwright,*[12] making right to counsel mandatory in all serious criminal cases, was the triumph of his dissent in *Betts v. Brady.*[13] His influence is evident in the protection now available for defendants.[14] And finally, his dissent in *Colegrove v. Green*[15] was not only accepted in *Baker v. Carr,*[16] but has influenced subsequent leading decisions in the reapportionment field.[17]

It is of course true, as even a casual observance of his last four or five Terms reveals, that by the end of his career Justice Black was no longer the leader of the Court. In First Amendment cases he was chargeable with retreat from absolutism.[18] His later record on search and seizure,[19] wiretapping,[20] and collateral review,[21] seemed to be a withdrawal from his earlier willingness to invoke Bill of Rights guarantees on behalf of persons accused of crime. Restrictive readings of the Due Process and Equal Protection Clauses raised doubts about his willingness to continue to extend constitutional protection to minorities and to the poor.[22] Nevertheless, he continued to articulate his absolutist interpretation of the First and Fifth Amendments,[23] as well as his strong defense of Bill of Rights protection for persons accused of crime.[24]

How are these last few years to be understood? Did they reveal a change toward conservatism, possibly associated with old age? Did they indicate arbitrary inconsistency? Or did these changes reveal a basic misconception about the underlying premises of his entire career? In summarizing his colleague's achievements in 1956, Mr. Justice Douglas praised Justice Black for ."consistently . . . construing the laws and the Constitution so as to protect the civil rights of citizens and aliens, whatever the form of repression may be."[25] If this assessment is accurate, then Justice Black is, at best, inconsistent. There is much evidence, however, now that his entire career is before us, that he maintained a strong internal consistency and that the popular view of his work is inaccurate. In addition, the fact that Black retained most of his early views — as well as his early passion — to the end in significant areas of constitutional law, suggests that simplistic explanations are inadequate. In this connection, too, it is worth reflecting on Professor Kurland's observation that, although Justice Black was enormously successful in influencing Court positions, he never succeeded in having his basic doctrine accepted.[26] This anomalous fact casts doubt on the validity of the popular understanding of Justice Black's basic doctrine.

A closer look at Justice Black's entire record will support the conclusion that he was consistent. Examination of his last few years will reveal a misunderstanding of his underlying constitutional doctrine rather than inconsistency in his position. This examination will reveal, too, the paradoxical nature of Justice Black's legacy: a general constitutional doctrine of judicial power and protection of individual rights that has had practically no influence on the Court's doctrine, combined with the articulation of positions on specific individual rights that remains of enormous influence.

Justice Black's constitutional understanding: limited government and absolute rights

Fostering increasing sensitivity toward human rights and large conceptions of equality under law is not the same thing as always favoring claims of individual liberty against governmental authority. But to foster these ends does necessitate a general openness to such claims which, in the context of American constitutional law, encompasses two broad commitments. The first commitment is to a liberal reading of the Bill of Rights and other limits on governmental powers, particularly the Due Process and Equal Protection Clauses of the Fourteenth Amendment. Implicit in this liberal reading is the assumption that as societal needs change over time, constitutional provisions need reexamination and interpretation in light of their basic purposes. The second commitment is to a vigorous use of judicial power—a power accepted as legitimate in a democratic regime. While Justice Black always supported broad protection of individual rights, he never accepted either of these commitments. Nor did he ever focus on protection of individual rights as a primary political goal, to be sought as a good in itself. For Justice Black protection of individual rights was always linked to a specific conception of democratic government. This conception of democratic government, like the basic qualities of his opinions, is straightforward and without significant subtlety. Democracy is conceived exclusively in terms of governmental responsiveness to popular will. To make this responsiveness effective, government must be subject to certain limits. Among the more important limits are those on behalf of individual rights, and, among these, First Amendment limits are central.

The intellectual freedom secured by the First Amendment insures a thorough canvassing and dissemination of views, the necessary precondition for the emergence of a genuinely free popular will. Freedom of association joined with constitutionally protected voting rights implements this intellectual freedom by facilitating the transmission of popular will into public policy. True responsiveness is incompatible with any exception or qualification of this process. Critical limits must be absolutely enforced. This absolutism, furthermore, is anchored in the language of the Constitution, particularly in the unequivocal command of the First Amendment.

Justice Black spoke often of the primacy of the First Amendment. It is the "heart of the Bill of Rights,"[27] and "the foundation upon which our government structure rests and without which it could not continue to endure as conceived and planned."[28] More striking than this, however, was the extent to which he viewed other limits on behalf of individual rights as subordinate to this same end of maintaining unfettered intellectual and political exchange:

> For the fears of arbitrary court action sprang largely from the past use of courts in the imposition of criminal punishments to suppress speech, press, and religion. Hence the constitutional limitations of courts' powers were, in the view of the founders, essential supplements to the First Amendment.[29]
>
> [Persecution following the attempt to exercise First Amendment rights inevitably involved] secret arrests, unlawful detentions, forced confessions, secret trials, and arbitrary punishments under oppressive laws. Therefore it is not surprising that the men behind the First Amendment also insisted upon the Fifth, Sixth, and Eighth Amendments. . . . If occasionally these safeguards worked to the advantage of an ordinary criminal, that was a price they were willing to pay.[30]

Just as genuine intellectual freedom demands absolute enforcement of the first Amendment, so, too, there must be absolute enforcement of those other provisions which serve this same end. In like manner, the unqualified language of the First Amendment is duplicated in the language of the "essential supplements to the First Amendment," the Fifth and Sixth Amendments.[31]

Absolutism is not only the key to effective limitation of legislative and executive power, but, equally important, it serves to limit the judiciary as well. In a properly run democratic regime, no branch may interfere with the popular formation of public policy. Should the judiciary take upon itself the task of broadly interpreting and updating constitutional provisions, it would, according to Justice Black, be taking upon itself an essentially policymaking role. For the exercise of judicial power to be acceptable, constitutional provisions must be self-executing; their entire meaning must be contained in the text, and be applicable for all time:[32]

> Had the drafters of the Due Process Clause meant to leave judges . . . ambulatory power to declare laws unconstitutional, the chief value of a written constitution, as the Founders saw it, would have been lost. . . . A written constitution, designed to guarantee protection against governmental abuses, including those of judges, must have written standards that mean something definite and have an explicit content.

In addition to the First, Fifth, and parts of the Sixth Amendments[33] only two other major constitutional limits possess the requisite self-executing clarity necessary for absolute enforcement. These are the Due Process Clause of the Fourteenth Amendment, understood as meaning no less than and no more than the specific guarantees of the Bill of Rights, and the Equal Protection Clause, understood as reaching only certain limited kinds of discrimination.[34]

Other provisions of the Bill of Rights, on the other hand, are either qualified or imprecise. They cannot be said to carry their meaning in their words. Limited democratic government demands judicial deference to interpretation of these clauses made by the responsible branches. Chief among these are the Fourth Amendment's ban on unreasonable searches and seizures; the Sixth Amendment's guarantee of an impartial jury; the Due Process Clause understood as meaning either less or more than the Bill of Rights; and the Equal Protection Clause, loosely construed as a mandate to strike down governmental distinctions:[35]

> Some constitutional provisions are stated in absolute and unqualified language such, for illustration, as the First Amendment. . . . Other constitutional provisions do require courts to choose between competing policies, such as the Fourth Amendment which, by its terms, necessitates a judicial decision as to what is an "unreasonable" search or seizure.

Justice Black's constitutional understanding was never presented as his own interpretation but rather as a faithful rendering of the Founders' intentions. History and language were the only acceptable standards for interpretation. Standards such as justice, fairness, or reasonableness were impermissible. The constitutional text, enforced as Justice Black argued its language dictated, *is* fairness and justice.[36] Failure to follow this standard would be undemocratic. In the course of interpreting the words of the Constitution under standards such as justice and fairness, the judiciary would inevitably introduce its own conceptions of justice and fairness, and thus unjustly arrogate to itself the people's policy-making functions:[37]

> It can be . . . argued that when this Court strikes down a legislative act because it offends the idea of "fundamental fairness," it furthers the basic thrust of our Bill of Rights by protecting individual freedom. But that argument ignores the effect of such decisions on perhaps the most fundamental individual liberty of our people — the right of each man to participate in the self-government of his society.

Moreover, acceptance of such standards prepared the way for the kind of judicial abuse which culminated in the New Deal Court crisis.[38] Finally, this "accordion-like" method of adjudication would likely result in a contraction of Bill of Rights protection at some point. It is inevitable that the judicial conception of fairness or justice will, at times, be less strict than the absolutist reading of the First, Fifth, and parts of the Sixth Amendments.[39]

This understanding resolves a good many of the apparent contradicitons in Justice Black's judicial career. It explains, for example, how he could argue for both literal adherence to the words of the text, and a liberal, rather than niggardly reading of specific guarantees. It is only for those constitutional provisions whose language is unqualified that judges are to give a liberal or an absolute reading. In practice this means that these limits are to be enforced to the furthest extent that language permits. Individual rights claims are always to take precedence over a demand for governmental action. This is what he meant when he said that the Founders did the balancing for us. All of Justice Black's ringing defenses of individual rights, all of his exhortations to the judiciary to live up to its responsibilities, all of his memorable defenses of minorities and dissidents, occurred in the context of absolutely protected rights, as he defined them. He differed from the libertarian position mainly in Fourth Amendment cases, in due process cases that did not involve specific Bill of Rights guarantees, and in equal protection cases that did not involve confrontation with the criminal process, certain kinds of racial discrimination, or voting rights questions. These departures from the liberal creed are traceable to the beginning of his career.[40]

Justice Black's vision of a free, democratic society was that of a completely automatic and self-regulating mechanism. The heart of the mechanism, the market place of ideas, was to be self-regulating and self-perpetuating. He expected a fully informed populace to reject any political alternative that would destroy the freedom of the market place itself.[41] The real source of danger to the free market place of ideas is the failure to allow it to operate as intended. The judiciary's responsibility is to thwart such attempts by enforcing the clear limits of the Constitution. The judiciary's role is thus also essentially automatic; it exercises no genuine judgment but merely enforces commands whose meanings are manifest from history and the words themselves.

For Justice Black, the constitutional limits provided by the Founders were sufficient to perpetuate this self-regulating system. Should the people conceive themselves threatened by a danger that could not be met by the existing guarantees, the remedy is available through amendment of the Constitution. There is no warrant for the judiciary to arrogate to itself the power to decide what is crucial to liberty, or how to meet a new danger:[42]

> I realize that many good and able men have eloquently spoken and written, sometimes in rhapsodical strains, about the duty of this Court to keep the Constitution in tune with the times. The idea is that the Constitution must be changed from time to time and that this Court is charged with a duty to make those changes. For myself, I must with all deference reject that philosophy. The Constitution makers knew the need for change and provided for it. Amendments suggested by the people's elected representatives can be submitted to the people or their elected agents for ratification. That method of change was good for our Fathers, and being somewhat old-fashioned I must add it is good enough for me.

Justice Black frequently expressed his admiration for the Constitution and alluded to the adequacy of the Bill of Rights to protect liberty.[43] At no time did he indicate need for additional protections.

Justice Black's constitutional understanding rested on three dubious propositions: (1) Absolute or liberal enforcement of the precise and unqualified provisions of the Bill of Rights is sufficient to maintain a free regime. (2) This position is a faithful statement of the Founders' intentions and not his own judicial policymaking. (3) The unqualified provisions of the Bill of Rights are, in fact, unambiguous in meaning.

I shall postpone discussion of the first proposition to the end of this paper. To come fully to terms with the historical argument it would be necessary to go over the entire ground. That has already been done well elsewhere. Justice Black's reading of history drew extensive and highly literate criticism, even from those sympathetic to his constitutional interpretation.[44] He never satisfactorily answered his critics, except by repeating his original argument. On this record, he has not made his case. Given Justice Black's stress on the clarity of the text and the single-mindedness of the Founders, the mere existence of reasonable and cogent disagreement over the Founders' intentions weakens his position. At best, it is possible to reach meaningful agreement only on the most general intentions of the original document. The "intentions of the Founders" simply do not lend themselves to the kind of detailed guidance Justice Black claimed for them.

The third proposition deserves lengthier treatment. To do justice to Justice Black's literalism it is necessary to open the larger question of judicial review, democracy, and the activism–self-restraint controversy.

Democracy and judicial power

Justice Black's literalism reflected his dissatisfaction with the major attempts to reconcile the exercise of judicial review with democracy. In the aftermath of the New Deal–Court controversy there was widespread agreement that vigorous exercise of judicial review entailed judicial policy-making that was incompatible with democratic government. Two main responses arose to this challenge. The first, judicial self-restraint, conceded the basic illegitimacy of judicial review and counseled judicial restraint in all areas of constitutional adjudication. The second, judicial activism, argued that the exercise of Court power in one sphere, individual rights adjudication, did not invade the policy prerogative of the people but actually enhanced it by keeping open the processes of democracy and increasing access to decision-making.[45] The legitimacy of such adjudication was supported with argument that it involved more a legal judgment than a political one. In practice this legal judgment was reduced to linking the democratic exercise of judicial review with a presumption on behalf of the minority litigant.[46] The core of activism, however, remained the proposition that judicial action safeguarding individual rights against popular passion or bureaucratic willfulness enhanced, rather than interfered with, the democratic process.

While Justice Black was clearly the leader of the activist bloc during the 1950s and 1960s, he never accepted this broad proposition exempting individual rights adjudication from the sphere of illegitimate judicial policy-making. His individual rights adjudication rested entirely on activism's subordinate proposition, namely, its legal or technical character. Furthermore, his exclusive reliance on history and language committed him to this proposition more fully than was the case for any other member of the Court.[47] Justice Black's literalism constituted a rejection of the dominant justifications for the exercise of judicial power and an attempt to make that exercise more secure by resting it on a revived form of the declaratory theory of law. Difficulties with declaratory theory had contributed to the Court crisis of the 1930s and Justice Black's attempt at revival compounded these difficulties.

To understand this attempt it is helpful to turn first to Chief Justice Marshall, the leading American expounder of the declaratory theory. For Marshall, judicial review rested on the legal character of the Constitution and the judiciary's responsibility to apply and thereby to interpret the law. The text and intent of the Framers were two starting points in Justice Marshall's constitutional interpretation, an interpretation obviously culminating in judicial judgment, which was distinguished from judicial will. He strove to legitimize this exercise of judgment by his efforts to remain faithful to the text and historical intent, by avoidance of overt partisanship, and by the high quality of his judgments.

Over the years the distinction between judicial judgment and will began to lose its force. History and language were increasingly regarded simply as vehicles for the expression of judicial will, and judicial judgment was perceived to be more a reflex of a Justice's values than a thoughtful interpretation of the text to meet important political needs. In the face of the overt partisanship and clear abuse of judicial power by the economic activists, the distinction disappeared completely. Save for the exception made by the libertarian activists, all significant judgment was widely seen as mere will. Justice Black, however, did not find the grounds for this exception persuasive, nor was he willing to relinquish Court power to the extent demanded by the proponents of self-restraint. He sought instead to find something to replace Justice Marshall's judgment, and in so doing returned to history and language alone, asserting their complete clarity and sufficiency for all significant purposes. There was to be no need for any judgment whatever.

This attempt has proved less than serviceable. History is too inconclusive and words too ambiguous to bear the burden Justice Black would impose on them. Even in statutory interpretation, but certainly in constitutional interpretation, the judicial task is constantly to give new meaning to the same words, in response to changing circumstances. The contention surrounding so many of Justice Black's constitutional positions reflects the breadth of disagreement over the meaning of the text and fatally undercuts his assertion that he is merely enforcing the plain meaning of plain words and agreed-upon intent of the Framers.[48]

Although he never retreated from his position, he was not unaware of the problems it involved. On two occasions he confronted the issue fairly directly, and acknowledged the impossibility of obliterating the need for all judgment. Tacitly accepting the widespread equation of judgment with will, he proposed literalism as the optimal solution for keeping that will within tolerable limits:[49]

> Of course I realize that you can never do away with, or indeed would I want to do away with, an individual justice's judgment. But I think there is something to our people's aspirations for a government of laws and not of men. And I cannot accept a Due Process Clause interpretation which permits life-appointed judges to write their own economic and political views into our Constitution. I earnestly believe that my due process interpretation is the only one consistent with a written constitution in that it better insures that constitutional provisions will not be changed except by proper amendment processes.

Justice Black had made the same suggestion, in a somewhat fuller form, once before, in his *Adamson* dissent:[50]

> Since *Marbury v. Madison* . . . was decided, the practice has been firmly established, for better or worse, that courts can strike down legislative enactments which violate the Constitution. This process, of course, involves interpretation, and since words can have many meanings, interpretation obviously may result in contraction or extension of the original purpose of a constitutional provision, thereby affecting policy. But to pass upon the constitutionality of statutes by looking to the particular standards enumerated in the Bill of Rights and other parts of the Constitution is one thing; to invalidate statutes because of application of "natural law" deemed to be above and undefined by the Constitution is another. "In one instance, courts proceeding within clearly marked constitutional boundaries seek to execute policies written into the Constitution; in the other, they roam at will in the limitless area of their own beliefs as to reasonableness and actually select policies, a responsibility which the Constitution entrusts to the legislative representatives of the people."

This explanation, however, did not resolve his difficulties. In the process of "seek[ing] to execute policies written into the Constitution" he strained certain clauses beyond recognition, while downgrading others to the point of virtually eliminating them from judicial scrutiny. It is simply not true that such an approach "execute[s] policies written into the Constitution," or demonstrates a meaningful faithfulness to the Constitution's original language or purpose. Rather, Justice Black's solution became an exercise of judicial will which, within his own framework, he could not justify. This difficulty was particularly acute because of the demonstrated activism of his literal approach. Incorporation, First and Fifth Amendment absolutism, and Justice Black's reapportionment position simply belie any claim that literalism is to be preferred because it serves "to execute policies written into the Constitution." If anything, such activism, coupled with the insistence that this was merely enforcing the clear words of the text, invited cynicism about the judicial function.

Justice Black's position, in fact, failed to win over a single adherent among his colleagues and has been completely bypassed by the changes in both activism and self-restraint that have taken place during the last decade. While the practice of judicial activism has not abated, its underlying justification has undergone a substantial shift. By the late 1960s there was little vitality left in the old categories of activism and self-restraint. This shift evolved in the course of debate over Professor Wechsler's critique of activism[51] and despite the generally negative reception this critique received. While rejecting Professor Wechsler's criticism of leading individual rights decisions, commentators made no serious effort to distinguish the unique character of individual rights adjudication or to link the democratic exercise of judicial review with support for minority litigants.[52] Without intending to do so, Professor Wechsler nonetheless made it impossible to deny that protection of individual rights is a problematic, value-laden task, rather than a largely legal or technical one. He thus undermined the libertarian activist position and effectively destroyed its subordinate position, the only one, as we have seen, to which Justice Black adhered. In the process of defending itself from Professor Wechsler's criticism, libertarian activism lost whatever reliance it once placed on the explicitness of the constitutional text, and increasingly rested on the ground that such adjudication is good policy, that it is conducive to worthwhile ends.[53] At the same time, there has also been an increased willingness to defend judicial review without linking it to particular ends, and without apologizing for its supposedly undemocratic attributes.[54]

With Justice Harlan's emergence as leader of the old self-restraint bloc, that bloc too underwent important changes. Self-restraint in Justice Harlan's hands became a necessary instrument of, but not identical with, sound constitutional interpretation. He fully accepted the judiciary's power to make final constitutional determinations and boldly and jealously guarded that power.[55] Justice Frankfurter's agonizing self scrutiny in the flag salute[56] and *Dennis*[57] cases was not repeated. Sounding more like Chief Justice Marshall, Justice Harlan rested judicial review on the judiciary's assigned task of deciding cases.[58] Even when sustaining a challenged exercise of governmental power, the Court placed more stress on its assessment of constitutionality than on the need to defer to judgments made by the responsible branches.[59] Harlan accepted the inevitable need for judgment that grows out of this task, and turned first to history and tradition as guides in the exercise of that judgment:[60]

> [J]udicial self restraint . . . an indispensable ingredient of sound constitutional adjudication . . . will be achieved . . . only by continual insistence upon respect for the teachings of history, solid recognition of the basic values that underlie our society, and wise appreciation of the great roles that the doctrines of federalism and separation of powers have played in establishing and preserving American freedoms. . . . Adherence to these principles will not, of course, obviate all constitutional differences of opinion among judges, nor should it.

In expressing his own constitutional opinions he combined self-restraint with a consistent and successful endeavor to maintain a superior quality of judgment.

The demise of self-restraint has carried over into the Nixon Court. None of the new appointees can be meaningfully described as adherents of that position. In a certain sense everyone on the current Court is an activist. This general activism, of course, is no longer a libertarian activism and it does not carry with it any presumption on behalf of the minority litigant.

The current state of the controversy still leaves major questions unanswered. Neither side can be said to have resolved the dilemma of the legitimacy of Court power in a democracy. for Mr. Justice Douglas's wing this problem involves legitimizing the relatively overt policy-making of the nonelective, nonresponsive court. For Justice Harlan's successors, it involves, at a minimum, giving credibility to the distinction between judgment and will.

While resolution of such problems remains for the future, Justice Black's theses contribute nothing toward that resolution. He always was, and remained to the end, an advocate of self-restraint who fundamentally disapproved of extensive constitutional review. It is not surprising that in his last few years Justice Black began to sound increasingly like Justice Frankfurter, as Justice Harlan sounded less so. At the end, Justice Black was the only advocate of self-restraint left on the Court. He found some governmental practices abhorrent but reluctantly saw no judicial remedy.[61] And it was Justice Black who moved to a new position of lonely dissent, on an activist Court willing to use judicial power to go beyond specific guarantees of the Bill of Rights and to give broader meaning to the Due Process and Equal Protection Clauses.[62]

. . . .

Conclusion

Justice Black always strove for internal consistency in his work, and he was far more consistent than a superficial review of his record would indicate. Most of the charges of inconsistency arise from a misconception of his basic position. He never supported Court intervention on behalf of individual rights in general. Although he contributed enormously toward its realization, he cannot rightfully be regarded as the leader in the movement for "increasing sensitivity toward human rights, and large conceptions of equality under law." The goals of this movement are far broader than those of Justice Black. He always sought to restrain the Court from abusing power while enabling it to give significant meaning to the Bill of Rights. In practice this meant a liberal interpretation only of the specific guarantees of the Constitution, particularly the First, Fifth, and parts of the Sixth Amendments, and incorporation. He never supported liberal interpretations of the Due Process or Equal Protection Clauses, the two key clauses for implementing expanding conceptions of human rights and equality.

For the overwhelming number of cases in Justice Black's last five years in which he agreed with his former opponents, there are sufficient precedents for his work. By far the largest number of such cases involved Fourth Amendment questions, and his record here was never on the civil libertarian side. His unwillingness to extend due process protection beyond the specific provisions of the Bill of Rights was clearly stated in *Adamson* in 1947. As the incorporation struggle abated with the success of selective incorporation, new due process problems beyond the confines of the Bill of Rights were brought to the Court. In his positions in *Goldberg, Snaidach,* and *Winship,* as well as in his refusal to recognize a constitutional right to privacy, Justice Black was wholly faithful to his *Adamson* position.

Equal protection and First Amendment problems were the only areas that put a strain on Justice Black's internal logic. While incorporation allowed him to overcome the openness of the Due Process Clause without seeming to violate his own strictures on the appropriate use of judicial power, it was far more difficult to give any meaning to the Equal Protection Clause without being forced into the kind of strained distinctions he made, for example, between reapportionment and other voting rights cases. On First Amendment questions his tone and emphasis changed more than his votes.

There are, however, two aspects of Justice Black's work which raise important questions of consistency beyond the technical consistency already discussed. One was an obvious shift in tone and language reflecting a changed attitude toward political reform and society's obligations to, and the responsibility of, dissidents and minorities. The second, and more far-reaching, touches Justice Black's premises concerning the essentially self-regulating democratic process, which needs a judiciary only to enforce clear, written limits on governmental power in order to sustain itself.

The major part of Justice Black's career was marked by a passionate concern for the "poor, the ignorant, the numerically weak, the friendless, and the powerless."[63] In his last years this strong concern clearly abated. In some instances it seems to have disappeared entirely. He certainly did not view what he called, "the ordinary criminal," for example, in these terms, not did he regard him in any way as a victim of society. He was also unreceptive to accepting poverty as a suspect category in equal protection cases and showed himself unsympathetic to calls for judicial protection of welfare recipients.[64] As we have seen, his disparagement of protest movements and their leaders was without parallel in his long career.

Justice Black's official statements offer few clues to understanding these changes. In the end he claimed full support for his positions in the clear commands of the Constitution, without offering adequate explanation for the changes in his work or the genuine differences that clearly exist over constitutional interpretation. We may thus go beyond his writing to review his overall political views, in an attempt to gain additional understanding.

Justice Black was, in decisive ways, a product of the New Deal and of one strand of populism that fed into the New Deal. He was heir to that component of American reform which, while opposing concentrated power and wealth, never had any basic objection to capitalism, to competition as the central mechanism in economic relationships, or to individualism as the key to personal advance and satisfaction.[65] Opposition to concentrated power was aimed essentially at fostering competition and individualism rather than at replacing or qualifying it. Governmental regulation of the economy was encouraged as a necessary instrument in providing genuine equality of opportunity and in maintaining a competitive and productive economy in the face of new technology and new forms of economic organization.[66]

When Justice Black talked of political oppression he often conjured up an image of a distinct and powerful minority, divorced from society, oppressing the many.[67] An integral part of this conception was the supposition that the many are decent, hard-working, honest, and patriotic.[68] When government ceases to be a tool of the few, the need to concentrate on the underdog is vastly diminished; the underlying virtues of self-discipline, hard work, and individualism can be expected to come to the fore.

Justice Black's work during the last decade of his career suggests that he considered the New Deal and the postwar years successful in taking government out of the hands of the few and putting it at the service of the many. Equality of opportunity had been made a reality, thus ending the need for major political reform. Incorporation and the extension of Fourteenth Amendment protection to end de jure discrimination fulfilled the true promise of the Constitution and symbolized the conversion of the judiciary from a tool of the few into the agent of the many. No longer did he link poverty and ignorance with numerical weakness, friendlessness, or powerlessness. Justice Black's often noted patriotism, an extension of his own experience, was an expression of satisfaction with the course of American democracy.[69]

. . . .

The second inconsistency in Justice Black's judicial career casts doubt on the core of his doctrine: that democracy is essentially an automatic, self-regulating process that needs only judicial enforcement of clear, written limits in order to maintain itself. His fear of protest and its potential for degeneration into mob violence challenged his earlier confidence in the self-regulating market place of ideas. It challenged his expectation that successful democratic life is the by-product of enforced absolute limits on governmental power. In his earlier years Justice Black had pushed the market place concept virtually to absurdity. Yet the spoken premise of *Gregory* is that First Amendment cases present difficult problems that may not be subject to satisfactory resolution simply by applying the general principle embodied in the constitutional text. There emerged the recognition that there are — at least — two sides to First Amendment issues, and that the resolution of particular problems is difficult. Furthermore, the unspoken premise of *Brown* and *Gregory* is that more speech may not necessarily defeat bad speech and that the unregulated market place of ideas may not necessarily produce progress but may end in self-destruction.

In a sense, Justice Black never did rely on an automatic process to maintain liberty. If the foregoing analysis is correct, his fundamental reliance rested not with absolute limits but on the expectation that certain shared standards were operative in society and that these standards guided the market place and the nation toward salutary choices. It is impossible to know the extent to which he acknowledged the primacy of these standards to himself. He certainly never did so in his opinions. It is clear, however, that the difficulties with his First Amendment adjudication grew out of this conflict over the relative importance of underlying societal standards and values on the one hand, and constitutional limits on the other. In his First Amendment inconsistencies, seeking to maintain the primacy of judicially enforced guarantees while losing confidence in the accompanying values, Justice Black unwittingly began the critique of his own work.

The First Amendment states a general and important political principle. Supreme Court enforcement of that guarantee helps to reinforce the principle. But despite Justice Black's best efforts, it is obvious that all important provisions need continual interpretation in their application to particular circumstances. Part of that interpretation involves consideration of the conditions needed for the successful operation of the general principle.

Perhaps the most crucial condition for successful enjoyment of First Amendment freedoms is the existence of common standards by which various speech is judged. No intelligible discourse can take place without the capacity to distinguish honest inquiry, no matter how basic or exaggerated, from such attacks on meaningful public discussion as demagoguery, calculated slander, or systematic subversion. When this capacity is present, legal restraint becomes largely superfluous. When this capacity is absent, the law can contribute to its cultivation; when it is weak the law can help envigorate it. But if the law consistently denies validity of such distinctions, the public's capacity to make them can disappear. It is unrealistic to rely on the continual vitality of private choices while the standards for making these choices are publicly undermined.

Yet this is precisely where Justice Black's absolutism pointed, with its equation of all speech and its strident refusal to make judgments on the content of any speech. The problem is well illustrated in the current debate over libel of public figures. Until *New York Times v. Sullivan*, falsehood was punishable as libel. With the *New York Times* case, the requirement of actual malice was added. Statements made with the knowledge that they were false, or with reckless disregard for truth, were actionable; honest error was not. The decision reflected the judgment that to hold all falsehood libelous overly inhibits the cautious and subjects the careless but honest commentator to excessive restraint. These evils were considered more serious than the impact of honest error on political debate.

Justice Black concurred in the decision but advocated the extension of First Amendment protection to all speech, including the malicious and deliberate lie. Yet the distinction that he rejected is crucial for the vitality of First Amendment freedoms. It is an integral part of the public's capacity to maintain a democratic, to say nothing of a decent, society. Were Justice Black successful, it is at least as likely that "bad speech" — demagoguery, slander, subversion — would eventually drive out honest discourse.

All major First Amendment problems encompass similar considerations. It cannot be blandly assumed that all challenges to a democratic order will prove as ineffective as did the Communist challenge, the major national security issue during Justice Black's tenure. American economic conditions, coupled with basic political traditions, probably precluded a successful Communist appeal. But other such movements may meet more receptive conditions. The most obvious one at this time would be some antidemocratic movement exploiting racial fears and antagonisms. When needed most, "more speech" can succeed in curbing "bad speech" only if the public appeals to distinctions between worthwhile and worthless speech have genuine meaning. Other First Amendment problems would also be easier to handle if there were more acceptance of the legitimacy of judgments about the quality of speech and if there were more overt assessments of the threat of particular speech to other interests, such as fair trial, public peace, or institutional integrity.

If there is one underlying problem in all of Justice Black's work it is precisely his denigration of this kind of judgment. His literalism was fashioned to avoid recourse to it. First Amendment absolutism avoided the need for judgment. Justice Black's continual attack on the judiciary's attempt to give specific meaning to concepts of reasonableness, fairness, and justice extended the attack on judgment to other constitutional guarantees. He derided all such attempts, indicating that they involved "natural law" concepts, clearly a term of abuse as he used it. All departures from strict enforcement of explicit constitutional commands are lumped together as unacceptable exercises of judicial will.

. . . .

American courts, in the process of constitutional adjudication, play an enormous role in this debate, articulating and shaping basic values. In so doing they make as significant a contribution to a healthy society as they do in enforcing particular provisions of the Constitution. Whether or not *Miranda* remains law, for example, is less important than how the public and the police respond to the call for higher standards in law enforcement. The Equal Protection Clause cannot bring racial equality in the absence of sufficient popular commitment to racial justice. There can be no hope for maintaining workable and decent criminal procedures without ready acceptance of such judgments that proof beyond reasonable doubt is an essential part of fundamental fairness,[70] and that a conviction in a trial permeated by excessive publicity and a "carnival-like" atmosphere is a denial of justice.[71] If not related to meaningful conceptions of justice, judgments of constitutionality will not be able to survive.

Justice Black, of course, feared that a judiciary giving confident voice to such judgments would endanger liberty. He would have us believe that we have only two choices in constitutional adjudication—either to abandon ourselves to unrestrained subjective judgments or to uphold absolute rules whose meaning is irrevocably fixed by history and language. But Justice Black's choice is Hobson's choice. First, as we have seen, history and language do not fix the meaning of the constitutional text, and exclusive reliance on these standards results in arbitrariness, not objectivity. Secondly, Justice Black shifted our gaze away from the true political choice—it is not, as he said, between no standards or clear standards but between better or worse standards for public life.

The susceptibility for abuse inherent in the search for better standards has given strong appeal to any attempt to avoid recourse to such standards. The rule of law itself is testimony to the need for a system of rules, rather than case-by-case resolution of problems in light of abstract principles. Yet no system of rules can anticipate and provide for all situations. Justice Black went as far as possible in making an attempt to do just that. But he failed. No set of rules can provide in detail for the multiplicity of changing needs that must be judged as they arise. In addition to rules there must always be judgment. With respect to the necessarily broad rules of the Constitution, the need for judgment is even greater. That there is little likelihood of agreement on the worth of all judgments does not mean that no judgments are possible. Societies must continue to argue over and strive toward better judgments if they are not to succumb to the worst judgments. No judicial determination need end debate on the merit of a distinction that has been drawn. Public argument over alternative standards is far preferable to the denial of the possibility of defending any meaningful standard and the retreat to a legal objectivity and neutrality that is illusory.

There are some negative consequences of Justice Black's approach. We have already seen how overt reliance on the words of the text, in the face of obvious disagreement over the meaning of such words, resulted in arbitrariness. This, in turn, led to cynicism about the judiciary's work. In addition, there is simply no evidence for Justice Black's confidence that the Bill of Rights, as drafted by the Framers, meets all the needs of limited government. His incapacity to give satisfactory treatment to the problem of electronic surveillance, and of privacy in general, are major examples of the serious limitations of his approach.

Professor Kurland, in noting Justice Black's success in bringing the Court to his position, without thereby gaining converts to his basic doctrine, noted that this could not be pure coincidence.[72] It cannot be and it is not. What linked Justice Black with the majority he led was a concern for a limited government solicitous of individual rights. But for Justice Black, this goal was overwhelmed, as it never was for others, by a staggering fear of judicial abuse of power and a simplistic conception of the democratic process. Serious as these defects are, their danger is mitigated by their lack of power to compel. They also contain a negative virtue in that they clearly show the dead end that awaits the attempt to banish judgment from political life.

Despite the genuine problems in his work, however, Black shaped the major trends in contemporary constitutional law. He was the architect of incorporation, which has served to nationalize higher standards of police conduct. Although First Amendment absolutism is not likely to triumph, Justice Black was instrumental in narrowing the scope of libel, in tightening restraints on obscenity, and in generating greater acceptance of public protest, even over his own dissent. In addition, loyalty oaths, disbarment, and various penalties and disabilities for alleged subversion will undoubtedly have to survive stricter scrutiny than in the past. He is also the author of leading decisions, such as *Gideon* and *Griffin,* which, while they do not, as perhaps they cannot, eliminate the disadvantages of poverty in the criminal process, go far toward mitigating them. If not always for the soundest reasons, he made it more difficult to accept glib justifications for such practices as convicting a person in one jurisdiction for evidence compelled in another, and for making failure to disclose information a crime in one jurisdiction while that information is incriminating in another.

Justice Black achieved these ends through the forcefulness, power, and single-minded clarity of purpose of his opinions, rather than through exceptional analytic ability or subtle treatment of the many complexities of constitutional adjudication. His rhetorical force and consistent voting record, for the major part of his career, were instrumental in focusing attention on the Bill of Rights as legal protection for individual rights against undue governmental power. Even with all his shortcomings, the power of his opinions is such that it is still accurate to think of the judicial era just ended as that of "The Black court."

In Justice Black's law school yearbook, as he once recalled, it was said of him, "This fellow seems to possess but one idea, and that is a wrong one."[73] Justice Black's one idea is not so much wrong as incomplete. Insisting on judicial enforcement of the constitutional text can only be the starting point in making the Bill of Rights a legal limit on political power. But his insistence on fidelity to the text, with all its unresolved problems and incompleteness, has served to enhance the importance of basic constitutional guarantees. This same insistence on fidelity to the text can serve another worthwhile end, too. Justice Black's literalism constitutes a reminder of "our people's aspirations for a government of laws and not of men." While his literalism is an unsatisfactory and oversimplified attempt to fulfill this aspiration, it can serve a useful purpose amid stress on the openness of the constitutional text, the political character of the Court's work, and the suggestion that we accept the inevitability of the rule of men. For this too is an oversimplification, as is the contrast between a government of laws and one of men. A government of laws represents a singular achievement of men, while the Supreme Court's practice of judicial review is a unique manifestation of the rule of law. On the whole it has been successful in providing legal resolution for a significant area of political controversy and in elevating the quality of American political life. Constitutional law calls for a range of talent well outside that of traditional legal analysis and easily accommodates — if not demands — greater freedom in interpreting the legal text than do other branches of the law. Yet it remains one branch of legal analysis, and the court's success in its unique endeavor is intimately tied to its performance as a court of law. This makes fidelity to the text — for all its openness — a necessary part of constitutional adjudication.

Justice Black's "absolutism": notes on his use of history to support free expression

3

DWIGHT L. TEETER
MARYANN YODELIS SMITH

Only four months before his death on September 25, 1971, Justice Hugo Lafayette Black listened to oral arguments in the Pentagon Papers case.[1] Black, at 85, had served more than 34 years on the Supreme Court of the United States, the second longest tenure in the Court's history.

Although Justice Black was in failing health, his almost instinctive support for free expression remained undiminished as he considered the dispute between the United States Department of Justice and the press. The New York *Times* and the Washington *Post* had published excerpts from a secret report on the beginnings of United States involvement in Vietnam. The Justice Department had secured injunctions against publication of further excerpts, which meant that as the justices heard the arguments, prepublication censorship was in force against some of America's leading newspapers.

Solicitor General Erwin Griswold, a noted scholar and former dean of the Harvard Law School, spoke for the government near the end of the two-hour hearing in the Pentagon Papers case. Griswold declared that publication of the documents embarrassed the United States and made diplomatic negotiations aimed at ending the Vietnam conflict difficult if not impossible.

DWIGHT L. TEETER, JR., is professor and chairman of the Department of Journalism at the University of Texas. He holds the Ph.D. in mass communications from the University of Wisconsin-Madison. His research is concentrated on historical and legal study of freedom and restraint of the print and broadcast media. He is coauthor (with Harold L. Nelson) of *Law of Mass Communications,* now in second edition, and he is particularly interested in the origins of the First Amendment and of free press theory in the United States.

MARYANN YODELIS SMITH is associate professor in the School of Journalism and Mass Communication at the University of Wisconsin-Madison. She holds the Ph.D. in mass communication from the University of Wisconsin-Madison. She has published research on diverse communications law topics and on economic and legal restraints on the press during the revolution and the War for Independence.

Justice Thurgood Marshall voiced fear that a government triumph in the case would be a precedent for other requests for courts to use prior restraint by injunction as a weapon against the press. Marshall asked Griswold, "wouldn't we then, the Federal Courts, be a censorship board as to whether this does . . . ?"

Griswold interrupted Justice Marshall: "That is a pejorative way to put it, Mr. Justice. I do not know what the alternative is."

Justice Black interjected, "The First Amendment might be."[2]

With that deft thrust at Solicitor General Griswold, Black drew once again upon his long-held constitutional faith that the First Amendment means just what it says:[3] there shall be no abridgement of the freedom of speech and press. Black told Edmond Cahn in 1962, "I learned a long time ago that there are affirmative and negative words. The beginning of the First Amendment is that 'Congress shall make no law.' "[4] Justice Black added:

> Of course, some will remark that that is too simple on my part. To them, all this discussion of mine is too simple, because I come back to saying that these few plain words actually mean what they say, and I know of no college professor or law school professor, outside of my friend, Professor Cahn here, and a few others, who could not write one hundred pages to show that the Amendment does not mean what it says.[5]

In the James Madison Lecture at New York University in 1960, Black said: "It is my belief that there *are* 'absolutes' in our Bill of Rights, and that they were put there on purpose by men who knew what words meant and meant their prohibitions to be 'absolutes.' "[6]

I

Such statements were based on Justice Black's knowledge of and understanding of Anglo-American history bearing on freedom of expression. This essay explores some aspects of Black's use of history as precedent to support his interpretation of the First Amendment's protection of freedom of speech and press. After briefly considering a few cautionary notes about the limitations of history, we take up two interrelated themes in Black's use of history: his fondness for examples drawn from English history, and his assumption that he not only could know but also did know what the Founding Fathers meant where First Amendment protection of speech and press freedom was concerned. It is our judgment that Justice Black was a far better libertarian than he was historian.

One could ask, why does Justice Black's use of history have any importance? Black was a respected, even revered, interpreter of First Amendment guaranties. His reading of history was crucial to his stands on First Amendment cases. Beyond that, to a large — if little studied — extent, history is a dispositive underpinning for constitutional adjudication.[7] As attorney John G. Wofford noted, "The past may be only prologue, but for the

Supreme Court the prologue sometimes appears to direct the whole drama . . . [of] the interpretation of the words of the United States Constitution."[8]

Black's greatness, as both a person and as a Supreme Court justice, is acknowledged and is not at issue here. His death meant that the news media and those members of the public who are concerned about their rights to hear, read, view, criticize, and be informed doubtless lost as staunch an ally as they have had in this century. Nevertheless, it is here argued that if Black's use of history in defense of freedom of expression was a source of delight to civil libertarians, it could also be a source of despair to historians. Black, certainly one of the ablest justices, may nevertheless be said to have been guilty of a considerable amount of law-office history. Law-office history—the phrase is historian Alfred H. Kelly's—refers to "selection of data favorable to the position being advanced without regard to or concern for contradictory data or proper evaluation of the relevance of the data proffered."[9]

Although Black's historical scholarship may have been highly regarded in some quarters, and although he doubtless was more knowledgeable in Anglo-American history than many twentieth century justices,[10] unfavorable criticism of his historical scholarship is scarcely new.[11] Some of that criticism has been scathing. Justice Felix Frankfurter wrote a concurring opinion in *Adamson v. California* (1948)[12] on Black's use of history. Frankfurter called Black "one who may respectfully be called an eccentric exception" in his interpretation of the Fourteenth Amendment, particularly. In a massively long dissenting opinion, Black in *Adamson* contended that the Fourteenth Amendment was intended to incorporate the Constitution's first eight amendments in its sweep and apply them to the states.[13]

In 1963, Paul Murphy declared that Justice Black's scholarship in an opinion for the Court in a 1962 school prayer case was defective.[14] Murphy complained that Black "relied upon works which may be 'historical' given the length of time in the past they were written, but which modern scholars would hesitate to suggest an undergraduate rely upon as anything but a once important, although now outdated, view."[15]

II

History, of course, is a term that has many meanings—perhaps as many meanings as there are human beings. As Charles A. Beard was fond of saying, "A man sees that which is behind his eyes."[16] All of us, after all, base our daily lives on a personal kind of history; the pictures in our heads are conditioned by individual experiences. Beyond such day-to-day, personal, and reflexive uses of a kind of history, most, if not all, individuals live with historical facts and myths firmly in mind, which must naturally affect the way the world is viewed. Thomas A. Bailey has written that most Americans have too long lived with dangerous myths: the myth that Americans are God's chosen folk (with "In God We Trust" stamped even upon our pennies and nickels); that

Americans are militarily omnipotent (despite the War of 1812 and the Korean and Vietnamese conflicts), and that America is always righteous in its international dealings.[17]

The commonest — and perhaps vaguest — definition of history says, with deceptive simplicity, "history is the past of mankind." Such a broad definition includes, among other things, what actually happened (history as actuality); surviving records of what happened (history as record); and history as told (spoken or written history).[18]

History's goal may be truth, but that is an unattainable goal. History-as-actuality is gone beyond recall. Surviving records of what happened, moreover, will never create a one-to-one relationship with what actually happened. Not all events are observed, and most observed events are not recorded. And even if events are recorded with impressive accuracy, not all records survive. And even if records do survive, not all are noticed. If a historian does locate documents, are they authentic? That is, do they come from the time and place they purport to represent? Or are they forgeries? Do they come from another time and place? Even if surviving documents are authentic, are they credible? Are these documents verifiable? Can they be said to represent testimony of two independent witnesses who were in a position to tell the truth? And certainly history as told reflects these same shortcomings.[19]

Historians are thus the victims of a considerable amount of what might be termed involuntary sampling in the source material they use. As Louis Gottschalk has said, spoken or written history "is only the historians' expressed part of the understood part of the credible part of the discovered part of history-as-record. . . . In other words the 'object' that the historian studies is not only incomplete; it is markedly variable as records are lost or rediscovered."[20] So it is that the process of writing history is one of imaginative reconstruction or re-creation; the historian's personal beliefs and attitudes, along with that individual's level of knowledge, intelligence, training and intellectual honesty, will all affect the finished work of history. Historians, for the most part, work *adductively* in the sense of adducing answers to specific questions. The answers may be general or particular.[21]

This process of imaginative re-creation has many pitfalls. English essayist Samuel Butler said, since God himself cannot change the past, he is obliged to tolerate the existence of historians. Other cynics wonder why history is so dull when so much of it is obviously false.[22] Mark Twain's reaction to a museum's dinosaur skeleton as consisting of three bones and ten barrels of plaster should speak to historians who try to create too much history from too little evidence.

III

History, then, should be used by the Court — or by anyone — with great caution. Justice Oliver Wendell Holmes, Jr., who perhaps knew more legal history than any other twentieth century justice, indicated some mistrust of history as used in constitutional law. He wrote that he looked forward "to a time when the part played by history in the explanation of dogma shall be very small, and instead of ingenious research we shall spend our energy on a study of the ends sought to be attained and the reasons for desiring them."[23]

Disenchanted commentators who declare that history does not matter because it is "irrelevant" will find little comfort in reading Black's opinions dealing with freedom of expression. History was alive for Black; for him, the present was the cutting edge of the past. Many of his opinions made obvious his reliance upon history as precedent. Time and again, he returned to a line of argument that became a kind of trademark for him: the lessons to be drawn from Anglo-American struggles for freedom of expression. As Charles A. Miller noted, Black often relied on a "parade of horribles" approach: he often wrote of repression of speech and press in England from the sixteenth century onward. The thrust of such argument by historical example was that the American colonists revolted against England to be free from such oppression. "Justice Black, in fact [could] scarcely write an opinion in the entire area of civil liberties without adverting unfavorably to British history and favorably to the beliefs of the Founding Fathers, particularly Madison and Jefferson. History, in sum, tells us what to avoid and whom to accept."[24] In *Talley v. California,* Black writing for the Court held unconstitutional an ordinance forbidding distribution of unsigned materials:

> Anonymous pamphlets, leaflets, brochures and even books have played an important role in the progress of mankind. Persecuted groups and sects from time to time throughout history have been able to criticize oppressive practices and laws anonymously or not at all. . . . The old seditious libel cases in England show the lengths to which government had to go to find out who was responsible for books that were obnoxious to the rulers. John Lilburne was whipped, pilloried and fined for refusing to answer questions designed to get evidence to convict him or someone else for the secret distribution of books in England. Two Puritan ministers, John Penry and John Udal, were sentenced to death on charges that they were responsible for writing, printing or publishing books. Before the Revolutionary War colonial patriots frequently had to conceal their authorship or distribution of literature that easily could have brought down on them the prosecutions by English-controlled courts.[25]

Aside from doubts about the efficacy of pen names to conceal identities (the authorship of pseudonymous writings was often an open secret, even when the names chosen were less transparent than Thomas Paine's use of "Common Sense" to sign some of his writings), Black's statement about the English-controlled courts is open to some question. There were few seditious libel prosecutions involving the supposedly tyrannous common law courts. Without suggesting a causal relationship, it may be said that after the Zenger trial of 1735, there were evidently no more jury trials for seditious libel in the American colonies. Restraints imposed by colonial legislative bodies seemed to be a much greater threat because the assemblies provided more instances of prosecution and punishment than did the courts.[26]

Historian Thomas A. Bailey was sufficiently concerned about the misuse of history by politicians and government officials that he used his address as president of the Organization of American Historians to warn: beware of anyone who says, "History teaches. . . ."[27] One of the key distinctions in dealing with history—any kind of history—is the difference between "the history" and "a history." It is doubtful that *the* history could ever be written about any topic of human endeavor. All that can ever be said is that a writing is *a* history. This more modest phrasing assumes that subsequent historians, who may have access to additional records or the benefit of additional scholarship, may be able to improve on any historical writing, no matter how worthy that writing may be. Such caution was not characteristic of Justice Black's writings or opinions. This man, who was most tolerant of diverse viewpoints, more than once revealed a belief that he knew *the* history of freedom of expression. Speaking in 1960 at New York University, he said:

> The whole history and background of the Constitution and Bill of Rights, as I understand it, belies the assumption or conclusion that our ultimate constitutional freedoms are no more than our English ancestors had when they came to this land to get new freedoms. The historical and practical purposes of a Bill of Rights, the very use of a written Constitution, indigenous to America, the language the Framers used, the kind of three-department government they took pains to set up, all point to the creation of a government which was denied all power to do some things under any and all circumstances, and all power to do other things except precisely in the manner described.[28]

In the same year, his dissent in *Konigsberg v. State Bar of California* expressed the same sort of absolutism, the same sort of confidence in his understanding of the First Amendment: "The history of the First Amendment is too well known to require repeating here except to say that it certainly cannot be denied that the very object of adopting the First Amendment, as well as the other provisions of the Bill of Rights, was to put the freedoms protected completely out of the area of any congressional control. . . ."[29]

Justice Black's use of history often seemed to go beyond an intellectual construction into the realm of a religiously held belief. In delivering the Carpentier Lectures at Columbia University School of Law in 1968, Black explained how his reading of history was the basis of his constitutional faith.

> It is of paramount importance to me that our country has a written constitution. This great document is the unique American contribution to man's continuing search for a society in which individual liberty is secure against government oppression. . . .
>
> The American Constitution is no accident of history, but is the evolutionary product of man's strivings throughout past ages to protect himself from tyrannical kings, potentates, and rulers.[30]

No accident of history? Black's words revealed a faith that the past was not a random succession of events but instead had at least a kind of form or pattern. The Constitution was a product of humanity's upward strivings toward perfectibility.[31] His confidence that his reading of history was *the* correct one may not have been justified. Black, it is emphasized, was little better or worse than other Supreme Court justices in his use of history; he merely made more use of history than most of his brethren. Lawyers and judges (like the politicians they frequently are or wish to become) often use history-based assertions as if they were immutable truths. Such quasi history, or parahistory, often is used in situations where it is not helpful — and might even be downright misleading — in ways reminiscent of what Abraham Kaplan has called the law of the instrument. "Give a small boy a hammer," said Kaplan, "and he will find that everything he encounters needs pounding."[32]

IV

A rather lengthy example of Justice Black's use (and misuse) of history occurred in his dissent in a 1960 case known as *Communist Party v. Control Board.* Some 20 pages of Black's 32-page dissent spoke to the Anglo-American history of suppression of political dissent. Black discussed, among other things, religious persecution in England, the 1799 English "Act for the more effectual Suppression of Societies established for Seditious and Treasonable Purposes; and for better preventing Treasonable and Seditious Practices." He compared that impressively titled act to the United States' Subversive Activities Control Act.[33] Thus warmed up, he declared — with little if any convincing evidence to back him up — that the First Amendment had done away with seditious libel in America.[34] Seditious libel simply means making criticism of government a crime.

Black had a major obstacle to overcome in support of his assertion that the First Amendment, adopted in 1791, had outlawed seditious libel: the Alien and Sedition Acts of 1798. He wrote:

> The enforcement of these statutes, particularly the Sedition Act, constitutes one of the greatest blots on our country's record of freedom. Publishers were sent to jail for writing their own views and for publishing the views of others. The slightest criticism of Government or policies of government officials was enough to cause biased federal prosecutors to put the machinery of Government to work to crush and imprison the critic. . . . Members of the Jeffersonian Party were picked out as special targets so that they could be illustrious examples of what could happen to people who failed to sing paeans of praise for current federal officials and their policies.[35]

Not only did Justice Black denounce the 1798 Sedition Act, he reached backward more than 160 years to pronounce that law unconstitutional. "I regret, exceedingly regret," wrote Black, "that I feel impelled to recount this history of the Federalist Sedition Act because, in all truth, it must be pointed out that this law — which has since been almost universally condemned as unconstitutional—did not go as far in suppressing the First Amendment freedoms of Americans as do the Smith Act and the Subversive Activities Control Act."[36] Charles A. Miller is one historian who has challenged Justice Black's convoking the " 'court of history' . . . to set at rest the question of the constitutionality of the Sedition Act and the historical meaning of freedom of expression." Miller added:

> To the historian, the constitutionality of the Sedition Act ought to depend on evidence of the time, not on the reaction of subsequent generations. To the judge, the practice of determining constitutionality retrospectively creates the appearance of attempting to halt the process of constitutional development: for while it is justifiable to argue that what might have been valid a century ago is void today because of the nature of ongoing history, it is a baffling and literal anachronism to remove an uncontested law from the stream of history just long enough to declare it unconstitutional, and then replace it in order to enjoy the illusory satisfaction that the act had been notoriously invalid all the time.[37]

Running through Black's use of history is an innocently optimistic view of the men who wrote the Constitution and those who presented the nation with its Bill of Rights. His reading of history seemed to be through lenses that might have been given him by nineteenth century historian John Fiske. Fiske saw the Founding Fathers as patriots of spotless principle who wrought a quite possibly divine document in the Constitution.[38] Black's view of history ignored historians who saw the Founding Fathers as men subject to human frailties, including the distortions accompanying economic and political ambitions.[39]

Speaking in 1968, Black declared that

> a critically important factor in considering the basic purpose of the Constitution is the disappointing experience of the thirteen new states under the Articles of Confederation. Each state had been too jealous of its own power to give enough authority to the national government to form a unified country. Men like Washington, Jefferson, Madison, Hamilton, and Adams saw this weakness in the Articles and knew that a national government with sufficient powers to protect and defend itself had to be established if a real country was to be created.[40]

First, it should be noted that Jefferson was not even in America during the period of the framing and ratification of the Constitution; he was in France. Given the slowness of trans-Atlantic communication in the late 1780s, Jefferson had only scanty and dated information about what the Constitutional Convention was doing.

Second, such "critical period" history is history according to the winning—or Federalist—side. Justice Black, in company with many of his colleagues on the bench, has recited a veritable Federalist catechism. The Federalist Papers, now articles of political belief, were once only one side of a political argument—an internal political revolution with decidedly antidemocratic overtones accomplished in the infant United States in the late 1780s.

Although little attention is now paid to Antifederalist writings such as those of "Centinel" (Pennsylvania politician Samuel Bryan), those outspoken attacks on the motives of the members of the Constitutional Convention suggest strongly that what we now call the Constitution was of less than divine origin.[41] In fact, James Madison's journal stated: "Mr. Pinckney was for a vigorous Executive, but was afraid the executive powers of the existing Congress might extend to peace and war &c; which would render the Executive a monarchy of the worst kind, to wit, an elective one." This was typical fare in the constitutional debates.[42]

Black indeed had a Constitutional faith, a faith which no revisionist historians ever shook. He declared:

> My experiences with and for our government have filled my heart with gratitude and devotion to the Constitution which made my public life possible. That Constitution is my legal bible; its plan of government is my plan and its destiny my destiny. I cherish every word of it, from the first to the last, and I personally deplore even the slightest deviation from its least important commands.[43]

V

It seems, however, that Justice Black's faith was founded at least in part on a highly selective reading of history. Hugo Black, according to one of his sometime law clerks, " 'trusted in the wisdom and justice of the masses.' "[44] Even so, Black paid no discernible attention to statements such as those of Edmund Randolph and Alexander Hamilton showing distrust if not outright contempt for majority rule. Consider Randolph:

> "[O]ur chief danger arises from the democratic parts of our constitutions. It is a maxim which I hold incontrovertible, that the powers of government exercised by the people swallows up the other branches. None of the [state] constitutions have provided sufficient checks against the democracy [the lower house of a state's legislature]. The feeble Senate of Virginia is a phantom. Maryland has a more powerful senate, but the late distractions in that State have discovered that it is not powerful enough. The check established in the constitution of New York and Massachusetts is yet a stronger barrier against democracy, but they all seem insufficient.[45]

Consider Alexander Hamilton, who spoke for the Federalists when he declared that "[a]ll communities divide themselves into the few and the many. The first are the rich and well-born, the other the mass of the people. . . ." The people, Hamilton added, seldom judge rightly.[46]

The traditional view of the adoption of the First Amendment in particular and the Bill of Rights in general, the view adhered to by Justice Black, celebrates the intent of the "Framers" or the "Founding Fathers" as a triumph of libertarian principle. Black told Edmond Cahn:

> I believe when our Founding Fathers . . . wrote the [First] Amendment they . . . knew what history was behind them and they wanted to ordain in this country that Congress . . . should not tell people what religion they should have or what they should believe or say or publish, and that is about it. It [the First Amendment] says "no law," and that is what I believe it means.[47]

Black had heroes and was fond of quoting James Madison, sometimes referred to as "the father of the Constitution," and Thomas Jefferson.

> Thomas Jefferson, the great strategist of the campaign to bring about the adoption of the Bill of Rights, a campaign which he began even before the Constitution was adopted, said as to one of the guaranties of the First Amendment: 'The basis of our governments being the opinion of the people, the very first object should be to keep that right; and were it left to me to decide whether we should have a government without newspapers or newspapers without a government, I should not hesitate a moment to prefer the latter.'[48]

That oft-quoted bit of Jeffersoniana was written before Jefferson was President. After going through some bitter press wars, Jefferson took a different tack. Writing to Governor Thomas McKean of Pennsylvania in 1803, Jefferson said that the Federalists who had failed to destroy press freedom with their Sedition Act, were now "pushing it's [sic] licentiousness & it's [sic] lying to such a degree of prostitution as to deprive it of all credit." Jefferson added:

> the press ought to be restored to it's [sic] credibility if possible. The restraints provided by the states are sufficient for this if applied. And I have therefore long thought that a few prosecutions of the most prominent offenders would have a wholesome effect in restoring the integrity of the presses. Not a general prosecution, for that would look like persecution; but a selected one.[49]

Black perhaps never saw evidence of that facet of Jefferson, or if he did, he put it aside. Actually, Jefferson's irate letter to McKean may well have reflected accurately freedom of the press as Jefferson then understood it. After all, Jefferson was not writing in the twentieth century. Freedom of the press then seemed to mean, most often, something Blackstonian: "The liberty of the press is indeed essential to the nature of a free state: but this consists in laying no *previous* restraints upon publications, and not in freedom from censure for criminal matter when published."[50]

Careful attention should be paid to the wording of the First Amendment:

"*Congress* shall make no law. . . ." That does *not* say that states might not make laws abridging freedom of the press. The First Amendment, and indeed the entire Bill of Rights, may be viewed as a political device proffered to secure ratification of the Constitution. Historian Irving Brant, certainly no revisionist, has written:

> The cry for a Bill of Rights came loudest from state-minded politicians who hoped to defeat the Constitution altogether, or had dreams of a second convention in which Congress would be denied the power to lay taxes or to regulate commerce. However, their expressions of alarm would have had no force if they had not touched a sensitive nerve among the masses of the people throughout the thirteen states.[51]

What then of the "intent of the Framers" where the freedoms of speech and press are concerned? The best recent scholarship on the topic sees the impetus for a Bill of Rights in the context of practical politics: what guaranties against central government encroachment did the Federalists have to promise in order to secure ratification of the Constitution?[52] As Leonard Levy has declared, "There is even reason to believe that the Bill of Rights was more the chance product of political expediency on all sides than of principled commitment to personal liberties."[53]

Wittingly or unwittingly, Justice Hugo Black—and many of his colleagues on the Supreme Court—turned to history, finding what John P. Roche terms "retrospective symmetry." That is, the past has been interpreted—and on occasion twisted—in order to give sanction to twentieth century civil liberties.[54] Such selective argumentation out of the past is not without dangers. Civil liberties are needed now, in full measure, regardless of what the Revolutionary generation "meant" or "intended" by phrases such as freedom of speech or freedom of the press. Also, if decent judges and rulers use history for what we perceive to be "good" ends, could not corrupt judges or rulers use history to oppress? As Charles A. Miller points out, American history is not a history forced upon its citizens by political authorities. "While American history is often made use of for official purposes, it does not have to be made up for these occasions."[55] Even so, purposive use of selective history does have dangerous overtones. Perhaps "it can't happen here," but Miller took pains to remind his readers of the Party slogan from George Orwell's *1984*: "Who controls the past controls the future; who controls the present controls the past."[56]

VI

This essay on a great jurist's use of history in support of his most cherished political and societal value, freedom of expression, gives rise to a rather disquieting question. Are the basic purposes of history and law at least to some extent mutually exclusive? Or, to put it another way, is serious factual distortion inevitable when history is used for contemporary legal purposes? The distinguished federal judge, Edward Dumbauld, himself a respected historian, insists that history as used by lawyers and judges "must be both accurate and reliable."[57] But why is the lawyer or judge using history? To seek truth, or to win or decide a case? Judge Dumbauld, with disarming candor, has said that the lawyer's use of history "is entirely pragmatic or instrumental. His history may be fiction, from the standpoint of a scholarly historian, but if it produces victory, it has served its purpose."[58]

Justice Black, like most if not all of his colleagues on the bench, cannot be given high marks for his use of history in legal argument. His history, and his system of values, came from another, earlier United States. As legal historian James Willard Hurst has noted, American constitutional law began in a practical setting; the "Framers" now so revered

> fought over and adopted the first state constitutions and the Federal Constitution in an atmosphere of the utmost political realism. They saw they were dealing with the balance of power between interests, and they were frankly skeptical of the permanency of what they had done. The sanctity that came to surround the idea of constitutional principles was the growth of years and of many influences. It was fostered by the logic and prose of *The Federalist*, Marshall, and Webster; by the reverential histories of Fiske, Hildreth, and Bancroft; by the gathering of emotion and tradition about symbols by which generations fought their political battles.[59]

Less than a year after Black's death, Anthony Lewis of the New York *Times* published a revealing anecdote about the Justice. Black had read a book by one of his former law clerks, *The Greening of America* by Charles Reich. One passage in the book dealt with what Reich called "Consciousness I"—Reich's term for the traditional American view of society. Reich said that Consciousness I "believes that the American dream is still possible and that success is determined by character, morality, hard work and self-denial."

Justice Black wrote in the book's margin: "I still do."[60]

Dimensions of First Amendment "absolutes": a public interview

EDMOND N. CAHN

On April 14, 1962, the biennial convention of the American Jewish Congress, held in New York City, culminated with a banquet to honor Justice Hugo L. Black and to celebrate his completion of 25 years of service on the United States Supreme Court. Justice Black, who had consented to be interviewed at the banquet by Professor Edmond Cahn of New York University School of Law, expressly declined, in the interest of fair dealing with the public, to receive advance information of the nature or content of the questions. The following transcript, which was not submitted to Justice Black for correction, presents, first, Professor Cahn's Introduction and, second, the questions and answers of the Interview.

The introduction

CAHN: I have the function of revealing the secret of the greatness of this great jurist and American, and that is the theme of the remarks I am about to give you. Probably no word in the English language has been cheapened so much by indiscriminate use as the word "great." For this reason, I usually dole it out with a caution approaching miserliness. When, therefore, I tell you unreservedly that Hugo Black is a great judge, you may be certain that I intend to employ a full superlative and am prepared to give particulars.

Reprinted by permission from 37 (1962) N.Y.U.L. REV. 549.

EDMOND N. CAHN was professor of law at New York University from 1948 until his death in August, 1964, at age 58. He held A.B. and law degrees from Tulane University and was a practicing attorney in New York City from 1927 to 1950. Among his books are *Sense of Injustice, The Moral Decision,* and *The Predicament of Democratic Man.* Many of Cahn's speeches and writings were published in *Confronting Injustice: The Edmond Cahn Reader,* edited by his widow, Lenore, with a Foreword by Hugo L. Black.

There are two respects in which he ranks clearly among the foremost and best in our judicial annals. I refer, on the one hand, to his sense of injustice and deep concern for the oppressed and, on the other hand, to his professional skill and technical acumen. In each of these he is not surpassed by anyone. But I do not think it is they that make him unique.

What does make Hugo Black one of the few authentically great judges in the history of the American bench? I believe I have found the answer. He is great because he belongs to a certain select company of heroes who, at various crises in the destiny of our land, have created, nurtured, and preserved the essence of the American ideal. It is interesting to look back on our history and see the same phenomenon appearing time and time again. As a crisis approaches, some man, who might otherwise remain relatively unimportant and obscure, discovers a word, a phrase, a sentence in a basic text that history and legal tradition have placed in his hands. He reads, kindles, ignites, and bursts into flames of zeal and resolution. The torch of his spirit leads first a few, then the vast majority of his countrymen — like a pillar of cloud by day and a pillar of fire by night — toward freedom, equality, and social justice.

This is what happened at the very birth of our country. Our founding fathers and revolutionary heroes examined the charters that had been granted to the colonies by the Crown of England. There they read the King's solemn promise that they were to possess and enjoy the "rights of free-born Englishmen." This became their fundamental text. Beginning in the 1760's, their insistence on this promise inflamed them to rebellion, revolution, and national independence.

It was the same kind of inspiration that later gave us our national Bill of Rights. As you know, the original Constitution, drafted at the Philadelphia Convention, contained no bill of rights. The Federalists contended that though bills of rights might be necessary against emperors and kings, they were needless in a republican form of government. They argued that the people ought to repose trust in popularly chosen representatives. But Thomas Jefferson indignantly referred them to the words of the Declaration of Independence which announced that governments derived their just powers from the consent of the governed: words to be taken literally, absolutely, and without exception. He declared, "A bill of rights is what the people are entitled to against every government on earth." His demand succeeded, and a Bill of Rights was added to the Constitution. The Bill of Rights protects us today because Jefferson stood firm on the inspired text.

Then there is the next momentous episode, the series of court decisions in which Chief Justice John Marshall held that acts of legislation that violated the Constitution of the United States were null and void. What was the clause on which Marshall relied in asserting this awesome power for the Supreme Court? It was the provision, to which all Americans had pledged themselves, that the Constitution of the United States must be "the supreme law of the land."

President Lincoln also drew guidance and inspiration from a single basic text. He opposed the institution of slavery because, as he said, the country was dedicated to the proposition that "all men are created equal." Our own epoch has again demonstrated the explosive validity of that proposition.

What does one see happening in each of these historic instances? The majority of people, at least at the beginning, are wont to say that though the basic text may embody a fine ideal, it cannot work in practical application. They say it is utopian, visionary, unrealistic. They remark condescendingly that any experienced person would know better than to take it literally or absolutely. Accepting the words at face value would be naive, if not simple-minded. In 1776 Worldly Wisemen of this kind said that while the colonists might be entitled to the rights of Englishmen, they ought to put their trust in the King and Parliament and submit to a few convenient adjustments in the interest of imperial security. In 1788 they said that while a bill of rights might be desirable in theory, the people must learn to show confidence in their rulers. Why not leave it all to a majority, whether in Congress or in the Supreme Court? In every generation, the lesser minds, the half-hearted, the timorous, the trimmers talked this way, and so they always will. Ours would be a poor, undernourished, scorbutic freedom indeed if the great men of our history had not shown determination and valor, declaring, "Here are the words of our fundamental text. Here are the principles to which we are dedicated. Let us hold ourselves erect and walk in their light."

It is to this rare company of inspired leaders that Hugo Black belongs. He has been inflamed by the political and ethical ideals that Jefferson, Madison, and other libertarians of the 18th century prized the highest. Child of the 18th century Enlightenment and champion of the 20th century Enlightenment (that is how I think of him), he draws his highest inspiration from the First Amendment in the Bill of Rights, which forbids the Government to abridge our freedom of speech, freedom of press, freedom of religion, and freedom of association. Since his appointment to the bench in 1937, he has incessantly called on the state and federal governments to respect these freedoms literally, completely, and without exception. They are, to him, the meaning and inner purpose of the American saga.

Justice Black's major premise and point of departure is the text of the Constitution, which he emphasizes in all his decisions. He believes that the main purpose of the Founders, in drafting and adopting a written constitution, was to preserve their civil liberties and keep them intact. On their own behalf and on ours, they were not satisfied with a fragment or fraction of the basic freedoms; they wanted us to have the whole of them.

Some people display a curious set of values. If government employees were to come into their homes and start slicing off parts of the chairs, the tables and the television set, they would have no doubt that what was happening was absolutely wrong. Not relatively or debatably, but absolutely wrong. But when the same Government slices their civil liberties, slashes their basic freedoms or saws away at their elementary rights, these people can only comment that the case is too complicated for a doctrinaire judgment, that much can be said on both sides of the matter, and that in times like these the experts on sedition, subversion, and national security know what they are doing.

(Sometimes I wonder whether it is quite fair to assume that the experts know what they are doing; perhaps it would be more charitable to assume that they do not know.)

Justice Black's uncompromising zeal for freedom of speech, press, religion, and association might not have seemed so urgently necessary in previous periods of our history. In Lincoln's day, men naturally felt more excited about emancipation from slavery; in Franklin D. Roosevelt's day, more excited about food, employment, and social welfare. But today, when democracy stands here and on every continent presenting its case at the bar of destiny, our supreme need is to share Hugo Black's devotion to the First Amendment and his intrepid defense of the people's rights.

The American covenant was solemnly inscribed on the hearts of our ancestors and on the doorposts of our political history. It is a covenant of freedom, justice, and human dignity. Through keeping it in a quarter-century of judicial decisions, he has proved himself a great jurist. Through keeping it in all the transactions of our public life, we can prove ourselves a great and enlightened nation.

The interview

CAHN: Let me start by explaining the purpose of this interview. Two years ago, when you delivered your James Madison Lecture[1] at New York University, you declared your basic attitude toward our Bill of Rights. This was the positive side of your constitutional philosophy. Tonight I propose we bring out the other side, that is, your answers to the people who disagree with and criticize your principles. The questions I will ask, most of them at least, will be based on the criticisms. As you know, I consider your answers so convincing that I want the public to have them.

Suppose we start with one of the key sentences in your James Madison Lecture where you said, "It is my belief that there *are* 'absolutes' in our Bill of Rights, and that they were put there on purpose by men who knew what words meant and meant their prohibitions to be 'absolutes.' " Will you please explain your reasons for this.

JUSTICE BLACK: My first reason is that I believe the words do mean what they say. I have no reason to challenge the intelligence, integrity or honesty of the men who wrote the First Amendment. Among those I call the great men of the world are Thomas Jefferson, James Madison, and various others who participated in formulating the ideas behind the First Amendment for this country and in writing it.

I learned a long time ago that there are affirmative and negative words. The beginning of the First Amendment[2] is that "Congress shall make no law." I understand that it is rather old-fashioned and shows a slight naivete to say that "no law" means no law. It is one of the most amazing things about the ingeniousness of the times that strong arguments are made, which *almost* convince me, that it is very foolish of me to think "no law" means no law. But what it *says* is "Congress shall make no law respecting an establishment of religion," and so on.

I have to be honest about it. I confess not only that I think the Amendment means what it says but also that I may be slightly influenced by the fact that I do not think Congress *should* make any law with respect to these subjects. That has become a rather bad confession to make in these days, the confession that one is actually for something because he believes in it.

Then we move on, and it says "or prohibiting the free exercise thereof." I have not always exercised myself in regard to religion as much as I should, or perhaps as much as all of you have. Nevertheless, I want to be able to do it when I want to do it. I do not want anybody who is my servant, who is my agent, elected by me and others like me, to tell me that I can or cannot do it. Of course, some will remark that that is too simple on my part. To them, all this discussion of mine is too simple, because I come back to saying that these few plain words actually mean what they say, and I know of no college professor or law school professor, outside of my friend, Professor Cahn here, and a few others, who could not write one hundred pages to show that the Amendment does not mean what it says.

Then I move on to the words "abridging the freedom of speech or of the press." It *says* Congress shall make no law doing that. What it *means*— according to a current philosophy that I do not share — is that Congress shall be able to make just such a law unless we judges object too strongly. One of the statements of that philosophy is that if it shocks us too much, then they cannot do it. But when I get down to the really basic reason why I believe that "no law" means no law, I presume it could come to this, that I took an obligation to support and defend the Constitution as I understand it. And being a rather backward country fellow, I understand it to mean what the words say. Gesticulations apart, I know of no way in the world to communicate ideas except by words. And if I were to talk at great length on the subject, I would still be saying— although I understand that some people say that I just say it and do not believe it— that I believe when our Founding Fathers, with their wisdom and patriotism, wrote this Amendment, they knew what they were talking about. They knew what history was behind them and they wanted to ordain in this country that Congress, elected by the people, should not tell the people what religion they should have or what they should believe or say or publish, and that is about it. It says "no law," and that is what I believe it means.

CAHN: Some of your colleagues would say that it is better to interpret the Bill of Rights so as to permit Congress to take what it considers reasonable steps to preserve the security of the nation even at some sacrifice of freedom of speech and association. Otherwise what will happen to the nation and the Bill of Rights as well? What is your view of this?

JUSTICE BLACK: I fully agree with them that the country should protect itself. It should protect itself in peace and in war. It should do whatever is necessary to preserve itself. But the question is: preserve what? And how?

It is not very much trouble for a dictator to know how it is best to preserve his government. He wants to stay in power, and the best way to stay in power is to have plenty of force behind him. He cannot stay in power without force. He is afraid of too much talk; it is dangerous for him. And he should be afraid, because dictators do not have a way of contributing very greatly to the happiness, joy, contentment, and prosperity of the plain, everyday citizen. Their business is to protect themselves. Therefore, they need an army; they need to be able to stop people from talking; they need to have one religion, and that is the religion they promulgate. Frequently in the past it has been the worship of the dictator himself. To preserve a dictatorship, you must be able to stifle thought, imprison the human mind and intellect.

I want this Government to protect itself. If there is any man in the United States who owes a great deal to this Government, I am that man. Seventy years ago, when I was a boy, perhaps no one who knew me thought I would ever get beyond the confines of the small country county in which I was born. There was no reason for them to suspect that I would. But we had a free country and the way was open for me. The Government and the people of the United States have been good to me. Of course, I want this country to do what will preserve it. I want it to be preserved as the kind of Government it was intended to be. I would not desire to live at any place where my thoughts were under the suspicion of government and where my words could be censored by government, and where worship, whatever it was or wasn't, had to be determined by an officer of the government. That is not the kind of government I want preserved.

I agree with those who wrote our Constitution, that too much power in the hands of officials is a dangerous thing. What was government created for except to serve the people? Why was a Constitution written for the first time in this country except to limit the power of government and those who were selected to exercise it at the moment?

My answer to the statement that this Government should preserve itself is yes. The method I would adopt is different, however, from that of some other people. I think it can be preserved only by leaving people with the utmost freedom to think and to hope and to talk and to dream if they want to dream. I do not think this Government must look to force, stifling the minds and aspirations of the people. Yes, I believe in self-preservation, but I would preserve it as the founders said, by leaving people free. I think here, as in another time, it cannot live half slave and half free.

CAHN: I do not suppose that since the days of Socrates a questioner ever got answers that were so cooperative.

In order to preserve the guaranteed freedom of the press, are you willing to allow sensational newspaper reports about a crime and about police investigation of the crime to go so far that they prejudice and inflame a whole state and thus deprive the accused of his right to a fair jury?

JUSTICE BLACK: The question assumes in the first place that a whole state can be inflamed so that a fair trial is not possible. On most of these assumptions that are made with reference to the dangers of the spread of information, I perhaps diverge at a point from many of those who disagree with my views. I have again a kind of an old-fashioned trust in human beings. I learned it as a boy and have never wholly lost that faith.

I believe in trial by jury. Here again perhaps I am a literalist. I do not think that trial by jury is a perfect way of determining facts, of adjudicating guilt, or of adjudicating controversies. But I do not know of a better way. That is where I stand on that.

I do not think myself that anyone can say that there can be enough publicity completely to destroy the ideas of fairness in the minds of people, including the judges. One of the great things about trials by jury in criminal cases that have developed in this country—I refer to criminal cases because there is where most of the persecutions are found in connection with bringing charges against unpopular people or people in unpopular causes—we should not forget that if the jury happens to go wrong, the judge has a solemn duty in a criminal case not to let an unfair verdict stand. Also, in this country, an appellate court can hear the case.

I realize that we do not have cases now like they had when William Penn was tried for preaching on the streets of London. The jury which was called in to send him off quickly to jail refused to do so and suffered punishment from the judge because they would not convict a man for preaching on the streets. But that is a part of history, and it is but one of thousands of cases of the kind. Those people had publicity; that is why they would not convict William Penn. They knew, because the people had been talking, despite the fact that there was so much censorship then, that William Penn was being prosecuted largely because he was a dissenter from the orthodox views. So they stood up like men and would not convict. They lost their property, some of them their liberty. But they stood up like men.

I do not myself think that it is necessary to stifle the press in order to reach fair verdicts. Of course, we do not want juries to be influenced wrongfully. But with our system of education we should be in better condition than they were in those days in England, when they found that the jury was one of greatest steps on their way to freedom. As a matter of fact, Madison placed trial by jury along with freedom of the press and freedom of conscience as the three most highly cherished liberties of the American people in his time.

I do not withdraw my loyalty to the First Amendment or say that the press should be censored on the theory that in order to preserve fair trials it is necessary to try the people of the press in summary contempt proceedings and send them to jail for what they have published. I want both fair trials and freedom of the press. I grant that you cannot get everything you want perfectly, and you never will. But you won't do any good in this country, which aspires to freedom, by saying just give the courts a little more power, just a little more power to suppress the people and the press, and things will be all right. You just take a little chunk off here and a little bit there. I would not take it off anywhere. I believe that they meant what they said about freedom of the press just as they meant what they said about establishment of religion, and I would answer this question as I have answered the other one.

CAHN: Do you make an exception in freedom of speech and press for the law of defamation? That is, are you willing to allow people to sue for damages when they are subjected to libel or slander?

JUSTICE BLACK: My view of the First Amendment, as originally ratified, is that it said Congress should pass none of these kinds of laws. As written at that time, the Amendment applied only to Congress. I have no doubt myself that the provision, as written and adopted, intended that there should be no libel or defamation law in the United States under the United States Government, just absolutely none so far as I am concerned.

That is, no federal law. At that time—I will have to state this in order to let you know what I think about libel and defamation—people were afraid of the new Federal Government. I hope that they have not wholly lost that fear up to this time because, while government is a wonderful and an essential thing in order to have any kind of liberty, order, or peace, it has such power that people must always remember to check them here and balance them there and limit them here in order to see that you do not lose too much liberty in exchange for government. So I have no doubt about what the Amendment intended. As a matter of fact, shortly after the Constitution was written, a man named St. George Tucker, a great friend of Madison's, who served as one of the commissioners at the Annapolis Convention of 1786 which first attempted to fill the need for a national constitution, put out a revised edition of Blackstone. In it he explained what our Constitution meant with reference to freedom of speech and press. He said there was no doubt in his mind, as one of the earliest participants in the development of the Constitution, that it was intended that there should be no libel under the laws of the United States. Lawyers might profit from consulting Tucker's edition of Blackstone on that subject.

As far as public libel is concerned, or seditious libel, I have been very much disturbed sometimes to see that there is present an idea that because we have had the practice of suing individuals for libel, seditious libel still remains for the use of government in this country. Seditious libel, as it has been put into practice throughout the centuries, is nothing in the world except the prosecution of people who are on the wrong side politically; they have said something and their group has lost and they are prosecuted. Those of you who read the newspaper see that this is happening all over the world now, every week somewhere. Somebody gets out, somebody else gets in, they call a military court or a special commission, and they try him. When he gets through sometimes he is not living.

My belief is that the First Amendment was made applicable to the states by the Fourteenth. I do not hesitate, so far as my own view is concerned, as to what should be and what I hope will sometime be the constitutional doctrine that just as it was not intended to authorize damage suits for mere words as distinguished from conduct as far as the Federal Government is concerned, the same rule should apply to the states.

I realize that sometimes you have a libel suit that accomplishes some good. I practiced law twenty years. I was a pretty active trial lawyer. The biggest judgment I ever got for a libel was $300. I never took a case for political libel because I found out that Alabama juries, at least, do not believe in political libel suits and they just do not give verdicts. I knew of one verdict given against a big newspaper down there for $25,000, and the Supreme Court of Alabama reversed it. So even that one did not pan out very well.

I believe with Jefferson that it is time enough for government to step in to regulate people when they *do* something, not when they *say* something, and I do not believe myself that there is *any* halfway ground if you enforce the protections of the First Amendment.

CAHN: Would it be constitutional to prosecute someone who falsely shouted "fire" in a theater?

JUSTICE BLACK: I went to a theater last night with you. I have an idea if you and I had gotten up and marched around that theater, whether we said anything or not, we would have been arrested. Nobody has ever said that the First Amendment gives people a right to go anywhere in the world they want to go or say anything in the world they want to say. Buying the theater tickets did not buy the opportunity to make a speech there. We have a system of property in this country which is also protected by the Constitution. We have a system of property, which means that a man does not have a right to do anything he wants anywhere he wants to do it. For instance, I would feel a little badly if somebody were to try to come into my house and tell me that he had a constitutional right to come in there because he wanted to make a speech against the Supreme Court. I realize the freedom of people to make a speech against the Supreme Court, but I do not want him to make it in my house.

That is a wonderful aphorism about shouting "fire" in a crowded theater. But you do not have to shout "fire" to get arrested. If a person creates a disorder in a theater, they would get him there not because of *what* he hollered but because he *hollered*. They would get him not because of any views he had but because they thought he did not have any views that they wanted to hear there. That is the way I would answer: not because of what he shouted but because he shouted.

CAHN: Is there any kind of obscene material, whether defined as hardcore pornography or otherwise, the distribution and sale of which can be constitutionally restricted in any manner whatever, in your opinion?

JUSTICE BLACK: I will say it can in this country, because the courts have held that it can.

CAHN: Yes, but you won't get off so easily. I want to know what you think.

JUSTICE BLACK: My view is, without deviation, without exception, without any ifs, buts, or whereases, that freedom of speech means that you shall not do something to people either for the views they have or the views they express or the words they speak or write.

There is strong argument for the position taken by a man whom I admire very greatly, Dr. Meiklejohn, that the First Amendment really was intended to protect *political* speech, and I do think that was the basic purpose; that plus the fact that they wanted to protect *religious* speech. Those were the two main things they had in mind.

It is the law that there can be an arrest made for obscenity. It was the law in Rome that they could arrest people for obscenity after Augustus became Caesar. Tacitus says that then it became obscene to criticize the Emperor. It is not any trouble to establish a classification so that whatever it is that you do not want said is within that classification. So far as I am concerned, I do not believe there is any halfway ground for protecting freedom of speech and press. If you say it is half free, you can rest assured that it will not remain as much as half free. Madison explained that in his great Remonstrance when he said in effect, "If you make laws to force people to speak the words of Christianity, it won't be long until the same power will narrow the sole religion to the most powerful sect in it." I realize that there are dangers in freedom of speech, but I do not believe there are any halfway marks.

CAHN: Do you subscribe to the idea involved in the clear and present danger rule?

JUSTICE BLACK: I do not.

CAHN: By way of conclusion, Justice Black, would you kindly summarize what you consider the judge's role in cases arising under the First Amendment and the Bill of Rights?

JUSTICE BLACK: The Bill of Rights to me constitutes the differences between this country and many others. I will not attempt to say most others or nearly all others or all others. But I will say it constitutes the difference to me between a free country and a country that is not free.

My idea of the whole thing is this: There has been a lot of trouble in the world between people and government. The people were afraid of government; they had a right to be afraid. All over the world men had been destroyed — and when I say "government" I mean the individuals who actually happened to be in control of it at the moment, whether they were elected, whether they were appointed, whether they got there with the sword, however they got there — the people always had a lot of trouble because power is a heady thing, a dangerous thing. There have been very few individuals in the history of the world who could be trusted with complete, unadulterated, omnipotent power over their fellowmen.

Millions of people have died throughout the world because of the evils of their governments. Those days had not wholly passed when the Pilgrims came over to this country. Many of them had suffered personally. Some of them had their ears cut off. Many of them had been mutilated. Many of their ancestors had. Some of your ancestors came here to get away from persecution. Certainly, mine did.

There had been struggles throughout the ages to curb the dangerous power of governors. Rome had a sound government at one time. Those who study it carefully will find that, except for the slave class, they had, so far as most of the people were concerned, a good form of government. But it turned, and then they had Augustus and the other Caesars, and the Neros and the Caligulas and Tiberiuses.

One of the interesting things about Tiberius is that in all the history I have read he is about the only man of great prominence who ever defended informers. He made the statement that the informers were the guardians of Rome. Recently I have heard that said here once or twice.

When our ancestors came over here and started this country, they had some more persecutions of their own. It was not limited to any one religion. A lot of my Baptist brethren got into trouble; a lot of the Methodist brethren got in trouble; a lot of the Episcopal Church got in trouble, the Congregational Church—each of them in turn. A lot of the Catholics got in trouble. Whichever sect was in control in a state for a time, they would say that the others could not hold office, which is an easy way of getting rid of your adversaries if you can put it over. Even for half a century after the Constitution was adopted, some of the states barred the members of certain faiths from holding office.

Throughout all of this—as the Jewish people know as well as any people on earth—persecutions were abroad everywhere in the world. A man never knew, when he got home, whether his family would be there, and the family at home never knew whether the head of the family would get back. There was nothing strange about that when Hitler did it. It was simply a repetition of the course of history when people get too much power.

I like what the Jewish people did when they took what amounted to a written constitution. Some of the states did it before the time of the Federal Constitution; they adopted written constitutions. Why? Because they wanted to mark boundaries beyond which government could not go, stripping people of their liberty to think, to talk, to write, to work, to be happy.

So we have a written Constitution. What good is it? What good is it if, as some judges say, all it means is: "Government, you can still do this unless it is so bad that it shocks the conscience of the judges." It does not say that to me. We have certain provisions in the Constitution which say "Thou shalt not." They do not say, "You can do this unless it offends the sense of decency of the English-speaking world." They do not say that. They do not say, "You can go ahead and do this unless it is offensive to the universal sense of decency." If they did, they would say virtually nothing. There would be no definite, binding place, no specific prohibition, if that were all it said.

I believe with Locke in the system of checks and balances. I do not think that the Constitution leaves any one department of government free without there being a check on it somewhere. Of course, things are different in England; they do have unchecked powers, and they also have a very impressive history. But it was *not* the kind of history that suited the people that formed our Constitution. Madison said that explicitly when he offered the Bill of Rights to the Congress. Jefferson repeated it time and time again. Why was it not? Because it left Parliament with power to pass such laws as it saw fit to pass. It was not the kind of government they wanted. So we have a Bill of Rights. It is intended to see that a man cannot be jerked by the back of the neck by any government official; he cannot have his home invaded; he cannot be picked up legally and carried away because his views are not satisfactory to the majority, even if they are terrible views, however bad they may be. Our system of justice is based on the assumption that men can best work out their own opinions, and that they are not under the control of government. Of course, this is particularly true in the field of religion, because a man's religion is between himself and his Creator, not between himself and his government.

I am not going to say any more except this: I was asked a question about preserving this country. I confess I am a complete chauvinist. I think it is the greatest country in the world. I think it is the greatest because it has a Bill of Rights. I think it could be the worst if it did not have one. It does not take a nation long to degenerate. We saw, only a short time ago, a neighboring country where people were walking the streets in reasonable peace one day and within a month we saw them marched to the back of a wall to meet a firing squad without a trial.

I am a chauvinist because this country offers the greatest opportunities of any country in the world to people of every kind, of every type, of every race, of every origin, of every religion—without regard to wealth, without regard to poverty. It offers an opportunity to the child born today to be reared among his people by his people, to worship his God, whatever his God may be, or to refuse to worship anybody's God if that is his wish. It is a free country; it will remain free only, however, if we recognize that the boundaries of freedom are not so flexible; they are not made of mush. They say "Thou shalt not," and I think that is what they mean.

Now, I have read that every sophisticated person knows that you cannot have any absolute "thou shalt nots." But you know when I drive my car against a red light, I do not expect them to turn me loose if I can prove that though I was going across that red light, it was not offensive to the so-called "universal sense of decency." I have an idea there are some absolutes. I do not think I am far in that respect from the Holy Scriptures.

The Jewish people have had a glorious history. It is wonderful to think about the contributions that were made to the world from a small, remote area in the East. I have to admit that most of my ideas stem basically from there.

It is largely because of these same contributions that I am here tonight as a member of what I consider the greatest Court in the world. It is great because it is independent. If it were not independent, it would not be great. If all nine of those men came out each Monday morning like a phonograph speaking one voice, you could rest assured it would not be independent. But it does not come that way. I want to assure you that the fact that it does not come that way does not mean that there is not a good, sound, wholesome respect on the part of every justice for every other justice.

I do hope that this occasion may cause you to think a little more and study a little more about the Constitution, which is the source of your liberty; no, not the source—I will take that back—but a protection of your liberty. Yesterday a man sent me a copy of a recent speech entitled "Is the First Amendment Obsolete?" The conclusion of the writer, who is a distinguished law school dean, was that the Amendment no longer fits the times and that it needs to be modified to get away from its rigidity. The author contends that the thing to do is to take the term "due process of law" and measure everything by that standard, "due process of law" meaning that unless a law is so bad that it shocks the conscience of the Court, it cannot be unconstitutional. I do not wish to have to pass on the laws of this country according to the degree of shock I receive! Some people get shocked more readily than others at certain things. I get shocked pretty quickly, I confess, when I see—and this I say with trepidation because it is considered bad to admit it—but I do get shocked now and then when I see some gross injustice has been done, although I am solemnly informed that we do not sit to administer justice, we sit to administer law in the abstract.

I am for the First Amendment from the first word to the last. I believe it means what it says, and it says to me, "Government shall keep its hands off religion. Government shall not attempt to control the ideas a man has. Government shall not attempt to establish a religion of any kind. Government shall not abridge freedom of the press or speech. It shall let anybody talk in this country." I have never been shaken in the faith that the American people are the kind of people and have the kind of loyalty to their government that we need not fear the talk of Communists or of anybody else. Let them talk! In the American way, we will answer them.

Do you swear to tell the truth, the whole truth, and nothing but the truth, Justice Black? He does.

5

JOHN MEDELMAN

The corridors of the Supreme Court Building are ghostly white, and silent. Through them move black messengers—banker-suited, heavy-jowled, middle-aged—carrying abstract words about the abstracted cases of abstract plaintiffs. Court visitors, their gait touched by the rigor mortis of awe, herd past benevolently abstracted guards; the shuffling sounds of their feet dissolve instantly, absorbed by space. Closed oak doors appear now and then along the halls. Behind each is a justice—an aging man retired from violent law or politics and encouraged to write long notes on social problems.

Yet the judges who pore over old casebooks behind these doors have a potent and unlikely role. They are philosophers with power. They pronounce unappealable decisions on issues ranging from the water rights of states to the legality of singing on jail driveways. Their decisions have left one elderly man stranded—for the rest of his life, as far as they knew—on Ellis Island, have deprived Mormons of surplus wives, have obliged policemen to expand their classic, "You are under arrest," into a brief oration. Once appointed, the judges seem to shed the atherosclerosis brought on by previous work and occupy their chairs forever. Their present senior member is an eighty-two-year-old Alabaman named Hugo Black.

Reprinted by permission of Curtis Brown, Ltd. from ESQUIRE MAGAZINE, June 1968, with special assistance from the author to whom we are grateful.

JOHN MEDELMAN is assistant professor of English and journalism at the University of Wisconsin (Stout) where he teaches expository writing and mass communications. His fiction and articles, covering diverse themes and topics, have appeared in a number of magazines, including *Harper's*, *Playboy*, and *Esquire*.

Justice Black is a wiry, medium-sized man, bowed and constricted by the tight joints and shrunken tendons of his age. When he moves — with a surprisingly rapid gait, almost a trot — to his high-backed chair behind the bench, he seems frail, an afterimage of issues and fervors which have become history. His translucent white hair is nearly gone. His face, the skin thickened by eighty years of sun, has an expression fixed and blank, yet watchful. It is a judge's face, the face of a judge grown old under public scrutiny; it offers nothing, it implies nothing, and behind it any thoughts — or none — might be concealed.

Beneath this facial impassivity Justice Black sits badly. His foot taps; one hand punches the other; he tilts forward and then folds back; his body seems eager to rise and move something with his muscles.

Then, when he begins to speak, that bodily energy pours into his face; its warmth melts off twenty of his years. His blue eyes — his whole visage — gleam with a tough good humor which suddenly and openly transmits to a gleaming anger, or to scorn. His voice is studded with the idioms and elisions of the small-town South. Possessing no unusual volume or sharpness, it is a voice that carries. He developed it giving campaign speeches — folk orations from the beds of wagons. He was a Southern politician — and Southern politics, wrote a historian, was "an arena wherein one great champion confronted another or a dozen, and sought to outdo them in rhetoric and splendid gesturing. It swept back the loneliness of the land, it brought men together under torches, it filled them with the contagious power of the crowd."

The farmers spit tobacco and applauded when Black spoke; the papers wrote of his "silver tongue." Now the robed justices listen impassively to his words. But behind their dignity they are frequently caught up as intensely as the farmers were. Black has the unexpectedness of the self-educated man; each term he produces opinions to excite conservative, liberal, moderate, and zealot — and there is still much of the orator in his delivery. A friend remembers the "cold steel with which he impaled the Solicitor General" in his first *Dennis* Case dissent. (Eugene Dennis, a Communist, had been convicted of contempt of Congress by a jury which had among its members seven government employees. "Government employees," said Black, "have good reason to fear that an honest vote to acquit a Communist . . . might be considered a 'disloyal' act which could easily cost them their job. . . .")

Beyond the doors visiting law professors are wondering how to label Black for their classes.

"*Today our subject is 'Hugo LaFayette Black, Historic Liberal.'*"

"*But, sir, hasn't he come out for police eavesdropping and against sit-ins?*"

"*All right. Hugo Black, conservative in so many ways. . . .*"

"*But, sir, hasn't he fought McCarthyism and press censorship?*"

"*As a corporate colleague of mine says, 'Luckily Justice Black has kept away from important issues.' We will devote this hour to Corporate Mulctation and Tax Escapement.*"

But Black is not really so hard to label. He was born in Clay County,

Alabama—scrub cotton land still desolate from the Civil War. It was 1886; Scarlett O'Hara would have been forty-one years old; Confederate veterans were everywhere—fierce, resentful, ready to resume shooting. Black grew up in the psychology of the time. Men were to be courteous but unyielding; they were to act from principle, paying no more than polite attention to peer groups, interacting-others, or any of the yet-uninvented euphemisms for pressure. They were kind to women, horses, good darkies, children, and old friends. They were implacable to opponents—of whom they cultivated many.

Of the occupations, law and politics had the most prestige. Following the lead of an older brother, Black tried medicine for a time, going through two years of medical school in one. He enjoyed it, as he has enjoyed anything he's ever studied. But medicine was still a kind of trade, a place for kindhearted, unimaginative fellows not troubled by ambition; it was obviously too mild and morose a trade for him; he quit it for the two-year law course at the University of Alabama. "I won't say whether Black is the best student in the school or not," said one of his professors. "I will say he has learned the most. He had the most to learn."

Graduating, he chose law's classic form; dramatizing accidents and murders before provincial juries. There was none of the business lawyer's urbane squeezing rigmarole in his practice. He represented people, mostly piteous or vicious ones, elementally, in the traditional trial lawyer's fashion. Brimingham, where he now lived, was elemental; at the time it was said to have the highest homicide and venereal-disease rates in the nation. He remembers nostalgically the clash and action of its courts:

The time he tried the marshal of Pinckney City for the murder of Gus Goolsby . . .

The time he tried Louis Walton, a merchant of "birth and breeding," for shooting a business associate through the head. "Isn't it true, Mr. Walton," he demanded, "that the whole corporation was arranged to take out accident insurance on this young man? And that if the young man died, you got ninety-nine percent of the total insurance? And isn't it true you murdered this young man to get that insurance money?" "Answer him! Answer him!" cried the judge. Two jurymen voted for acquittal. Before the case could be retried, Walton bought accident insurance and dynamited himself to pieces in the men's room of a train.

The Bessemer torture-chamber case—in which Black announced to a Grand Jury, "We find that a uniform practice has been made of taking helpless prisoners, in the late hours of the night, into a secluded room . . . and there beat them until they were red with their own blood." These beatings "are dishonorable, tyrannical and despotic, and such rights must not be surrendered to any officer or set of officers, so long as human life is held sacred and human liberty and human safety of paramount importance."

While flies were struggling languidly on hot noonday flypaper and murderers were drowsing in the county jail, he had been reading Thomas Jefferson in his office.

The Bessemer case took place fifty-three years ago; Black's prose style has not changed. He works to keep it—the ring, the indignation, the simplistic philosophy. He and his clerks—recent law-school graduates—go over each new opinion when he has finished writing it in longhand on a pad. The clerks read and Black listens. The opinion must sound right, cracking along in a style that the layman "can understand and the press cannot misquote." "How long is that sentence?" he will ask. If it runs over four lines he may cut it. His style draws on the simple styles of tractists whose ears and tongues and noses were chopped off three hundred years ago. It resembles the style of *Pilgrim's Progress.* Could he title his opinions himself, instead of accepting the traditional *Smith v. Texas* or *Ex Parte Kawato,* Black might hand down opinions on *Preacher-Spread-the-Faith v. City of Destruction* and *Sheriff-Floy-a-Back v. Martyr-Poor-Man.* His Petitioner, like Bunyan's Christian, plods through a wrong-thinking, hostile world.

From the McCarthy era on he advised young lawyers their safest course was to "scrupulously avoid association with any organization that advocates anything at all somebody might possibly be against"; "but that is the present trend, not only in the legal profession but in almost every walk of life. Too many men are being driven to become government-fearing and time-serving because the government is being permitted to strike out at those who are fearless enough to think as they please and say what they think."

For himself, Black has generally spoken out. After World War I, when he began courting Josephine Foster (who would become his first wife) his prospective in-laws considered him "that young Bolshevik." At the height of his courtroom practice, when he was making $50,000 a year, he ran against four strong contenders for the U.S. Senate. "SENSATIONAL!" read one of his ads, "THE EVIL POWER SCHEME REVEALED! HEAR HUGO BLACK, CANDIDATE OF THE MASSES!"

He won and went to Washington, where he introduced a heretical bill to shorten the work week to thirty hours. (The bill, considerably modified, survives as today's minimum-wage law.) He conducted fiery investigations of the airline industry (and the support given it by the government) and the utilities trusts, once sending a Senate messenger to drag a utilities executive from his office without warning. After the captive had disappeared into the committee room, Black emerged and said cheerily to the assembled newsmen, "Come on in, boys, the show is about to begin."

Except for a few publications (*Labor,* the organ of the Railroad Brotherhoods; the *Madison* (Wisconsin) *Capital Times*) the press reviled him when Roosevelt appointed him to the Court. The *New York Herald Tribune* cried, "Senator Black's record at the bar offers not the slightest qualification for the high office to which the President would elevate him. His real qualification is plainly the intensity of New Deal support." The paper spluttered on, "Lack of judicial spirit," "scorn of constitutional restraints . . . the nomination is as menacing as it is unfit."

To the nation, Black seemed another of the Southern demagogues who now and then arrive in Washington from canebrake—politicians as mediocre as Willy Loman and as ambitious as Macbeth. When the newspapers revealed that he had been a member of the Ku Klux Klan, even Roosevelt seemed to waver in his support. Law professors saw themselves delivering lectures on decisions with words like "nigra" in the text. A Gallup poll showed that most Americans thought Black should resign—even before he had been fitted for his robes.

Max Isenbergh, a Harvard Law student who would become Black's third clerk, realized that Black had proved himself decent and able in the Senate. "And I thought he had explained his Klan connections adequately," says Isenbergh today. "To succeed professionally in the South, one joined the Klan. But I didn't see how this man from Clay County, Alabama—without any real education, with a country prosecutorship for a law background, would be able to cope with the issues decided by the Supreme Court." Isenbergh mentioned his misgiving to one of his professors, Felix Frankfurter, who said, "Wait, Black will become a great Justice."

Frankfurter was not saying this a few years later, when he and Black had begun to clash. But by that time others, including Isenbergh, were. Black has always seemed a few skirmishes ahead of popular opinion. In the days when the majesty of business was exceeded only by its rapacity, he was business's chief judicial critic. "Laws are made to protect the trusting as well as the suspicious," he wrote about a fraudulent advertising campaign. About an insurance company that was avoiding taxation as a "person," he wrote, "I do not believe the word 'person' in the Fourteenth Amendment includes corporations. . . .Corporations have neither race nor color."

When government informers were finding Communists in the psychology departments of girls' colleges and among young men taking bar examinations, Black wrote, "Anyone who takes a public position contrary to that being urged by the House Un-American Activities Committee should realize that he runs the risk of being subpoenaed to appear at a hearing in some far-off place, of being questioned with regard to every minute detail of his past life, of being asked to repeat all the gossip he may have heard about any of his friends and acquaintances, of being accused by the Committee of membership in the Communist Party, of being held up to the public as a subversive and a traitor, of being jailed for contempt if he refuses to cooperate with the Committee in its probe of his mind and associations, and of being branded by his neighbors, employer and erstwhile friends as a menace to society *regardless of the outcome of that hearing.*"

When pornographers were using dots and euphemisms to describe life's elemental pleasures, Black was pointing out that part of the First Amendment which reads, *"Congress shall make no law abridging freedom of the press."* I understand that it is rather old-fashioned and shows a slight naiveté to say that 'no law' means no law," he said in one of his rare public talks. "It is one of the most amazing things about the ingeniousness of the times that strong arguments are made, which almost convince me, that it is very foolish of me to think 'no law' means no law." In the Ginzburg, Mishkin, *Fanny Hill* pornography cases he refused to read the books in question, insisting that no matter what was in them, publishing them was legal.

When many of the first freedom marchers were still children, Black was writing his school desegregation decisions; these made him so unpopular in Alabama that his son, Hugo Jr., felt he had to leave the state. In the late forties, after a dinner in his honor followed by a Marian Anderson concert, an N.A.A.C.P. official said, "Negroes sought Mr. Justice Black's autograph more than that of any other person except Marian Anderson herself. People have an uncanny instinct for recognizing their friends."

Now Black is often voting with the conservative middle class—upholding the trespass convictions of demonstrators, upholding eavesdropping by local police, upholding the right of homeowners to refuse to sell to Negroes if they choose. Perhaps he is again moving out ahead of the press, the courts, the conventional politicians—determined this time to protect those middle-class people whose tax money, whose small-business profits and property values are being conscripted for the uplift of the looter classes. Perhaps he feels that the reforms of the New Deal have gone too far, that the torpid, the unlettered and unskilled crying, "Give to me!" have already taken power beyond their right or their capacity for use.

Black himself has no comment; on most touchy subjects he speaks only in his Court opinions. Particularly, he has no comments for reporters. He once wrote in a dissent: "Freedom to speak and write about public questions is as important to the life of our government as is the heart to the human body. In fact, this privilege is the heart of government. If that heart be weakened, the result is debilitation; if it be stilled, the result is death." But he was less ringing in a private letter: "Evidently my work on the Court has not been altogether bad, since I continually receive repeated criticisms from the daily press. My observation has been that when this occurs, a man is more than likely to be rendering a public service."

From his record it seems the private Hugo Black might be a cranky terror. But privately he is mild and cheery—"so free of malice it seems he must be shamming," says a legal scholar. He smiles readily, makes small jokes at parties, and whistles as he half-trots down the Supreme Court corridors in the morning. "He still walks faster than any other man I know," says one of his recent clerks. Arriving at work, he goes through his outer office, which is commanded by a sturdy, well-groomed secretary, whose imperiousness—thrusting through her charm—would halt a platoon of assassins at the door. This office is elegantly stark, with a bank of wood-grained metal filing cabinets against one wall. These hold opinions which, at the end of each term, go unceremoniously off to storage. "Bring up a container about the size of a whiskey box," said his secretary to a Court messenger last term. "We'll wrap up the Judge's opinions and get them out of the road."

The outer office is clearly set up for work; there are none of the framed degrees, letters, or miscellaneous honors which hang so frequently in such offices, to convince visitors of the grandeur of the man who occupies the inner.

In his inner office, which is comfortable and simple, Black gives a cheery good morning to his two clerks—unless, as is the case more often than not, he arrives at the office before they do.

"From the window of my apartment," says a former clerk, "I could see the Judge's office. But somehow, I rarely succeeded in arriving before he did. Facing him early in the morning through bleary eyes I could hear his whistle before I could focus on his features. No sooner had I settled down to work when his head would appear at my door asking me whether I needed help. . . . Noon found him standing in line with the rest of us at the Court cafeteria."

Black has a strong personal relationship with his clerks. Every so often he holds a banquet for them, past and present. "In a sense," he has told them, "you are all my sons." He has arranged their introductions to pretty girls, advised them to get married, advised them to have children, boarded them in his home, and taught them to play tennis.

Their chief function is to argue with him. He likes to talk before he starts to write. If he plans to vote for a petitioner he wants to hear every argument that can be offered for the opposition. He often takes a side and presents it so vigorously that his clerks, being lawyers, are forced into fierce rebuttal. They rarely know which side he is really on.

"One such situation that occurred during my first term with the Judge," recalls George L. Saunders Jr. in *Confessions of the Law Clerks*, a booklet of recollections fondly prepared for Justice Black's eightieth birthday, "arose when several other members of the Court sought to overrule *Wolf v. Colorado*, in which the Judge had specially concurred. [In *Wolf*, evidence had been obtained by "unreasonable search and seizure," and the Court had ruled that such evidence was admissible in state courts.] For weeks prior to the time an appropriate case arose, the Judge took every opportunity to attack the position of the dissenters in *Wolf*. Larry Wallace [Black's other clerk] and I dutifully rose to their defense and presented every argument we could think of on why the case was dead wrong, but, in all honesty, I must admit that the Judge devastated them all. The law, whether judged from the standpoint of history, language, or logic, was simply dead set against putting the exclusionary rule on a constitutional basis, and even I began to have my doubts.

"At that time Larry and I had no idea that an effort was being made to overrule *Wolf*, much less that the Judge, who seemed more unreconstructed than ever on the subject, was entertaining thoughts of joining in. When the truth emerged and the Judge wrote a brilliant, if not definitive, answer to his own misgivings, Larry and I were as shocked and surprised as Mr. Justice Frankfurter."

Black has read determinedly for forty years, making up for the fact that he went to a two-year law school instead of college. When Earl Warren began his first term on the Court, he came tentatively into Black's chambers asking if there were not some book on the writing of opinions. "There's one book," said Black, "which is by far better than anything published before or after: Aristotle's *Rhetoric*."

Half-suspecting he was being hazed, the new Chief Justice ordered the book from the Library of Congress, and studied it until midnight. As he read, recalls one of Black's former clerks, "the puzzled feeling of the afternoon turned to one of pleasure and admiration and this comforting feeling continued to grow throughout the year."

Black's clerks get discourses on the Constitution, on English history, on the history of civil rights, on the Greek wars, on Roman government, on seditious libel, on New Deal politics, on tyranny. These are not dispassionate lectures; they are statements of belief, with pointed references to the present. "Tiberius is about the only man of great prominence who ever defended informers. He made the statement that the informers were the guardians of Rome. Recently I have heard that said here once or twice."

One of his clerks, planning to practice a proper, icy sort of law, once scornfully rejected a petition against a railroad, made by the attorneys and parents of a three-year-old girl who had been killed after wandering onto the tracks. Since not giving railroad money to people killed by trains is a historic function of American courts, the clerk was right.

But Black gave him a little talk. He made the clerk see the girl as she tottered across the gravel of the roadbed, see her as she wandered with her infant's uncoordination between the rails, made him hear the hoot and rattle of the train, the hiss of its brakes, the splashing thud as she was hit. He made him consider the grieving parents, the courteously indifferent railroad officials, the cold railroad lawyers. He demonstrated why in the twenties the Alabama Supreme Court has said of awards he had wrung from juries for disabled workmen, "We cannot avoid the suspicion that the jury has been too liberal with the money of the defendant." He also said of another award, "Passion and not reason dictated the amount of the verdict." The latter, said the clerk, "would have had all but the most hardhearted juror reaching for his handkerchief." He thereafter tossed aside such petitions with solemnity rather than scorn.

The law, says Black, has been his life. He works almost constantly, with a capacity that is still prodigious. He works in his office, and late into the night at home. When the Court is recessed he calls in regularly, asking what new business has arrived. If the load is light he is obviously disappointed. When he has no work to do he is restless, does much abrupt walking back and forth. But he does have one institutionalized interruption. Each day he breaks off to play tennis on the clay court in his backyard. "His faith in the therapy of tennis is absolute," says a friend. A skipped tennis session or a session of clumsy play brings him closest to bad temper. When someone once told him he would die if he kept playing tennis he answered that, on the contrary, he would probably die if he did not.

His tennis court is surrounded on three sides by leafy vines; magnolias and fruit trees give off a warm and misty scent. He wears regulation tennis whites, which give him a dried, knobbed, but curiously imposing look. He suggests a pioneer tool — a hand ax or an adz. His usual opponents are his clerks, who, his friends half-seriously insist, are chosen for their ability to play tennis. Black and his wife fondly remember Drayton Nabers, a 1965 clerk who had been an intercollegiate tennis champion. "Now he gave us a good game," says Mrs. Black.

Black does not seem to move rapidly on the court, but he has a way of being there when the ball hits, and of whapping it with an intent easiness that sends it whirring and spinning across the net to some inconvenient corner. In

1966, he and Mrs. Black, a fortyish-looking beauty who was then sixty, beat Black's clerk and his wife, a pair of young and athletic Texans. Those players Black cannot beat he wears down. Thin and dry, he pumps on and on in the moist dense heat. Drayton Nabers recalls a summer game:

"One afternoon (quite possibly the hottest of all that summer) while the four of us were warming up, someone, I've forgotten whom but know it was not the Judge, mishit a ball, arching it high into the heavy vines that entangled the high fence on the south side of the court. The ball was replaced by another; the warm-up continued and soon the four contestants were hard at battle. The play was quite even. One set followed another, but neither side was willing to end the torture until the other was soundly thrashed. Finally, at the end of five sets, Mrs. Black who was no more pooped than Jim or I, but more honest, pleaded that she had 'had it' and could go no further. We all, totally exhausted, immediately sank into the court-side chairs. Suddenly 'we all' realized that we were only 'we three' and that the Judge had vanished. To me it was quite logical that someone whose age was thrice mine should seek the cover of a cool house after three hours of tennis in the most blistering of Washington's summer suns. But Mrs. Black, who was more accustomed to the Judge's habits than I, knew that he needed no rest and laughed aside my notions of the Judge's whereabouts. Shortly thereafter Jim and I pushed ourselves from our chairs and began looking for the mysteriously absent Judge to see if we could be of any help. We found him in an Atlas-like posture with a ten-foot aluminum ladder hoisted on his back. 'I'd better get that ball down out of the vines before it slips my mind,' he explained. At once I understood more clearly the work that would be expected of me that year."

Climbing a ladder to retrieve an old tennis ball is a characteristic act for Black. He is likely to examine a photograph frame carefully, to make sure it is worth the $2.50 it has cost, and to dicker firmly about the price of an air conditioner for his Buick. His consuming habits can be regarded either as upper-aristocratic, a status his Court post gives him—or as those of the son of a Reconstruction storekeeper, which he also is.

Justice Black lives just across the Potomac from Washington, in the slow, lovely, garden-sprinkled town of Alexandria, Virginia. His house is an antebellum sea captain's house. The neighborhood is part restored Williamsburg, part Catfish Row.

Inside, the house has the atmosphere of those rooms displayed intact at the Smithsonian Institution. It is meticulously clean, with pillars sweeping up beside doorways, with wide varnished stairs and polished floors. The rugs are lean and worn; the furniture is dark and old, giving off gleams like polished coal. Black's is a position beyond the most imaginative of American status scurryings; he values his possessions only for their utility, or because they have some personal meaning in his life. Old tennis balls are useful and worth the trouble of retrieving. He likes good cars and his black Buick pleases him. But the only thing differentiating it from the black Buicks of ten thousand small-town lawyers is the "United States Supreme Court, Official" card near the windshield. Said his first wife, who died in 1951, "All it takes to make Hugo happy are a good car and plenty of good steaks." But in his mind "good" is separated in a most un-American way from pretentious. One year he formed a car pool with one of his clerks, and commuted happily in a Volkswagen.

Outside his home office is a framed enlargement of a newspaper cartoon in which four Negroes, pressed upon by Hatreds, Persecutions, and Bigotry, are finding refuge in the Supreme Court.

In the office are his books— *The Lives of the Twelve Caesars, The Federalist,* Aristotle's *Rhetoric. . . .* They are annotated, marked; many of them are half-memorized.

In a downstairs bedroom, transported carefully from Clay County is the bed he was born in. *This* is the sort of possession that arouses his possessiveness. Among the trophies carried away from the family home by Black, his brothers, and his sisters, was a red, grey, and black coverlet, which his mother had made after spinning the wool herself. She had given it to Black's oldest brother, who had given it to his daughter. Recalls the daughter:

"Of course I brought the wool coverlet with me to Washington after Cutler and I were married. Uncle Hugo found that we had it and told Cutler his mother had given it to *him,* since he was her baby. He had a grey and blue wool coverlet, which he said was supposed to be Papa's, and the red, grey and black coverlet was his. When the argument came up about the two coverlets, I immediately wrote to Mama and Papa, and they wrote me that Uncle Hugo was mistaken; Grandma had definitely given the red, grey, and black wool coverlet to them as a wedding gift six weeks before they were married. Well, Uncle Hugo and I are both pretty stubborn people; so we both believed we were right in our beliefs about the two coverlets. Cutler was working in his office at that time; so Uncle Hugo would tell him not to come to work without the coverlet, and I would tell him not to come home without the coverlet. Poor Cutler! He would take the coverlet to work and bring it home each night. I believe he did this for a week or more. The outcome of the argument is that Cutler and I still have our beautiful red, grey, and black coverlet and I suppose Uncle Hugo still has his blue and grey. The matter hasn't been mentioned between us in years."

Black is a family-centered man; most of his family relationships are amiable and easy. A former secretary remembers one of her first days on his staff. Black and his clerk were drafting a last-minute dissent. "It was late afternoon. I was told we would probably work late that night. The Judge emphasized he wanted no interruptions. As the clock in the outer office shifted, the silence was broken only by the sound of the pencil sharpener as the Judge's supply was replenished. Suddenly the phone rang. I hurried to answer it, glad to have something useful to do. A feminine voice came over the wire. The caller insisted on speaking to Justice Black, saying with an air of dismissal, 'Oh, he always takes *my* calls.' With some hesitation and considerable misgiving I gingerly buzzed the Judge. Then I settled down to worry. A minute later the Judge's door flew open. He emerged on the double, heading straight for the coatrack.

" 'I've got to go pick up Jo-Jo,' he exclaimed with finality. 'She's stranded at school. She needs a ride home. We'll have to knock out that dissent in the morning.' "

Jo-Jo is his daughter, Josephine, now in her early thirties and married to a child psychiatrist. When she entered the Black home after her father's official eightieth-birthday party, the orchestra (made up of Max Isenbergh, a former clerk, and Thomas Corcoran, a lawyer who was once accused of writing Black's opinions) struck up a fast tune from the forties. Black strode to her, put out his arms, and the two of them began to jitterbug.

At such parties Black often sings in a clear, true voice; in his repertoire are obscure songs of the Civil War such as *I Am a Dirty Rebel.* "I don't think he remembers them from the war," says a friend.

Black's son Sterling is a lawyer and state legislator in New Mexico. The lawyer aspect of his son's work is fine with Black, who believes that lawyers are the clearest-thinking, the most socially aware and reform-minded men in their communities. But he did try to talk Sterling out of politics.

His other son, Hugo Jr., who left Birmingham because of the hostility to his father's desegregation decisions, is a lawyer in Miami. He shares his father's faith in exercise and runs a mile each day, trailed by his wife and children. (The Judge took to running himself recently, when a series of cataract operations forced him to give up tennis for a time. To keep fit during that period, he ran forty times each day between his bedroom and his den.)

Beneath Black's informal warmth is a dignity that never melts. He was always kind and reasonable with his children, and believes now that it would have been possible to bring them up without raising his voice. His authority was never in doubt. But there is some interference between the patriarch and the latest generation. One of his grandsons, a four-year-old, was sobbing beside a swimming pool one day, afraid to go in, outraged because his mother had left him to go in herself. Black took his hand and led him outside the pool enclosure. "Now you cry as much as you please," he said. "I never knew anyone to die of crying." They stood there, Black willing to stand all day if that would help give the child a sense of the uselessness of his noise — unwilling to engage in any act he would consider coddling.

One of the boy's aunts, melting under the howls, came out with a piece of candy and pressed it into his hand. As the noise stopped, Black gazed at the aunt for fully a minute, much as he sometimes gazes at the Solicitor General when he feels the government has won a case that will hurt the country. He then gave his judgment.

"Bribery!" he said, and turned away in outrage.

The period immediately following the death of his first wife was the lowest one in Black's life. "Silence became a part of this lonely man," says a niece. His children were gone, the McCarthy era was in full swing; many of his best opinions were dissents. And no matter how it rings, a dissent is only "an appeal to the brooding spirit of law, to the intelligence of a future day, when a later decision may possibly correct the error into which the dissenting judge believes the court to have been betrayed."

In 1957 he married Elizabeth DeMeritte, his former secretary, an

Alabaman about twenty years younger than himself. "I think my father spoke against Hugo when he was running for the Senate," she says, "but I'm not sure. I wasn't really old enough." The new Mrs. Black dutifully took up tennis; according to a recent clerk she is now a better player than the Judge. A vivacious woman, she seems to regard her husband with kind and friendly awe. "She realizes his place in history," says a family friend.

One night during his lonely years Black was awakened by a noise. His dog, Jigger, was trying to devour someone at a side window. Black could have called the police; he could have locked his bedroom door; he could have opened a window and roused the neighbors. In his late sixties, alone, the target of much pro-McCarthy paranoia, he stood up and roared with indignation, "Who is trying to break into my house?"

It was only his clerk, trying to get in without a key. Had it been an intruder Black probably would have joined the dog in the attack. When fighting is authorized, he fights; when it is not, he does something else. This has become his major recent philosophy: the Constitution does not give anyone the right to substitute force for law.

It might be his last important view. The one intruder he has been fighting all his life — with tennis, with other exercise — is now beneath his window. Before long it will get in. But then Justice Holmes was on the Court until he was ninety-one, and wrote some of his best opinions after he was eighty. Perhaps Black does have time to formulate some new theme. Not long ago his wife wrote to his niece: "Your Uncle Hugo is hard at work when he's not hard at play or hard at resting. Right now he has his yellow pad at his makeshift desk where he is writing. Every now and then I hear him erase and blow away the crumbs. But for the most part he just writes steadily away."

Black on Libel:
so firm . . . in his foundation

DAVID L. GREY

The fundamental assumptions underlying the law of libel are inconsistent with the fundamental assumptions of a system of free expression.[1]

Justice Hugo Black could not have agreed more with these words of First Amendment scholar Thomas I. Emerson. Emerson, of course, had listened to and pondered Black's words, such as these in the now classic 1962 interview with the Justice by Edmond Cahn: "I have no doubt there should be no libel or defamation law . . . just absolutely none,"[2] or these in his revealing and vehement dissent in the 1952 *Beauharnais v. Illinois* case:

I think the First Amendment, with the Fourteenth, "absolutely" forbids such laws [group libel] without any "ifs" or "buts" or "whereasas."[3]

As one might suspect, it was in the landmark 1964 *New York Times v. Sullivan* decision that Black probably made his position most clearly, pointedly, and with long-lasting impact. Many passages could be cited but the one that perhaps says the most was his:

This Nation, I suspect, can live in peace without libel suits based on public discussion of public affairs and public officials. But I doubt that a

DAVID L. GREY is professor of journalism at San José State University. He holds a Ph.D. in mass communication from the University of Minnesota, with a political science minor. He has specialized in research and teaching in mass media and society, mass communication law, reporting of public affairs, and the applications of communication theory and social science research methods to newswriting and reporting. Among published writings are books on *The Supreme Court and the News Media*, *The Writing Process*, and, as coeditor, *Handbook of Reporting Methods*.

country can live in freedom where its people can be made to suffer physically or financially for criticizing their government, its actions or its officials.[4]

Ten years later, if alive, Black would certainly have been unhappy with most of the language of the 5 to 4 decision (and division) of the 1974 Court in *Gertz v. Robert Welch, Inc.,* that ruled private citizens should be given greater leeway in libel suits.

An essay on Justice Black on libel might, at first glance, end here. What more is there to say? His views were so strong and clear that seemingly little can be added.

But to study Justice Black on libel turns out not to be so simple. A closer look at the cases in which the Justice discussed libel is only a beginning; in many ways, libel laws can be best understood through the words, beliefs, and convictions of the Justice.

Certainly Black's influence in the only recently evolved libel decisions of the U.S. Supreme Court (since the 1964 *Times* case) is one of his major contributions to United States constitutional law. His thoughts in such cases reveal much of his personality and background and philosophy—from his fighting instincts and commitment to the "little man" to his pragmatic and ideological resistance to big money lawsuits and the powers of big government. Black's antilibel arguments, so inflexible and often repetitious, help reveal why he revered the press so highly. Right or wrong, it was obviously Black's belief that the press had to be free from all libel constraints in order to do its job as watchdog and critic of those in positions of public power who also have the opportunity to abuse their power.

Trying to understand Justice Black's legal reasoning and thinking, however, is much more complicated. It merits full critical dissection in his spirit of vigorous debate.

I

Unlike many areas of law, libel is relatively simple to define, if not always easy to resolve in court. It is written defamation, an attack upon one's reputation and good name. Libelous words tend to diminish the esteem, confidence, and goodwill with which others view you. Libel laws are designed to protect against personal injury, against the effects of an assault of words.[5] These words can, at times, expose a person to hatred, ridicule, contempt, loss of personal or professional standing. Libel laws are intended to protect the individual against *unfair* damage to reputation where, for instance, there might be outright lying, maliciousness, reckless disregard for the truth.

Civil libel is designed to protect the individual's interests. (Criminal libel, infrequently used in court today, is designed to protect society's interests; it falls closer to contempt and other judicial or statutory actions, such as sedition, that can be used in the name of protecting the "dignity and obligations" of the court or of the state.) As Emerson pointed out, libel laws have their historical roots in protections of individuals or governments against *unfair* criticism, attack, or whatever the damage of words may prove to be.[6]

Slander is oral or spoken defamation; it tends to be less serious, and damages are often harder to prove than in libel cases because of the absence of documents providing firm evidence of causality, which are more likely to be available in libel disputes.[7]

A closely related question is the definitional difference between libel and privacy. Constitutional law scholar Milton Konvitz has offered one of the better clarifications: "Libel and slander differ from violation of the right of privacy in that privacy protects a person in his spiritual interests—the publication of his private affairs hurts him in his estimation of himself, in his own feelings, while libel or slander hurts him in the estimation of his fellows. . . ."[8]

But as Emerson stressed, libel and privacy decisions cannot be much separated; many of the issues involved in libel cases were also discussed in *Time, Inc. v. Hill,* 1967, the main privacy case of the Supreme Court in the still muddied field of privacy law.[9]

Libel laws sometimes can be best understood in the reasonings against them. Justices Black and William Brennan have articulated the fuller and more complex antilibel issues, which, in turn, open up many of the prolibel protection issues. It is at this point that Black's views merit detailed attention as one of the best means of determining why and how libel law has evolved to the point where the news media are mostly unrestricted and confident when taken to court in libel suits by *public officials* and *public figures.*

II

Black's attachment to the U.S. Constitution has been a "passionate one . . . [it is] his guide, his compass, his sheet, his anchor."[10] These words by former Chief Justice Earl Warren summarize much of Black's feelings about the First Amendment and especially its protection of freedom of speech, press, and religion. (Assembly did not get Black's devoted attention, and in his later years he wavered when more than just speech was involved, in the so-called speech-plus cases.)

Black's philosophy, according to scholar Charles Reich, was that the spirit of the Constitution was the "spirit of limitation" on government.[11] Or as interpreted by former Black law clerk John McNulty, the Justice believed that the Bill of Rights was meant to give freedom to the individual and that the government has no power to intrude into this freedom until the written Constitution is amended.[12]

Black (and Justice William Douglas) clearly gave the First Amendment a most preferred position. It is not inappropriate to say they stood in awe of the Bill of Rights.[13]

But Black did more than just "stand." As Reich observed, Black "was one of the first to see the Bill of Rights issues of his time, and he was a pioneer in demanding that the court deal with them."[14]

Reich's view is that the Court's concern for liberty owes much to the Justice who was willing to take on constitutional issues and to dissent and comment in denials of certiorari by the Court.[15] Even then it was not until the 1964 *Times* case that libel was advanced to a major constitutional question from a mere tort (basically a civil dispute between individuals). There have been many libel cases but only a very few have ever reached the U.S. Supreme Court. The most "important" of these were clustered in the 1964–1967 period. Some refinements and modifications have been made since—in the 1970s during Black's twilight years and since his death.

Black was a self-proclaimed "chauvinist" about the greatness of the Supreme Court and its independence.[16] As a serious lover of freedom, like Justice Felix Frankfurter, he could become doctrinaire at times in his defense of liberty and such institutions as the press.[17] In fact, Black seemed convinced it was a sign of weakness to control speech.[18] The Bill of Rights was meant not to protect the freedom of silence (as Frankfurter argued) but, instead, was to permit freedom of thought.[19] And Black believed every person had a right to express his or her own thoughts.

The philosophy most often identified with Black is his own statement that "I believe words to mean what they say—so that in the First Amendment no infringement of free speech means *exactly* that."[20] This proposition has been debated among legal scholars and has been usually labeled as either "absolutism" or "literalism." Black often used the word "absolute" or implied it; in many ways, however, "literalism" may be a better way to explain his thinking. (Still other labels might be "rigidness" or "inflexibility" or whatever best fits one's ideological bias.)

But these labels tend to oversimplify Black's position, especially in libel cases. Other forces may have been as much at work in his mind or, when accumulated, may have been of equal significance.

Black had his own system of weighing and balancing, despite his protests to the contrary.[21] Clearly, when the dangers involved loss of free press or speech, he leaned far toward the First Amendment.

Black was roundly critical of case-by-case adjudication, particularly when First Amendment interests were involved; stopgap measures were not enough, either, when fundamental liberties were involved.[22]

Even more, he was opposed to the kinds of punishments levied in libel suits; he did not see how any "injury to reputation" could merit large sums of judgments or "reward." Here Black might have agreed with a part of the majority holding of the Court in *Gertz v. Robert Welch, Inc.*, 1974, which, while giving more libel recourse to private citizens, constrained most libel judgments to actual or proven compensatory damages and strongly discouraged possible punitive damages. But, in general, Black would have dismissed the majority holding.[23]

Black was also flatly unsympathetic to governmental officials' cries of being hurt by words critical of their performance of public duties. He certainly would not have supported any right-of-reply legislation for politicians or court decisions favoring "forced access" to newspaper columns.[24]

An important fact that many overlook is that Black's views on free speech grew slowly; some of his most important positions sometimes have been misstated or even overlooked.[25] For instance, in the 1962 Cahn interview is a revealing but seldom noted comment by the Justice: "Buying the theater tickets did not buy the opportunity to make a speech there." The point, Black said, is that constraint of speech could be possible in such a situation not because of "what [was] shouted but because [it was] shouted."[26] In other words, there were appropriate times and places for speech. And, as one might interpret Black, what better place than in the press?

Once evolved, Black's views of libel never wavered. He stood firm, it seems now, because he felt so strongly about the appropriateness of the forum. Newspapers and other media offered, for good and bad, the marketplace for ideas. And, as Black would remind us, we had better remember libel's history. He had read widely within parts of history and often referred to such periods as 1750–1800; thus came forth views such as this in the Cahn interview:

> Seditious libel, as it has been put into practice throughout the centuries, is nothing in the world except the prosecution of people who are on the wrong side politically; they have said something and the group has lost and they are prosecuted. . . .
>
> There had been struggles throughout the ages to curb the dangerous powers of governors. . . .
>
> Government cannot control the individual. He cannot be jerked by the back of the neck by a government official. . . .[27]

Both "outdated" seditious and "contemporary" civil libels have been ways to do this; therefore, Black argued that a vigorous free press would be one means for controlling power and its potential abuses at the hands of the governors. Here entered Black's belief in the basic goodness and will of the common people and in the checks of public debate and knowledge about the governors. There is nothing special in this observation, but the roots of such thinking go much to the man, his background, his personality, his more-than-legal philosophies about life. In libel, these heritages became basic to the way he thought and decided issues.

III

"No law" means no law, Justice Black frequently said, and he sometimes added such a phrase as "being a rather backyard country fellow, I understand it to mean what the words say."[28]

Here is the fighter, the advocate, the self-educated Southerner mixing charm, directness, ambition, and political savvy.[29] High on his list of convictions was a mistrust of many judges; he had seen them at work during his early Alabama days as an attorney.[30]

Black "passes a major test for a great judge on free speech issues. He displays the requisite passion." Black was a man of "intense energies, zeal to reform and intense moral commitment." These evaluations from legal scholars Harry Kalven, Jr., and Paul Freund are not shared by all, but they tell much about the man and his positions on libel.[31]

So does his pragmatic side.[32] For example, in his dissent in the 1970 *Ginzburg v. Goldwater* denial of certiorari by the Court, Black stressed that it was "incomprehensible" to think of $75,000 in damages when no provable harm could be demonstrated.[33] The money issue mattered very much, especially in *New York Times v. Sullivan*. Six times in his concurring opinion in that case he mentioned the size of the judgment: $500,000. His very first words were, "I concur in reversing this half-million-dollar judgment. . . ."[34]

Equally helpful in understanding the man is a look at his relative lack of interest in privacy issues; this position has puzzled some students of the Court but on balance it should not be considered strange.[35] Public officials, as Black saw them, should not have the chance to hide behind cloaks of privacy; and even the ordinary citizen should not be worried about it—in large part, because "a man's private life is a spiritual asset."[36]

And Black believed in the human spirit. He had been raised in rural Alabama where there were few secrets and even fewer places to hide. If a man had been libeled or had his privacy invaded, he could simply speak up and fight back. Here Black seemed to be deliberately confronting Justice Frankfurter and the idea that either privacy or libel protections mattered much. "Sticks and stones may break my bones but words can never hurt me" seemed to be an operating philosophy for the Justice, and it seemed to be based as much on personal convictions as on legal or constitutional reasoning.

Certainly these patterns in Black's thinking help explain why he was so firm and unbending on libel issues and yet why in his later years he would not protect in the same way many speech-plus and symbolic speech issues or activities. There could be real harm when more than words were used. And, certainly, the cautious Southerner at times believed there were right places and times for speech. Libel? It was, for him, little or no problem.

Several other personal factors are also important in understanding Black's thinking about libel. He worked on words, often for dramatic effect; at times his opinions contained more repetition and themes-and-variations than new ideas.[37] He became, especially in his later years, an impatient and restless "winner," as in the *New York Times* ruling. He fought in libel as well as in other areas with many concurring and dissenting opinions.[38] As early as the mid-1950s and the McCarthy and post-Rosenbergs era, there were many signs of going-it-alone (with, of course, Justice Douglas frequently joining in). And there were signs of alienation and bitterness over many civil rights issues.[39] Part of the struggle was clearly won during the years of the Court under Chief Justice Warren. But still there was Black the battler, fighting brethren such as Frankfurter and remembering the period of the Truman Court and the Era of Fear.[40]

IV

Not all of Justice Black's thinking on libel shows up in his libel opinions. In fact, some of Black's strongest views on libel can be found in other First Amendment commentaries.

Several are worth brief but pointed attention before moving on to the decisions of the Court directly related to libel. All are in Black's words:

> It is a prized American privilege to speak one's mind, although not always with perfect good taste on all public institutions. *Bridges v. California,* 314 U.S. 252, 270 (1941).

> There are grim reminders all around this world that the distance between individual liberty and firing squads is not always as far as it seems. *Braden v. U.S.,* 365 U.S. 431, 446-447 (1961).

> In my view it is unfortunate that some of my Brethren are apparently willing to hold that the publication of news may sometimes be enjoined. Such a holding could make a shambles of the First Amendment. "Pentagon Papers" decision, *New York Times v. U.S.,* 403 U.S. 713, 715 (1971).

These do not reflect any wavering in Black's position on the press. It is important, however, that in such cases as *Estes* (television in the courtroom) and *Sheppard* (fair trial-free press) Black thought of the press as mostly the print media.[41] To him, radio and television seemed to be latter-day categories of print. Protection for them was less clear-cut. Certainly his arguments in many of most of the administrative law decisions involving the media and such agencies as the Federal Trade Commission and the Federal Communications Commission indicate that he was able to recognize—in his own mind at least—degrees of speech involved in the issues.

His views on religious freedom and obscenity issues hardly wavered; but (in his later years) he defined freedom of assembly more cautiously. Black's reasoning was relatively simple and maybe even simplistic: pure cases of freedom of speech and press were different and merited full protection. While there is debate about his consistency in certain areas of civil liberties, Black's stance on libel stood so firm that it could be called inflexible. But in his attitudes toward libel, this "inflexibility" could be interpreted as positive—a compliment to the Justice by his followers and an admission by his detractors of his sincere conviction, at least. Even those who disagreed with Black's extreme position on libel had to respect his vigor and ponder his words carefully.[42]

V

Black's dissent in *Beauharnais v. Illinois* in 1952 is probably his most revealing commentary — not only because it set (forever?) the stage for his later views in *New York Times v. Sullivan* but also because it revealed so early his position.

With Douglas concurring, Black simply stated that group libel laws (now, for all practical purposes, extinct) were a constant threat to freedom of the press. He said many things in the 1952 case with vigor and apparent great clarity:

> My own belief is that no legislature is charged with the duty or vested with the power to decide what public issues Americans can discuss. I reject the holding that either state or nation can punish people for having their say in matters of public concern.[43]

> Unless I misread history the majority is giving libel a more expansive scope and more respectable status than it was ever accorded even in the Star Chamber. . . . [The] Act sets up a system of state censorship which is at war with the kind of free government envisioned by those who forced adoption of our Bill of Rights. . . .[44]

Black stressed that he found the racist "fighting words" of Beauharnais to be offensive personally to him yet he held fast to the view that Beauharnais had a right to speak up, even if Negroes were to be defamed as "niggers." Black was very sensitive to the explosive issues his position, had he won, would have permitted. He seemed to sense the racial, social, and political conflicts ahead:

> The motives behind the state law may have been to do good. But the same can be said about most laws making opinions punishable as crimes. . . .
> Ironically enough, Beauharnais, convicted of crime in Chicago, would probably be given a hero's reception in many other localities, if not in some parts of Chicago itself. Moreover, the same kind of law that makes Beauharnais a criminal for advocating segregation in Illinois can be utilized to send people to jail in other states for advocating equality and nonsegregation. . . . What Beauharnais said in his leaflet is mild compared with usual arguments on both sides of racial controversies.[45]

As a final warning and near-prophecy of things to come, Black ended with his often-used touch of irony and the dramatic:

> If there be minority groups who hail this holding as their victory, they might consider the possible relevancy of this ancient remark: "Another such victory and I am undone."[46]

The leap from criminal group libel in 1952 to the all-important civil libel decisions in *New York Times v. Sullivan* in 1964 and beyond is not easy to explain (it certainly stretches outside the boundaries of this essay). There were many libel cases in the intervening years but nothing reached the Court for commentary until 1964. Either the Court was uninterested in libel or was so unsure of itself that it could offer little or no guidance. It may simply have wanted to wait for the "right" case. Whatever the reasoning behind the silence, the *Times* case did provide the opportunity for a swift, bold, suddenly expanded ruling — greatly increasing press protection against many libel suits or judgments. Whether the Supreme Court had been waiting for the clear-cut and relatively easy issue in this case is not certain, but the *Times* decision obviously was able to start the fast-moving expansion of protection for the press against libel constraints.

Black, in his theme-and-variation style, contributed his own extra punches to the decision in his concurring opinion:

> An unconditional right to say what one pleases about public affairs is what I consider to be the minimum guarantee of the First Amendment.[47]

> [S]tate libel laws threaten the very existence of an American press virile enough to publish unpopular views on public affairs and bold enough to criticize the conduct of public officials.[48]

But then Black went after his brethren in the majority opinion:

> I regret that the Court has stopped short of this holding indispensable to preserve our free press from destruction.[49]

Black concurred in reversing the decision against the *New York Times* but not in sending the case back to a lower court; although not explicitly stated here, the fighting Justice often saw such remanding as a form of "cop out" when First Amendment issues were involved.[50] The Court should not have merely "delimited"; the state's power to award damages to public officials against critics of their official conduct should be completely prohibited.[51]

> "Malice," even as defined by the Court, is an elusive, abstract concept, hard to prove and hard to disprove. The requirement that malice be proved provides at best an evanescent protection for the right critically to discuss public affairs and certainly does not measure up to the sturdy safeguard embodied in the First Amendment. Unlike the Court, therefore, I vote to reverse exclusively on the ground that the Times and the individual defendants had an absolute, unconditional, constitutional right to publish in the Times advertisement their criticisms of Montgomery [Alabama] agencies and officials.[52]

Black's assault on the so-called *Sullivan* rule had begun. In the *Time, Inc., v. Hill* privacy decision, the Justice vehemently expressed unhappiness with the *Times* holding:

The words "malicious" and particularly "reckless disregard" can never serve as effective substitutes for the First Amendment words.[53]

In the criminal libel case of *Garrison v. Louisiana,* 1964, he had said even more along the same sharp lines:

> Indeed, "malicious," "seditious," and other such evil-sounding words often have been involved to punish people for expressing their views on public affairs. Fining men or sending them to jail for criticizing public officials not only jeopardizes the free, open discussion which our Constitution guarantees, but can wholly stifle it.[54]

The *Garrison* decision did dispel most of any doubts left in the *Times* decision that criminal libel laws might be outside First Amendment protections, but Black, as the "restless winner," clearly was accelerating his criticism.

Actual malice is "small protection," he said in *Rosenblatt v. Baer,* 1966. It was here that Justice Douglas, in particular, stressed that the question is not whether a public official was involved but whether there was a public issue. Black and Douglas were trying to accelerate their drive to extend the *Times* holding; *Rosenblatt v. Baer* also gave them the chance to protest the "impossible situation" of case-by-case review of libel decisions. This pragmatic approach (somewhat parallel to arguments that pushed the Earl Warren Court ahead in right-to-counsel cases) seemed to dominate as libel issues continued to come before the Court — at least in Black's time.[55]

In *Rosenblatt v. Baer* and in his dissent over denial of certiorari in *Ginzburg v. Goldwater,* Black started calling the *Times* (or so-called Sullivan) rules "totally inadequate." His bitterness started to show even more in the force of his words: "[T]he First Amendment bars in absolute, unequivocal terms any abridgment by the Government of freedom of speech and press."[56]

Even though professing to be against any balancing approach in the First Amendment, Black stressed that the "grave dangers" to free speech and press seems to more than outweigh any resulting gains from libel actions. Each person, Black (and Douglas) said, has "the unconditional right to print what he pleases about public affairs."[57]

The Court's denial of certiorari was ominous and repressive, Black stressed, in what also turned out to be an almost eerie, forward-looking wisdom in early 1970:

> The public has an unqualified right to have the character and fitness of anyone who aspires to the Presidency held up for the closest

scrutiny. Extravagant, reckless statements and even claims which may not be true seem to be an inevitable and perhaps essential part of the process by which the voting public informs itself of the qualities of a man who would be President.[58]

In this case, it was Senator Barry Goldwater who won in his suit against publisher Ralph Ginzburg and his *Fact* magazine. There is absolutely no evidence to suggest that Justice Black, had he been alive, would have felt differently about a Thomas Eagleton for the vice-presidency in the 1972 Democratic election struggle, or a Richard Nixon during the era of Watergate, 1972-1974, or an Edward Kennedy as a Democratic frontrunner for 1976 or 1980 or 1984. In fact, the feisty Justice might even have turned his pages back to his 1970 *Goldwater* dissent and said even more vigorously that he had told us so and we should have listened more carefully.

The major extension of the *Times* decision came, of course, in 1967 in the companion cases of *Curtis Publishing Co. v. Butts* and *Associated Press v. Walker*. Most directly put, in the spirit of Black and Douglas, *public officials* were not the only group left with little libel protection; *public figures* were to be added, too.[59]

The cases were decided together but had different outcomes because the AP was found not guilty by the Court of reckless disregard for the truth while Curtis was found guilty of actual malice. Black was very unhappy with what he saw as the seeming contradictions of the Court affirming one judgment and not another:

> I think it is time for this Court to abandon *New York Times v. Sullivan* and adopt the rule to the effect that the First Amendment was intended to leave the press free from the harassment of libel judgments.[60]

Black called the *Times* decision guidelines "wholly inadequate":[61]

> These cases illustrate, I think, the accuracy of my prior prediction that the *New York Times* constitutional rule concerning libel is wholly inadequate to save the press from being destroyed by libel judgments. . . .
> The main reason for this quite contradictory action [of upholding the AP but not the *Saturday Evening Post*], so far as I can determine, is that the Court looks at the facts in both cases as though it were a jury. . . . That seems a strange way to erect a constitutional standard. . . .

Black then attacked the case-by-case approach with his to-be-expected gusto:

> If this precedent is followed, it means that we must in all libel cases hereafter weigh the facts and hold that all papers and magazines guilty of gross writing or reporting are constitutionally liable, while they are not if the quality of the reporting is approved by a majority of us. In the final analysis, what we do in these circumstances is review the factual questions

in cases decided by juries — a review which is a flat violation of the Seventh Amendment (". . . no fact tried by a jury shall be otherwise re-examined in any Court").[62]

And finally, the Justice took an almost wild swipe at his colleagues:

> It strikes me that the Court is getting itself in the same quagmire in the field of libel in which it is now helplessly struggling in the field of obscenity.[63]

These extensive quotings are deliberate and important because they were the Justice's last major attacks on libel laws. He and Justice Douglas had maintained their consistency by dissenting in *Butts* and had added some biting words and warnings of their own. But except perhaps for his 1970 *Goldwater* denial-of-certiorari dissent, Black added little after these 1967 cases — in part because the libel issues seemed to have slowed down both in numbers and intensity during his last years on the bench and because the Justice himself was apparently starting his own slowing-down period.[64]

In *St. Amant v. Thompson*, 1968, for example, the Court (with only Justice Fortas dissenting) quickly and simply applied the actual malice rule of the *Times* case.[65]

In the 1971 case of *Rosenbloom v. Metromedia,* Justice Black concurred in the judgment (to be overturned barely in the 1974 *Gertz* decision) that almost any public figure or any issue of public interest deserved immunity from libel laws.[66] But he relied heavily on Justice Douglas' comments in the 1966 case of *Rosenblatt v. Baer.*[67]

By 1971 and beyond, Black had won most of his battle. The exceptions to total victory were, obviously, the continuing use of the *Times* standard and the realization that some of his final "extremist" words would never be fully accepted by historians of the Court nor future Courts (as, again, witnessed by the complex 1974 *Gertz* case). As illustration, in concurring in *Rosenbloom* in 1971, Black had gone all the way:

> The First Amendment does not permit the recovery of libel judgments against news media even when statements are broadcast with knowledge they are false.[68]

Black may some day turn out to be right in the sweep of his words, but as in so many First Amendment cases in his later years he was on the fringe with only Justice Douglas close by and only Justice Brennan consistently within what might be considered "calling distance."

VI

The Justice had achieved a major but only partial victory. By his standards he was not satisfied; the Court should have gone much further.

Through his belief in "breathing space" for both the courts and the press, Black had helped to alter the Supreme Court's views of libel; he had probably been the first, or certainly among the early few, to equate libel actions with the First Amendment. With the help of Chief Justice Warren and Justices Douglas and Brennan especially, he had helped extend the *Times* malice standard far beyond public officials — to public figures and sometimes public issues. He had fought and mostly succeeded in working out libel rules which were susceptible to effective and relatively clear administration.[69]

Yet Black also participated in the sharp divisions of the Court over libel (and other issues). His strong stance, with frequent dissents and concurring opinions, written often in seeming frustration, helped create what might be called the "balancing wars" of the Warren and Burger Courts of the 1960s and early 1970s; Black had to share some of the responsibility for the infighting and splintering of the Court.[70] His struggles with Frankfurter and at times with all his brethren (although seldom with Douglas) left Black pushing libel constraints his way but denied him the role of victor in developing the Court's restrictive libel position by the early 1970s. Probably any such title of leader or symbol of the Court's thinking during Black's later years belonged to Justice Brennan.[71]

Although Black's warnings about the dangers of big government and repressive public officials (and the need, therefore, for a vital and free press) appear wise and valuable in the 1970s, not all his predictions were on target. In fact, the fears he expressed about prosecutions under group libel statutes in *Beauharnais* in 1952 never came to pass.[72] In retrospect, his fears about group libel abuses were overstated. His warnings in *Butts* in 1967 about libel falling into the "quagmire" of obscenity turned out also to be overstated and probably wrong by the time he had left the Court[73] (although the 1974 *Gertz* decision suggests that he may yet be right in the long term).

And while possibly right about the inadequacy of the actual malice standard from the *Times* cases as press protection, Black was wrong to think of it as small protection; malice has turned out to be extremely difficult to prove in a jury trial.

His use of the term "press-destroying" or phrases closely parallel to it in such cases as *Ginzburg v. Goldwater, Rosenblatt,* and *Rosenbloom* turned out to be more expressions of First Amendment values than of the facts of libel.[74] Indeed, many of Black's sweeping statements about the threats of libel turned out to be a reflection or a reinforcement of his general First Amendment concerns. His passionate pleas against libel helped point the Court his way, but his worst fears never seemed to materialize. Black's rhetoric turned out to be less memorable in libel arguments per se than as a general defense of the First Amendment.

VII

Black contributed mightily to encouraging public debate and criticism in the press. His legacy was near absolute protection for the press against the use of libel laws by public officials and public figures.

Black was often ahead of his time. Again his warnings from his January, 1970 *Goldwater* denial-of-certiorari dissent anticipated events of the 1970s—the Thomas Eagleton affair of 1972 in which revelations that Eagleton had undergone psychiatric care forced him eventually from the vice-presidential position on the Democratic ticket, and the Richard Nixon/Watergate/Committee to Re-Elect the President crises of 1972-74. Black's words were at least two to four years ahead of their time:

> The decisions . . . in this case can only have the effect of dampening political debate by making fearful and timid those who should under our Constitution feel totally free openly to criticize Presidential candidates.[75]

> In our times, the person who holds that office [Presidency of the United States] has an almost unbound power for good or evil. The public has an unqualified right to have the character and fitness of anyone who aspires to the Presidency held up for the closest scrutiny.[76]

One obvious theme of Black's convictions was that in public affairs there are better means than libel for a redress of grievances.[77] For one example: the encouraging of almost any "appropriate" means, short of infringing upon press freedoms, for opening up the marketplace of ideas and debate. Or by controlling excessive speech problems through unfair campaign practices laws.

And while Black was "right" to call malice an almost impossible standard to work out satisfactorily, his rightness may not have been based on the strongest reasons: the problem with malice turned out to be the difficulty of proving "maliciousness" before a jury.[78] Only some of his fears for freedom of the press against libel constraints seemed well founded.

These reflections lead to one final attempt at assessment. Again, perhaps it helps to turn to Professor Emerson:

> There is no satisfactory judicial technique for weighing the interest in free expression against the interest of the individual in preserving his reputation.[79]

Justice Black, it seems fair to say, would have both agreed and disagreed. In pragmatic terms, the situation was, indeed, impossible to work with. On philosophical grounds, the answer was much easier. For Black, the balance was all toward free expression. Reputations are little matters; and even when the "little guy" is hurt, he can always fight back. The person with "power," especially those voluntarily in politics or in the public arena, such as the entertainer, has either little or no right to cry about criticism of performance, character, or whatever. So, in essence, Black tried to tell us that words on public matters are very important but cannot do much damage. About words mixed with actions, such as sit-ins, or symbolic speech, however, he felt much differently. Libel, in Black's mind at least, did not involve such complexities and, therefore, could be treated with simple and broad legal language.

One must wonder here about the real strength of Black's positions since they seemed to be based more on his feelings and his personal background than on evidence from possibly useful behavioral science literature — especially psychology and psychiatry — about the potential dangers to certain individuals from "mere words." Deep inside some people they may do real emotional damage. To say, as Black did, that there is little or no damage is not to resolve any of the problems in which there might be real damage to a few public figures and to private individuals caught up in perhaps "involuntary" incidents. If anything, Black's support of individualism suggests he might have considered more carefully private libel in an effort to understand better the differences between public and nonpublic words and issues. (His views in the field of privacy were, obviously, consistent with his general unconcern about private libel matters [disputes between individuals, say, without involving the media]. But, as with libel, are most public officials to be so hardened and able to withstand and ignore their critics that they become self-shielded and isolated political and administrative animals?)

So Black's lack of concern over the powerless individual vs. big business or big government invasions of privacy or defamation suits seems at odds with many of his stated and philosophical views. In the end, one must assume that Black simply saw all libel as libel. There were few distinctions within the field; and even if there were distinctions, they were not important enough to be worth worrying about — certainly not when balanced against constraints on a free press.

Black was also slow to provide support for the broadcast media. Although he had become involved in obscenity issues, he was not ahead of his time in granting the status to television and radio that he assumed for newspapers, magazines, books, and leaflets. His later decisions acknowledged the other media, but all the evidence indicates that his views concerning them were slow, almost hesitant, in emerging.

The true legacy of Justice Black may be that he fought for a vigorous, critical press. He sensed the constraints that could be imposed and he moved swiftly against the threat of libel as a stifling force. The irony is that while he was struggling to deal with other forms of free speech (speech-plus, or speech-plus-action and symbolic speech) he could not quite include them in his anti-libel law arguments. Black's later position, especially in libel cases, indicates that he may even have put a free *press* ahead of free *speech*.

The press has the sword and the heritage to fight those in power; in his passionate view there was no room to give even an inch to libel challenges. Black understood politics and power almost too well and he knew what they could do to people and to a democratic society. A totally free press was, to the Justice, both an essential offensive weapon and a defensive force in all matters of public concern — as it was, for example, in its role in exposing such issues as Watergate during the early and mid-1970s. Libel laws could do nothing but get in the way of that part of the First Amendment committed to a free press. In libel issues, Black simply gave the institution of the press the highest, never-look-back priority.

7 Black and the problem of privacy

DONALD M. GILLMOR

Justice Hugo Black would have wanted us to take him at his word. In a personal testament,[1] the literal-minded libertarian, noting that he would refuse to go farther in interpreting the Constitution than a specific provision can be taken under the Necessary and Proper Clause, said of privacy:

> I can find in the Constitution no language which either specifically or implicitly grants to all individuals a constitutional "right of privacy." . . .[And] even though I like my privacy as well as the next person, I am nevertheless compelled to admit that the states have a right to invade it unless prohibited by some constitutional provision.

That would seem to say it all for Black and privacy; yet there is at least a hint of ambivalence in the words, "unless prohibited by some constitutional provision."

In the final decade of his long Supreme Court tenure, the elderly and increasingly choleric activist had abandoned his liberal brethren in cases involving symbolic speech,[2] speech-plus,[3] and searches and seizures.[4] In Fourth Amendment cases particularly, Black seems to have been less sensitive to individual rights than his constitutional soulmates, notable the doctrinaire liberal Justice William O. Douglas and Justice William J. Brennan.

For a number of justices the searches and seizures provisions of the Fourth Amendment have generally subsumed privacy. For Black, however,

DONALD M. GILLMOR is professor of journalism and mass communication at the University of Minnesota, from which he received the Ph.D. degree. He is the author of *Free Press and Fair Trial* and coauthor (with Jerome A. Barron) of *Mass Communication Law: Cases and Comment.* He has also written numerous articles on communication law, the relationship between legal studies and the behavioral sciences, the economics of the press, popular culture and political theory, and mass communications and society.

the outline of the right was less clear and he was tempted to exclude privacy from the Constitution by a strict construction or narrow interpretation of that document's language.

Certainly the Court's improvisation in finding privacy broadly protected in the Fourth, Fifth, and Ninth Amendments in *Griswold*,[5] the 1965 Connecticut contraception case, provokes a claim for more precise legal reasoning — although in a sense all enumerated constitutional rights may protect privacy if by that concept we mean to uphold the integrity and inviolability of the individual personality.

Still denying the existence of a constitutional right of privacy, Black, instead of pinning down his position in that case, hedged in a dissenting opinion that found "guarantees in certain specific constitutional provisions which are designed to protect privacy at certain times and places with respect to certain activities." We assume his reference is to the Fourth Amendment. Black then chastised his liberal colleagues for giving the Fourth a niggardly, privacy-only interpretation instead of "the kind of liberal reading I think any Bill of Rights provision should be given." The problem, of course, is that just such a liberal reading of the Bill of Rights permitted his colleagues to sustain the notion of a right of privacy. And, to add to our perplexity, in the same dissent Black rejected broad interpretations because, he said, they "dilute" or "expand" constitutionally guaranteed rights by word substitution.

Black's opinion was indeed confusing, but *Griswold*, the first case to provide doctrinal substance to a right of privacy, gave the senior member of the Court an opportunity to elaborate his constitutional philosophy. Where specific language of the Constitution did not intervene, he argued, full reign must be given the legislature even though its policies may be irrational, unwise, or unfair. In a 1963 opinion for the Court, Black had written that "courts do not substitute their social and economic beliefs for the judgment of legislative bodies, who are elected to pass laws."[6] The only alternative to legislative mandate would be the process of consitutional amendment.

Black's dissent in *Griswold*, then, can be read as an argument for a doctrine of judicial restraint — at least where jurists cannot rely on an unambiguous dictate of the Constitution and are forced to fall back on what Black refers to as a vague natural law or due process rationale, as did Justice Arthur Goldberg in *Griswold*. Goldberg had rejected state legislation that he said violated "fundamental principles of liberty or justice," or is contrary to the "traditions and (collective) conscience of our people." Black did not appreciate such nebulous words and concepts, and he rebuked Goldberg for assuming that the Ninth Amendment, enacted to protect the residual powers of the state from federal infringement, could be used to prevent state legislators from passing laws they considered appropriate to the governance of local affairs. And Black recalled that similarly promiscuous interpretations of the Fourteenth Amendment's Due Process Clause had been used by an earlier Court to obstruct comprehensive social welfare legislation in the name of property rights, and were being used now to enforce the Court's current notions about personal rights.[7]

Yet much earlier the Court had found privacy protected by the Fourteenth Amendment's "liberty" provision, at least where the state had interfered with privacy by prohibiting the teaching of a foreign language.[8]

For Black, privacy qualified as one of those "mysterious and uncertain natural law concepts," broad, abstract and ambiguous, which he had identified in *Griswold* as lacking respectable constitutional antecedents. Nor was an invasion of privacy synonymous with eavesdropping, a practice as old as human society in Black's view and still useful in the detection and prosecution of crime.

Two years after *Griswold*, in *Berger v. New York*,[9] a decision overturning the 1928 *Olmstead* rule[10] which found no constitutional ban on wiretapping in the absence of a physical trespass, Black showed another dimension of his strictness in reading the Constitution. Here he stated a preference for the common law rule that relevant evidence is admissible in criminal trials even though obtained contrary to ethics, morals, or law, a position that finds favor with some recent appointees to the Court.

In *Berger*, Black also discovered a faulty syllogism based on the majority's failure to distinguish between unreasonable searches and seizures and privacy:

> The Fourth Amendment forbids invasion of privacy and excludes evidence obtained by such invasion;
> To listen secretly to a man's conversation or to tap his telephone conversation invades his privacy;
> Therefore, the Fourth Amendment bars use of evidence obtained by eavesdropping or by tapping telephone wires.

The syllogism was faulty because the Fourth Amendment says nothing about a broad and undefined right of privacy. Indeed, it was impossible for Black

> to think that the wise Framers of the Fourth Amendment would ever have dreamed about drafting an amendment to protect the "right of privacy." That expression, like a chameleon, has a different color for every turning. In fact, use of "privacy" as the keyword in the Fourth Amendment simply gives this Court a useful new tool . . . both to usurp the policy-making power of the Congress and to hold more state and federal laws unconstitutional when the Court entertains a sufficient hostility to them.[11]

But it is also difficult to imagine the Framers having anticipated the nature and the consequences of an ever-accelerating technology, though it is true that the process of constitutional amendment may have been their way of recognizing that no one possesses the gift of prophecy. Nevertheless Black's interpretation is too narrow and, short of the amending process, the Fourth Amendment has become the constitutional mainstay of a right of privacy.

Dissenting in *Katz v. United States,*[12] a ruling which concretely reinforced *Berger,* Black reiterated:

> I do not believe that it is the proper role of this Court to rewrite the Amendment in order "to bring it into harmony with the times." . . . While I realize that an argument based on the meaning of words lacks the scope, and no doubt the appeal, of broad policy discussions and philosophical discourses on such nebulous subjects as privacy, for me the language of the Amendment is the crucial place to look in construing a written document such as our Constitution.

It is difficult to know whether Black's position reflected an antipathy for the very idea cf privacy, a reluctance to define a concept which for him was vague and abstract, or a sincere effort to protect the Constitution's specific language from those who would bandy it about, making it a document for all seasons.

"The Fourth Amendment," Black contended in *Katz,* "protects privacy only to the extent that it prohibits unreasonable searches and seizures of 'persons, houses, papers, and effects.' No general right is created by the Amendment so as to give this Court unlimited power to hold unconstitutional everything which affects privacy." All three suppositions — antipathy for privacy, a failure to define it, and a desire to protect the integrity of the Constitution — may be valid to a degree, although the second and third are perhaps more congruent with the judicial values of one who courageously and dependably defended what he did believe the Constitution said about civil liberties.

Yet there is a disconcerting inconsistency in Black's vacillation between narrow and broad interpretations of Fourth Amendment freedoms.

In 1949 Black rejected Justice Wiley Rutledge's dissenting argument in *Wolf v. Colorado*[13] that evidence illegally seized cannot be used against a defendant (the exclusionary rule). By 1961 and the landmark Fourth Amendment case, *Mapp v. Ohio,*[14] he had come round to the view that the force of Rutledge's argument had become compelling with a more thorough understanding of the problem. There is little evidence in later cases as to what Black's "more thorough understanding" of the problem incorporates.

Concurring in *Mapp,* Black said that it seemed to him that the 75-year-old *Boyd* decision,[15] "though perhaps not required by the express language of the Constitution strictly construed, is amply justified from an historical standpoint, soundly based in reason and entirely consistent with what I regard to be the proper approach to interpretation of our Bill of Rights." Justice Joseph Bradley in *Boyd* had posited a close relationship between the Fourth and Fifth Amendments and had argued that constitutional provisions protecting the sanctity of the home and the privacies of life should be liberally construed. "A close and literal construction," Bradley declared, "deprives them of half their efficacy, and leads to gradual depreciation of the right, as if it consisted more in sound than in substance." That significant case became precedent for what has been called "propertied privacy," a luxury that had to be relinquished in the face of New Deal and Civil Rights legislation.[16]

Similarly in *Rochin v. People of California*,[17] a case in which a stomach pump was used to obtain evidence from a suspected narcotics violator, Black concurred in the reversal of Rochin's conviction. He based his argument on the ground that the Fourteenth Amendment made the Fifth Amendment's unconditional provision against self-incrimination applicable to the States. That provision, Black declared, given a broad rather than a narrow construction, barred the introduction of this "capsule" evidence just as much as it would have forbidden the use of words Rochin might have been coerced to use. Rochin, and the more recent abortion ruling,[18] based largely on the protection of liberty by the Due Process Clause of the Fourteenth Amendment, emphatically protect a limited right to the privacy of those elements of our bodily functions found in procreation,[19] marriage,[20] contraception,[21] and the rearing of children.[22]

Black's eclecticism in *Wolf, Mapp,* and *Rochin* was uncharacteristic. His flat denial of constitutional status for privacy while cogitating on whether those constitutional provisions that suggest it deserve a narrowly literal or liberal construction, and his certainty as to what privacy was *not* while admitting that it had never been properly defined, indicate confusion in his mind as to what constitutional formula would permit the resolution of urgent problems of privacy.

The question, of course, was simpler for Black when he perceived as First Amendment rights what others called privacy. In the peculiar case of *Public Utilities Commission v. Pollak*,[23] for example, Black saw no issue of privacy where music and advertisements were piped into city buses. He would have seen a violation of First Amendment rights were such a captive audience as bus riders subjected to news, views, public speeches, or propaganda of any kind. In contrast Justice Douglas saw in these circumstances a clear violation of privacy under the Due Process Clause of the Fifth Amendment.[24]

Also in *Stanley v. Georgia*,[25] a case in which police officers looking for evidence of gambling activities found obscene films in a bedroom dresser drawer, looked at them on Stanley's projector, then charged him under an obscenity statute, a majority of the Court saw significant implications for privacy and ruled through Justice Thurgood Marshall that the mere private possession of obscene matter cannot constitutionally be made a crime. For Black, *Stanley* was a case involving only the First and Fourteenth Amendments; privacy need not have been mentioned. And in *Kent v. Dulles*[26] the Court may have created a "right to travel" as part of the liberty which cannot be denied a citizen without due process of law under the Fifth Amendment. Black concurred only because he saw First Amendment issues there also.

In a major, and for privacy a retrogressive, ruling arising under New York's privacy statute, Black again found only First Amendment issues, and in a concurring opinion he wrote:

> If judges have, however, by their own fiat today created a right of privacy equal to or superior to the right of a free press that the Constitu-

tion created, then tomorrow and the next day and the next, judges can create more rights that balance away other cherished Bill of Rights freedoms.[27]

Justice Abe Fortas, joined by Chief Justice Earl Warren and Justice Tom Clark, dissented in the case, arguing strenuously that he did not believe that

> whatever is in words, however much of an aggression it may be upon individual rights, is beyond the reach of the law, no matter how heedless of other's rights—how remote from public purpose, how reckless, irresponsible, and untrue it may be. . . . The greatest solicitude for the First Amendment does not compel us to deny to a State the right to provide a remedy for reckless falsity in writing and publishing an article which irresponsibly and injuriously invades the privacy of a quiet family for no purpose except dramatic interest and commercial appeal.

Fortas and Black could hardly have been farther apart in their conceptions of how the First Amendment bears upon privacy.

II

In his book, *Privacy and the Press*, Don R. Pember, adopting Black's orientation, contends that throughout the years a distinct First Amendment philosophy has developed which places freedom of the press above the right of privacy. "Truth" and the notion of a "public interest" have become such overriding social values that privacy laws seem an impotent remedy. "Which is more important," Pember asks, "the protection of society by a free and unfettered press, or the individual's claim to personal solitude?"[28] Justice Black might have accepted this formulation of the question.

But mark well the way the question is put. One is reminded of how poorly free expression fared in the early post-World War II Communist conspiracy cases when, in a similar equation, speech was designated an individual right and set against society's interest in self-preservation.[29] Who could prefer the former given such a choice? Roscoe Pound cautioned those who would attempt such balancing when he said, "When it comes to weighing or valuing claims or demands with respect to other claims or demands, we must be careful to compare them on the same plane. If we put one as an individual interest and the other as a social interest we may decide the question in advance in our way of putting it."[30]

Balancing rights is hazardous at best, as Justice Black so fervently believed, and in the case of free press and privacy it may be futile. "The possibility that the right of privacy will overwhelm the rights of society is so remote that it is hardly cause for alarm," Thomas Emerson has observed. "Most of the forces at work press the other way."[31] It is these forces that Alan Westin and Arthur Miller examine in their separate works on privacy:[32] computer and microfilm technology, physical and psychological surveillance, data centers and other dossier systems, all intrusions upon personal solitude.

Pember would agree that electronic snooping by both the government and private corporations poses a greater threat to a free society than a hyperactive press, and that where the press is concerned courts will continue to be generous in applying the defense of "newsworthiness" against privacy claims. Prying journalism will nevertheless continue to be one of the pressures that wear against privacy, and it may eventually be necessary to differentiate the meanings of "newsworthiness" and "public interest."[33] The latter, an especially intricate concept, may be a central element of the idea of free expression. In the meantime, if privacy claims cannot be sustained against absolutist interpretations of speech and press, then privacy may also require absolute status and a definition narrowly demarcating an inner and inviolate core of personality. It might also be necessary to distinguish between the broad right of privacy and the narrower law of privacy.[34]

In 1967 for the first time, the United States Supreme Court invoked the First Amendment right of free press to defeat a privacy suit. The suit began in 1952 when James Hill, his wife, and their five children were held hostage in their suburban Philadelphia home by three escaped convicts. The Hills were not harmed; in fact they were treated courteously by the intruders.

A year later, a novel, *Desperate Hours,* purported to describe the real-life episode but with the fictionalized addition of a violent attack on the father and son, a "verbal sexual assault" on a daughter, and ultimately a heroic role for Hill. The novel led to a play and the play to a movie. The play was promoted by a picture story in *Life* magazine, and by that time the embarrassed Hill and his family had moved to Connecticut, in part to get out of the public spotlight.

Hill's lawsuit was based on the *Life* piece which had reviewed the play as "a heart-stopping account of how a family rose to heroism in a crisis." The Broadway production set duplicated the actual Hill home. Otherwise there was little similarity between the docile captivity of the family and the sensationalized story line of the play.

Hill's suit was based on New York's privacy statute. The family had involuntarily become subjects of public interest and under the statute would not have had a case had the *Life* portrayal of their experience been even a reflection of reality. But it had been seriously inaccurate, presenting Hill as the neighborhood commando waging war against the invaders of his home.

Hill won a $75,000 judgment in a New York trial court. In a new trial that judgment was reduced to $30,000 in compensatory damages. The New York Court of Appeals subsequently affirmed the award and Time, Inc. appealed to the United States Supreme Court, arguing that the rules pertaining to the standards of newsworthiness had not been measured by guidelines that satisfy the First Amendment. Justice Brennan, speaking for the Court, agreed and applied the *New York Times* standard of actual malice, a condition since 1964 for the award of damages in a libel suit in which public officials or public figures are the target of a libelous attack. That standard is "knowledge of falsity or reckless disregard of whether it was false or not."[35] So for the first time an "actual malice" test, originally designed for libel, was used to measure the legal status of privacy. The judgment for Hill was reversed.[36]

Black, in a concurring opinion, as has been noted, renewed his claim for unqualified First Amendment rights. Douglas contended that it would be irrelevant to talk of any right of privacy in the context of the Hill case, implying thereby that privacy rights could be found in other circumstances.

One legal scholar observed at the time that "the logic of *New York Times* and *Hill* taken together grants the press some measure of constitutional protection for anything the press thinks is a matter of public interest."[37] The effect of the ruling, said Arthur Miller, was to give the media substantial immunity from liability for invasions of privacy in order to provide "breathing space" for freedom of expression, and he added that the decision "partially had aborted the common law right of privacy's capacity for doctrinal growth."[38]

To be sure, the *Hill* case did not present the free press–privacy question squarely, and it dealt with only one dimension of privacy. Although Justice Brennan's mode of analysis may have been vulnerable, damage to the Hill family's privacy may not have been sufficient to overcome the public's right to know. Nor was the line between fact and fiction in the case always as clear as it might have been. But a central question remained and it was pleaded by Justice Fortas in his dissent: Where does privacy stand in our hierarchy of values?

III

Justice Black's crabbed view of privacy may also have been due partly to his historical impressions and partly to his lack of interest in the subject. His view and the view of others seemed to be that privacy was a judicially imagined legal right and that its development is "simply bad history and bad law."[39] Louis Brandeis's instructive dissent in *Olmstead*, in which he defined the right to be let alone as "the most comprehensive of rights and the right most valued by civilized men,"[40] reinforces this notion. Brandeis and Samuel Warren had given the concept increased momentum in their influential 1890 *Harvard Law Review* article in which they spoke of "inviolate personality"; and they may have been prophetic in their anticipation of "mechanical devices [that] threaten to make good the prediction: 'what is whispered in the closet shall be proclaimed from the house-tops.' "[41] But long before, in pre–Civil War America, others, among them Justice Story and Thomas Cooley, had recognized the fundamental nature of the right and its implications for freedom. Indeed, John Adams, decrying the British policy of issuing general search warrants against American colonists, maintained that from this invasion of individual privacy "the child of Independence was born."[42]

Since then privacy has found protection specifically in the First, Third, Fourth, Fifth, and Ninth Amendments and in the penumbras of the Bill of

Rights generally. Adding the privacy provisions of some state constitutions, at least five state statutes, a District of Columbia law, a new federal privacy statute, and recognition of the right by the courts of some 35 states, there has evolved a reasonably sophisticated system of privacy law.

Relying on Dean Prosser, courts now acknowledge four forms of the tort: (1) expropriation of a name or picture for commercial use without consent, (2) disclosure of embarrassing private facts about a person, (3) placing a person in false light, usually through fictionalization, and (4) intrusion upon one's solitude or seclusion by means of electronic (or in-person) surveillance.[43]

When privacy first became an implied argument in First Amendment cases it appeared as a defensible right of a householder to enjoy the quiet of his premises free from the raucous blast of sound trucks or the intrusion of door-to-door salesmen.[44] Privacy was thus a passive virtue that the Court invoked in order to place limits on an overactive freedom of speech.[45]

Justice Black, of course, dissented in these cases. But where he could find prior First Amendment questions he voted for associational privacy in a landmark 1958 case involving NAACP membership lists,[46] for political privacy in *Watkins*[47] and *Sweezy*,[48] and more recently in *Baird v. State Bar of Arizona*,[49] and for the privacy of anonymous publication in *Talley v. California*.[50] Black also supported the right of privacy between counsel and client,[51] the right of a householder to be free from warrantless health inspections,[52] the right to remain silent in the landmark self-incrimination rulings,[53] and freedom of thought in a series of loyalty oath cases.[54] In these instances he was clearly willing to stretch the language of the First Amendment to give it the broadest possible application. But with *Griswold v. Connecticut* Black left his liberal colleagues.

In the past 15 years the Fourth Amendment has emerged as the strongest foundation upon which to lay a claim of privacy, although it is still shot through with technicalities and qualifications.

One of the best legal briefs on the privacy implications of the Fourth Amendment is Justice Brennan's dissenting opinion in the *Lopez* case,[55] a dissent in which Justice Black did not join. Brennan denied that a ruling holding electronic eavesdropping to be within the reach of the Fourth Amendment amounted to a total ban on electronic surveillance or to a blocking of traditional investigative techniques of law enforcement. Instead he drew a picture of the terrifying growth of electronic bugging and tapping and its effects on constitutional liberties.

"Freedom of speech," he said, "is undermined where people fear to speak unconstrainedly in what they suppose to be the privacy of home and office." Brennan emphasized that the Fourth Amendment's guarantee against physical intrusion had been clearly outdistanced by new technology, and he saw privacy as well as other fundamental rights lost in the race.

Unfortunately Justice Brennan is still dissenting in Fourth Amendment cases. Professor Westin's expectation in 1968 that the Court might have been on the brink of a landmark ruling defining a comprehensive, positive right of privacy from unreasonable surveillance has not been realized in recent terms of the Court. On the contrary, in *Bivens v. Six Unknown Named Agents*[56] and in *Coolidge v. New Hampshire*[57] there are indications that the new Court may reappraise the basic tenets of the unreasonable searches and seizures doctrine and abandon altogether the exclusionary rule regarding evidence seized in violation of the Fourth Amendment.

And in the 1970 term, the Court declared evidence admissible that had been obtained by warrantless electronic eavesdropping—in this case a transmitter hidden in the clothing of an informer. Justice White, joined by the Chief Justice, and Justices Stewart and Blackmun, spoke for a majority. Justice Black concurred, basing his judgment on his dissent in *Katz*. Justices Douglas, Harlan, and Marshall dissented on the grounds that earlier cases, notably *Katz* and *Berger,* had clearly made search warrants in such circumstances mandatory.[58]

Government, of course, is not the only violator of privacy and other freedoms. The corporation—what Black called nongovernmental combinations in the *Associated Press* case[59]—the mob, and individual persons play their roles as well.

"Viewed in terms of the relation of the individual to social participation," says Westin, "privacy is the voluntary and temporal withdrawal of a person from the general society through physical or psychological means, either in a state of solitude or small-group intimacy or, when among larger groups, in a condition of anonymity or reserve."[60] Each person, considering his own social context, must find an acceptable balance between solitude and companionship, intimacy and broader social participation, anonymity and visibility, reserve and disclosure. A free society, Westin argues, leaves these choices to the individual, with only extraordinary exceptions allowed in the general interests of society.[61]

When conduct and associations are being put "on file," says Arthur Miller, the citizen is less willing to pursue his constitutional rights.[62] It is this fear that makes the Court's recent obliviousness to the effects of army surveillance so painful. The plaintiffs claimed that the army's activities had a chilling effect on political expression, protest, and dissent. Chief Justice Burger, speaking for a majority, could see no concrete harm in the situation,[63] a view that gives credence to the idea that a police state may indeed be a state of mind.

IV

One of Black's biographers, Charlotte Williams, wrote that Black may have been a populist with dogmatic eccentricities about the Bill of Rights.[64] It is certain that he believed in strong and positive government unless that government interfered with those sacred rights of the individual explicitly stated in the Constitution. Privacy was not included. Had Black ignored the concept altogether, his views on privacy would have been consistent and comprehensible. His philosophy, as expressed dramatically in *Griswold,* becomes a narrow philosophy of judicial self-restraint. His liberal cohorts, on the other hand, regarded the Bill of Rights as furnishing a minimal, not a preemptive, content to the Fourteenth Amendment.[65]

A year after *Griswold* a majority of the Court invalidated, on the ground that it violated the Equal Protection Clause of the Fourteenth Amendment, a Virginia statute that made a poll tax a condition of voting. Again Black dissented, objecting strenuously to the use of what he called "the old 'natural-law-due-process formula' to justify striking down state laws as violations of the Equal Protection Clause . . . to license this Court . . . and to roam at large in the broad expanses of policy and morals. . . ."[66]

Black's persistence in stating his position compels us to ask whether restricting the Court's authority in protecting human freedom to the literal specifics of the Bill of Rights may be more or less dangerous than the abuse of judicial power we risk where that power is used broadly and presumably in the name of freedom. That question has dominated much of the Court's doctrinal division and its answer may depend upon how adequately the freedom at issue has been defined.

When we attempt to define privacy we recognize the complexity of the concept; but we sense that we are dealing with a right close to if not part of the central core of freedom. It is also a right that appears to exist in an inverse relationship to modern technology and a right that may disappear in the advanced technological state of the future. Whether we speak of psychic area or space, self-image, self-expression, or personal autonomy we are dealing with what Paul Freund has called "a greedy legal concept,"[67] because it is implied in so many of our constitutional provisions. Modern man's vision of privacy will not fade away, and the Court's opinions in *Griswold,* in spite of the intellectual disorder they may have created, suggest a judicial resolve to give privacy constitutional status.

The ultimate question, and one not yet faced directly by the Court, is to what extent legislative power ought to be permitted to interfere with the inviolable person who is, the Court said as long ago as 1891, "as much invaded by a compulsory stripping and exposure as by a blow."[68]

Charles Black, Jr., in the foreword to a book about Justice Black, infers erroneously, I believe, that the Justice had taught that "there are closes of personality, walled gardens of human dignity, where this power may not enter."[69] Justice Black may indeed have felt that way and it would have been congruent with his judicial instincts to do so, but it is not possible in his opinions to find any such reverence for the concept of privacy per se, even in the absence of a compelling state interest to invade it. He labeled the Court's efforts in *Griswold* to find protection for privacy "shocking doctrine." Similarly in *Rochin* he exempted Fourth Amendment rights from his list of absolutes because of that provision's conditional language; the Court, he said, must choose between competing estimates of what is and what is not an "unreasonable search or seizure" — the key word being "unreasonable." Judicial restraint or balancing could provide acceptable solutions in such circumstances. But where First Amendment rights were involved, Black's system would permit no equivocation, no pragmatic weighing of values. But can the question of privacy be so simply put?

The Framers from their pastoral vantage points — Philadelphia was a city of 35,000, four long days from New York by carriage — could not have anticipated the plethora of technological and institutional pressures that now grind upon personal privacy. All of a living Constitution requires the opportunity for growth that Black has always granted the First Amendment. Even those on the Court farthest from Black in their judicial philosophies seem to have understood this. Liberty, said Justice John Marshall Harlan, "is a rational continuum which . . . includes freedom from all substantial arbitrary impositions and purposeless restraints. . . ."[70] "Great concepts like . . . 'liberty,' " said Justice Felix Frankfurter, "were purposely left to gather meaning from experience. For they relate to the whole domain of social and economic fact, and the statesmen who founded this Nation knew too well that only a stagnant society remains unchanged."[71] Our courts have not been deaf to appeals for privacy, and firmer constitutional supports may yet be constructed, especially where the invader is government.

In 1942 Justice Frank Murphy, dissenting in *Goldman v. United States*,[72] declared the right of privacy in the Fourth Amendment to be one of the greatest boons secured to the inhabitants of this country by the Bill of Rights. Justice Brennan in *Abel v. United States*[73] perceived the Fourth Amendment as protecting the individual's interest in privacy against the concentrated power of the executive branch of government. Justice Douglas, dissenting in *Poe v. Ullman*,[74] found the right of privacy emanating from the totality of the constitutional scheme under which we live. In *Griswold* Justice Goldberg discovered privacy in the Ninth Amendment, and Douglas in that case argued that "specific guarantees in the Bill of Rights have penumbras, formed by emanations from those guarantees that help give them life and substance. Various guarantees create zones of privacy." Douglas's penumbras may yet provide a conceptual framework for further constitutional analysis of privacy and its relation to personal dignity, individuality, and a sense of the inner person, all purposes for which a free society exists. As long as human freedom remains the goal, however ideal it may be, and other constitutional rights are not disturbed, such "tampering" with the Constitution does not seem to justify Justice Black's grave fears.

"It is at least a hypothesis worth testing," says Paul Freund,

> that privacy, though in its immediate aspect an individual interest, serves an important socializing function. An unwillingness to suffer disclosure of what has been discreditable in one's life, or of one's most intimate thoughts and feelings, reflects an intuitive sense that to share everything would jeopardize the sharing of anything. Complete openness in social life would encounter misunderstandings, inability to forgive, unlimited tolerance for differences. The inner sense of privacy, and mutual respect for it, may be a mechanism that helps to secure the condition for living fraternally in a world where men are not gods, where to know all is not to understand and forgive all.[75]

Freund may be suggesting that in situations where privacy must compete with other constitutional claims it can be defined as either a social or a personal right depending upon the circumstances. For those who would prefer to avoid the risks of balancing, privacy may be more resolutely defined as a set of countervailing rules that cut across any opposing rules of the collectivity and that constitute in Thomas Emerson's words "a sphere of space that has not been dedicated to public use or control."[76] Emerson would include in this space at least the privacy of one's bodily functions.

For Black there could be no protective shadows. Black's peculiar absolutism, his consistency in adhering to what he thought the Framers intended, required him to ignore the *law* of privacy; his sense of justice would not permit him to ignore a broader *right* of privacy. He equivocated and his equivocation became confusion. Privacy was a pressing constitutional problem which this great and humane Justice never succeeded in working out.

8 Black's view of obscenity as protected speech and press

KENNETH S. DEVOL

"The spectacle of a judge poring over the picture of some nude," Thurman Arnold once wrote, "trying to ascertain the extent to which she arouses prurient interest, and then attempting to write an opinion that explains the difference between that nude and some other nude has elements of low comedy."[1]

That statement surely must be one of the most insightful lines ever written about judicial impotence, and Arnold's assessment is accurate. It does indeed evoke chuckles — from the incongruity as well as from the futility of the undertaking.

Justice Hugo L. Black agreed with Judge Arnold's position, but was less generous in his criticism of the censorial role of the judiciary. In *Reidel*, a 1971 postal obscenity case, he foresaw his brethren "sifting through books and magazines and watching movies because some official fears they deal too explicitly with sex. I can imagine," he continued, "no more distasteful, useless, and time-consuming task for the members of this court than perusing this material to determine whether it has 'redeeming social value.' This absurd spectacle could be avoided if we adhere to the literal command of the First Amendment that 'Congress shall make no law . . . abridging the freedom of speech, or of the press.' "[2]

This was the last obscenity opinion written by Justice Black. But his colleagues on the Supreme Court paid as little attention to this final appeal as they did to his first stated position when he joined Justice William O. Douglas

KENNETH S. DEVOL is professor and chairman of the Department of Journalism at California State University (Northridge), where he has taught courses in law of mass communications since 1961. He received the Ph.D. from the University of Southern California in 1965 and is past national president of the Association for Education in Journalism. He is author of *Mass Media and the Supreme Court*, now in second edition.

dissenting in *Roth,* one of the Court's initial attempts to face the constitutional question of obscenity head-on. Time and again in the 14 years between *Roth* and *Reidel,* Justice Black admonished his brethren to accept the simple words of the First Amendment, chiding them at times with the label the "Supreme Board of Censors."[3]

But Justice Black's position relative to the First Amendment and obscenity was primarily philosophic. He was an "absolutist" or, as he called himself upon occasion, a "literalist." Ernst and Schwartz see his absolutist position as not "Constitution-made, but judge-made."[4] He believed simply that the Framers of the Constitution knew what words meant, could put those words together to form a meaningful sentence, and that "no law" as written into the First Amendment means just that — no law. There were, he pointed out, no qualifying words such as "unreasonable" as found in the Fourth Amendment, the "due process" qualification found in the Fifth Amendment, nor the word "excessive" found in the Eighth Amendment. The First Amendment plainly says "no law." Period. In a 1962 interview with Edmond Cahn, Justice Black was adamant:

> So we have a written Constitution. What good is it? What good is it
> if, as some judges say, all it means is: "Government, you can still do this
> unless it is so bad that it shocks the conscience of the judges." It does not
> say that to me. We have certain provisions in the Constitution which say,
> "Thou shalt not." They do not say, "You can go ahead and do this unless
> it is offensive to the universal sense of decency." If they did, they would
> say virtually nothing. There would be no definite, binding place, no
> specific prohibition, if that were all it said.[5]

Black used the same plain language he admired in the First Amendment. He relied little on legal jargon to make his points. David Grey of San José State University wrote before Black's death that "if a popularity poll of recent Courts were taken among newsmen, the justice[s] who would be . . . usually found easiest to read would include . . . Justice Black."[6] John P. Frank in *The New Republic* noted that "key elements of Black's method were his simplicity of thought, his simplicity of prose and his plain diligence."[7] Patrick McBride agreed:

> I would suggest that Black's opinions on the subject of censorship of
> obscenity are not only clear in theoretical application but also extremely
> convincing when judged by the result for which he argues. His opinions
> have a salutary crispness and clarity as they stand beside the vexing con-
> fusions of his brothers who continue their efforts to unravel the mysteries
> of the term "obscenity."[8]

Michael Ash hints at what may have been one of the influencing factors in Black's choice of simple language:

> There is Hugo Black — passionate advocate of unlimited free speech.
> This is the man whose basic understanding of social and political ques-

tions was instilled by speech in its most traditional sense, by old-fashioned orators perched on stumps in rural Alabama when Black was a lad.[9]

Ash claims that on matters involving freedom of expression, Black was "not merely a 'liberal' and an 'activist,' but a radical."[10] And in no area did he show more consistency in his advocacy — or "radicalism" — than in dealing with the perplexing questions of obscenity. While there is some debate relative to Justice Black's "retreat from liberalism" during his later years on the high bench, especially in the areas of dissent and assembly, his views on obscenity and government attempts to suppress it went unchanged during his tenure of the Supreme Court. He stood firm.

For 14 years Justice Black and the rest of the Justices wrestled with the obscenity problem — if, indeed, there is a "problem" other than one which is legislatively or judicially made. Only three other Supreme Court Justices sat with Black during the entire "obscenity period" (1957 to 1971). They were Justices Douglas, Brennan, and Harlan. By the start of the October 1971 term, only Brennan and Douglas remained from the days of *Roth.* Eleven other Justices served during those 14 years from *Roth* to *Reidel,* some staying for long periods (e.g., Chief Justice Warren from 1953 to 1969) and some stayed on the Court for only a brief time (e.g., Justice Goldberg from 1962 to 1965).

While Black was consistent in his dealing with obscenity, the Supreme Court as a body was not. From its first attempts at defining the indefinable, the Court zigged and zagged its way through a morass of obscenity decisions (or were they indecisions?) which pleased first liberals then conservatives. It attempted without success to draw a workable guideline so that writers, artists, photographers, and filmmakers could know before publication or showing whether their work met the Court's standards for First Amendment protection. The Court failed.

I

In 1957, the Supreme Court in *Roth v. United States* tried for the first time to define obscenity.[11] The case involved publisher Roth's conviction for sending obscene matter through the mails, a violation of federal law. His conviction was sustained by a divided Supreme Court which tried to justify obscene expression as being outside the protection of the First Amendment by claiming it was "utterly without redeeming social importance." This premise was heatedly debated at the time, just as it is today. "Obscene material," said the majority opinion, "is material which deals with sex in a manner appealing to prurient interest." Justice Brennan, who was to become the Court's "resident expert" on obscenity decisions during the Warren years by the frequency with which he spoke for the Court's majority, then suggested the following as a test for obscenity:

whether to the average person, applying contemporary community
standards, the dominant theme of the material taken as a whole appeals
to prurient interest.[12]

Two important points emerge from Justice Brennan's oft-quoted and
oft-criticized opinion of the Court. First, it acknowledged that much salacious
writing now could be free from prosecution, i.e., writing that met the test set
down by the Court and therefore received protection of the First Amendment.
The door was left ajar under certain ill-defined conditions, such as "redeeming social importance," whatever that is. Justice Black rather than leaving the
door ajar, would have taken it off the hinges.

Second, by trying to define the indefinable, Brennan and a majority of
his colleagues invited arguments that have continued to this day. How does
one exhibit a prurient interest? How prurient does one's prurient interest have
to be? By "contemporary community standards" does the Court mean local
standards? Is it implying that the Constitution means one thing in Iowa City
and another in New York City? Is there any literature or art that does not
have at least some redeeming importance to someone — to the artist if to no
one else? Should various esoteric groups be held to the nation's "average"
standards? How are these average standards measured? And on and on.

None of these dilemmas, of course, confronted Justice Black. He
repeatedly maintained that the government and the courts had no business
violating what he saw as an absolute constitutional prohibition against in-
terfering with free expression. Nor did these complexities concern Justice
Douglas, for he stood firmly with Black on these issues. The two, each on the
Court for nearly one-third of a century as the decade of the 1970s arrived,
took turns, as it were, agreeing with each other's absolutist positions as other
Justices attempted to justify their conclusions through verbal gymnastics. The
Black-Douglas tandem in dealing with obscenity is reminiscent of the Holmes-
Brandeis solidarity of a half-century earlier in dealing with sedition.

In each opinion of Black and Douglas the same line repeated itself: the
First Amendment absolutely prohibits governmental interference with free
expression, obscene or otherwise.

If the 1957 *Roth* decision opened the door to greater permissiveness
amongst the nation's writers and artists, *Smith v. California* opened it wider
for the distributor.[13] The Court unanimously held that a bookseller cannot be
convicted on obscenity charges unless he knows that the materials he is selling
are obscene. And the chipping away at the *Roth* foundation continued.

Three years after *Smith* the Court pushed the door farther open in
Manual Enterprises v. Day, this time allowing use of the mails for the
distribution of materials designed for homosexuals.[14] Finally, in the last of a
string of "liberalizing" decisions relative to censorship of alleged obscene
literature, the Supreme Court in 1966 overturned a lower court ruling that
the eighteenth century "classic" tale of a libertine named Fanny Hill was
obscene.[15] In what appeared at the time to be a major ruling by the Court,

Justice Brennan, delivering the opinion of the 6–3 majority, reemphasized the "redeeming social importance" dictum of *Roth*.

But that same day, two other obscenity decisions, handed down separately, signaled a new tack for the Court. In one, *Mishkin v. New York*, the Justices upheld the conviction of a publisher of sadomasochistic materials.[16] In the other, *Ginzburg v. United States*, the Court interjected a new test for obscenity — "pandering."[17] It involved an examination of the actions and intentions of the author or distributor of a work, rather than a decision based solely on the work itself. Black dissented vehemently in both decisions. In *Mishkin* he wrote:

> The only practical answer to these concededly almost unanswerable problems is, I think, for this Court to decline to act as a national board of censors over speech and press but instead to stick to its clearly authorized constitutional duty to adjudicate cases over things and conduct. Halfway censorship methods, no matter how laudably motivated, cannot in my judgment protect our cherished First Amendment freedoms from the destructive aggressions of both state and national government.[18]

In *Ginzburg* he threw up his hands in apparent despair, writing:

> As bad and obnoxious as I believe governmental censorship is in a Nation that has accepted the First Amendment as its basic ideal for freedom, I am compelled to say that censorship that would stamp certain books and literature as illegal in advance of publication or conviction would in some ways be preferable to the unpredictable book-by-book censorship into which we have now drifted.[19]

It is true that Chief Justice Warren, in a concurrence in *Roth*, suggested the "pandering" test, but few listened during the decade between *Roth* and *Ginzburg*. Warren in 1957 wrote that "it is not the book that is on trial; it is a person. The conduct of the defendant is the central issue, not the obscenity of a book or picture."[20]

An assessment of the progression of obscenity decisions, which peaked in *Ginzburg*, was offered in 1967 by Harry Kalven, Jr., of the University of Chicago:

> Prior to *Ginzburg*, one would have been tempted to observe that Justice Black was failing to note how with each succeeding case the constitutional law of obscenity was evolving by a common law process that added restrictive qualifications to the test, and that he was being too solemnly principled in opposition to a shrewd Court that was willing to hold in theory that obscenity was subject to regulation but was disposed in practice never again to find anything obscene. But the general sense of surprise attending the *Ginzburg* decision may suggest that his long view of the matter was sound after all.[21]

The corner apparently had been turned by the *Ginzburg* decision, which Justice John Harlan called "an astounding piece of judicial improvisation."[22] The path toward greater freedom to distribute salacious material had been blocked after nine years of growing—albeit uneven—liberalism. The Court seemed about to reverse field again the following year in *Redrup v. New York* when the Court in a brief, unsigned opinion emphasized that "girlie" magazines are not obscene per se.[23]

Still searching for the answer, the Court a year later, in 1968, said that states may enact laws prohibiting juveniles from being sold salacious literature that is constitutionally available to adults.[24] And the year following that, the Court handed down what appeared at the time to be a significant way out of the quagmire wrought by *Roth*. In *Stanley v. Georgia* the Court held that the possession of obscene matter for use within the privacy of one's home was constitutional.[25] This was the final obscenity decision of the Warren Court—a "last gasp" for liberalism, as it were. The Chief Justice retired following the close of that session. While the opinion written by Justice Thurgood Marshall was said not to negate *Roth*, it did hold firm views which, if allowed to develop further, would have reduced the effect of *Roth* significantly. In a beautifully turned phrase—one which could well have come from Black's pen as well—Marshall wrote for the majority:

> If the First Amendment means anything, it means that a State has no business telling a man, sitting alone in his own house, what books he may read or what films he may watch. Our whole constitutional heritage rebels at the thought of giving government the power to control men's minds.[26]

But tacking again, the Court in 1971 all but pulled back to "basic *Roth*" in two decisions handed down in May during the waning weeks of Justice Black's tenure on the high court. Many feel that these two federal decisions, one involving the Postal Service and the other the Customs, heralded a direction the Court would adhere to for some time, and all but eroded *Stanley* to footnote status.

In the postal case, *United States v. Reidel,* the Court held that the *Stanley* decision did not mean that the federal government had to be a party to the distribution of obscene matter.[27] Similarly, in *United States v. Thirty-Seven Photographs* the Court said that *Stanley* did not prohibit Customs officials from banning entry into the country of obscene matter destined for commercial distribution, in this case pictures intended for publication in book form.[28] One can only ponder what the Court might have done had the importer claimed his photos were for use in the privacy of his own home.

Dwight Teeter and Don Pember described the Court's action in *Reidel* as an "attempt to tidy up some of the judicial debris left behind by the *Stanley* and *Redrup* decisions."[29] Black and Douglas dissented in both these decisions and were joined by Justice Marshall in *Thirty-Seven Photographs*. Both decisions were handed down May 3, 1971, about one month before the Court was scheduled to adjourn for the term.

In what was to be his final written opinion regarding obscenity, Black once again chided his colleagues with the following insightful speculation:

> Since the plurality opinion offers no plausible reason to distinguish private possession of "obscenity" from importation for private use, I can only conclude that at least four members of the Court would overrule *Stanley.* Or perhaps in the future that case will be recognized as good law only when a man writes salacious books in his attic, prints them in his basement, and reads them in his living room.[30]

It was a good phrase for Justice Black to close with, because it illustrates the clarity of his thought, the simplicity of his phraseology, and the precision of his pen. It couldn't have been said better.

II

In questions of motion picture censorship, the Court demonstrated similar ambivalence. Originally, in 1915, the Court held that motion pictures were a "business pure and simple" and therefore were not among those expressions protected by the First Amendment.[31] Justice Douglas hinted at a reversal of that position in 1948. "We have no doubt," he wrote in his majority opinion, "that motion pictures, like newspapers and radio, are included in the press whose freedom is guaranteed by the First Amendment."[32]

Then in 1952 the Court firmly granted films First Amendment protection with its decision in the case of *The Miracle,* a film thought by some to be sacrilegious.[33] This protection was supported and widened in 1959 to encompass films dealing with sexuality—adultery in this case.[34] But it was not until 1961 that the Court addressed itself directly to the practice of licensing motion pictures prior to public showing. In *Times Film v. Chicago* the Supreme Court in a 5 to 4 decision said prescreening requirements and licensing were permissible under the Constitution.[35] But the Court vacillated as it did with the written word by modifying the *Times Film* decision in two cases decided in 1964 and 1965.[36] Finally, the Court echoed the *Ginsberg* decision involving literature by hinting in 1968 that it would accept "variable standards" of obscenity for youth and adults if the enabling legislation were written with care to protect First Amendment rights of adults.[37]

III

Through it all, Black stood firm, unbending at the quixotic winds blowing from a vote-conscious Congress, irate moralists, frustrated law enforcement officers, and rationalizing colleagues. He fought without wavering to protect the material he often claimed he hated. He did so because he felt the dictate of the First Amendment was clear.

Justice Black did not read or view material before the Court on obscenity questions. "I have not seen the picture," he wrote in a concurring opinion when the Court upheld the constitutionality of the film version of the D. H. Lawrence story *Lady Chatterley's Lover*.[38] Again, in the 1966 *Mishkin* decision: "Neither in this case nor in *Ginzburg* [handed down the same day] have I read the alleged obscene matter."[39]

In a CBS television interview with Justice Black in 1968 Martin Agronsky asked about this apparent dereliction of judicial duty:

> "There is an interesting aspect to your position on the obscenity cases in that you refuse yourself to even examine the evidence, as it were."
>
> "That's not peculiar," Black replied. "Why should it be peculiar?"
>
> "Well, one would think that a judge should examine the evidence."
>
> "Why?" was Black's retort. "Why should he if he doesn't think there is such a thing? Why should I go and look at those things—and I don't look at them—but why should I go and look at them when it doesn't make any difference what the talk is or what it is. I don't think it violates any law. Only those look at it think they're invested with the God-given power of looking at it and telling what's obscene—what's obscene enough so they won't let people see it. I don't feel that way."[40]

The line of consistency from *Roth* to *Reidel* can be seen in the following chronological excerpts from Justice Black's opinions:

In 1957:

> The standard of what offends "the common conscience of the community" conflicts, in my judgment, with the command of the First Amendment that "Congress shall make no law . . . abridging the freedom of speech, or of the press." Certainly that standard would not be an acceptable one if religion, economics, politics, or philosophy were involved. How does it become a constitutional standard when literature treating with sex is concerned? [*Roth,* Douglas, with whom Black joined, dissenting][41]

In 1959:

> My view is . . . that prior censorship of moving pictures like prior censorship of newspapers and books violates the First and Fourteenth Amendments. [*Kingsley International Pictures,* Black concurring.][42]

In 1961:

> I think the conviction of the appellant or anyone else for exhibiting a motion picture abridges freedom of the press as safeguarded by the First Amendment, which is made obligatory on the states by the Fourteenth. [*Jacobellis,* Black concurring.][43]

In 1966:

> I would reverse this case and announce that the First and Fourteenth Amendments taken together command that neither Congress nor the States shall pass laws which in any manner abridge freedom of speech and press—whatever the subjects discussed. [*Mishkin*, Black dissenting.][44]

In 1968:

> As I read the First Amendment, it was designed to keep the State and the hands of all state officials off the printing presses of America and off the distribution systems for all printed literature. [*Ginsberg*, Douglas, joined by Black, dissenting.][45]

And finally, in 1971:

> Despite the proven shortcomings of *Roth*, the majority today reaffirms the validity of the dubious decision. Thus, for the foreseeable future this Court must sit as a Board of Supreme Censors, sifting through books and magazines and watching movies because some official fears they deal too explicitly with sex. [*Reidel*, Black dissenting.][46]

But not everyone sees the First Amendment in such clear-cut terms. Harry Clor has rejected Black's absolutist theory:

> It is not true, as Justice Black asserts, that "the area set off for individual freedom . . . was marked by boundaries precisely defined." The words of the First Amendment do not define their own boundaries. Men must determine their scope and application by the exercise of judgments of fact, of law, and of value. This is not to say that First Amendment rights, having been adjudged to be such, will then be balanced against competing considerations. Rather, it is to say that we cannot define these rights, we cannot determine what specific rights are granted by the general terms of the First Amendment, without engaging in the kinds of intellectual operations which Justice Black seems to preclude. Judges will have to determine when a slight restraint upon speech constitutes an abridgment of the freedom of speech. This must involve judgments of value, as does any effort to define or apply terms which have ethical and political import. Such judgments may be more or less prominent, but they cannot be precluded. Thus the absolute language of the First Amendment does not of itself settle the problem of obscenity regulation.[47]

But Black would have countered with the argument that this "balancing" went on in the minds of the framers of the Constitution. And that, upon weighing the pros and cons, they opted for free speech—absolute free speech. "Censorship," Black said in *Smith v. California*, "is the deadly enemy of freedom and progress. The plain language of the Constitution forbids it."[48]

While most of the attention given to Black revolves around his absolutist position regarding First Amendment questions, during the half dozen years before his leaving the Court he increasingly braced his absolutist position with more pragmatic arguments. Most obscenity cases to come before the Supreme Court in the late 1950s and early 1960s resulted in a case-by-case common law trend toward greater freedom of expression. While Black and Douglas did not win the philosophical war, they were winning the individual battles. Obscenity convictions were being overturned by the Supreme Court and the lower courts, but not because the judges were convinced of the wisdom of Black's position. Still Black persisted.

But with the decisions in *Ginzburg* and *Mishkin,* the Court brought to a halt this trend toward liberalism. And with that change in direction, Black seemed to become more emotional and pragmatic in his arguments. He was convinced, apparently, that his "plain reading" of the "simple words" of the First Amendment would never be accepted by his colleagues. In his *Ginzburg* dissent, for example, he wrote about sex being a "fact of life" and urged that "its discussion ought not be made a crime."[49]

Michael Ash in 1967 commented:

> Typical of the Justice's new concerns during 1962-66, the argument raised an institutional question, the fitness of the federal judiciary to the task of censorship. Federal judges, Black argued in these cases, because of life tenure, constitute the most appropriate tribunal for marking out the boundaries of what government can and cannot do. The task of censorship—of "finally deciding what particular discussion or opinion must be suppressed"—however, is a horse of a different color. First, it is immensely time-consuming, involving a case-by-case assessment of social values and a more or less lengthy perusal of each piece of trash whose obscenity is contested. More important, it requires appointed officials, whose removal by the people is substantially impossible, to perform the kinds of duties traditionally left to elected legislatures.[50]

In his earlier writing, Black did touch upon the practical as well as the philosophical, but as the years moved on and the Court "faltered," he increasingly seemed to focus on this emphasis. Early hints of the pragmatic Black came from his concurrence in *Smith v. California* in which he wrote:

> While it is "obscenity and indecency" before us today, the experience of mankind—both ancient and modern—shows that this type of elastic phrase can, and most likely will, be synonymous with the political, and maybe with the religious unorthodoxy of tomorrow.[51]

Kalven questioned Black's fears. Referring to the quote immediately above, Kalven wrote:

> This seems to me an unpersuasive way to put the case against obscenity laws. The Court has shown a marked tendency not to expand the concept, as is evident from the refusal to permit its extension to

sadistic violence in *Winters v. New York,* or to sacrilege in *Burstyn v. Wilson,* or to thematic obscenity in *Kingsley Pictures.*[52]

In a 1962 interview with Edmond Cahn, Black acknowledged that the law allows arrests to be made for obscenity, but added that "it was the law of Rome that they could arrest people for obscenity after Augustus became Caesar. Tacitus says that then it became obscene to criticize the Emperor. It is not any trouble to establish a classification so that whatever it is that you do not want said is within that classification."[53]

Other early evidences of his pragmatism came in *Kingsley Pictures* when he wrote that "neither States nor moving picture makers can possibly know in advance, with any fair degree of certainty, what can or cannot be done in the field of movie making and exhibiting."[54]

Black's writing also became more forceful as time progressed. His dissent in the 1966 *Ginzburg* case:

> My conclusion is that certainly after the fourteen separate opinions handed down in these three cases today [*Ginzburg, Mishkin,* and *Memoirs*] no person, not even the most learned judge much less a layman, is capable of knowing in advance of an ultimate decision in his particular case by the Court whether certain material comes within the area of "obscenity" as that term is confused by the Court today.[55]

And in *Reidel,* Black wrote in a dissenting opinion that he "particularly" regretted the Court's revival of *Roth* as the test for obscenity. He noted that in the Court's many decisions involving questions of obscenity it had been extremely difficult for the judges — or for ordinary citizens — to agree on what is obscene. "After *Roth,*" he wrote, "our docket and those of other courts have constantly been crowded with cases where judges are called upon to decide whether a particular book, magazine, or movie may be banned. I have expressed before my view that I can imagine no task for which this Court of lifetime judges is less equipped to deal."[56]

Another reflection of Black's pragmatic view came during the 1968 interview over CBS. "Obscenity," said Black, "is wholly ambiguous. It means one thing to you, and another thing to you, and another thing to thee and another thing to me."

Newsman Martin Agronsky asked the Justice whether he could think of any time when restrictions against obscenity would not come into conflict with the First Amendment. Black's reply:

> I certainly couldn't. Of course, I understand that pornography sounds bad. It really sounds bad, but I never have seen anybody who can say what it is. Nobody. Now, some people say it's a-way over there and some people say it's a-way over here. If the idea is to keep people from learning about the facts of life as between sexes, that's a vain task. . . . How in the world can you keep people from learning who mix with others out on the streets and around in the various places? They're

going to learn. But that's not the reason I take that view. The reason I
take that view is that it's an expression of opinion. It refers to one of the
strongest urges in the human race — something that people have not
failed to talk about and they will not fail to talk about it.[57]

And Black is right. People never will stop talking about it. But where
does that leave the Supreme Court now that the strong voice for the First
Amendment is no longer heard in the chambers? Legal scholars have spotted
signs they believe point to one of two courses of action.

First is a prediction that the Court will tend to withdraw from the
obscenity hassle, tossing it back into the laps of state courts and legislatures by
refusing to hear state cases and thereby refusing to make "a federal case" out
of obscenity. Support for this view comes from (1) several recent decisions, (2)
the makeup of the Court with the four Nixon appointees who tend to favor
federal judicial restraint, (3) the Court's inability to agree on a meaning of the
"contemporary community standards" test as set down by *Roth,* (4) a general
frustration and dissatisfaction with the outcome of attempting to handle the
myriad state obscenity convictions on a case-by-case, First Amendment level,
and (5) the absence of Hugo Black from the bench.

Those who favor leaving such questions to the states can find support in
the writing of Black himself:

> I think the federal judiciary because it is appointed for life is the
> most appropriate tribunal that could be selected to interpret the Con-
> stitution and thereby mark the boundaries of what government agencies
> can and cannot do. But because of life tenure, as well as other reasons,
> the federal judiciary is the least appropriate branch of government to
> take over censorship responsibilities by deciding what pictures and
> writings people throughout the land can be permitted to see and read.
> When this Court makes particularized rules on what people can see and
> read, it determines which policies are reasonable and right, thereby per-
> forming the classical function of legislative bodies directly responsible to
> the people.[58]

Leaving obscenity decisions to the states would, of course, conflict with
Black's position on the absolutism of the First Amendment and his view that
only conduct should come under legislative restraints, never expression.
Nonetheless, Black did give support, conscious or otherwise, to those who
would like to move obscenity from the federal court calendars.

The second prediction relative to future Supreme Court action on
obscenity is that the Court might eventually draw a firm line between voluntary, adult exposure to salacious material and accidental or juvenile exposure
to such matter. Support for this position comes from (1) the Report of the
Presidential Commission on Obscenity and Pornography which suggests that
no relationship exists between adult exposure to salacious material and an-
tisocial behavior, thereby eliminating one strong argument of the censors,
i.e., that a "clear and present danger" does exist to society in the publication

of obscenity; (2) recent Supreme Court decisions involving postal regulation, privacy, and "variable standards" for adults and juveniles (e.g., *Stanley, Ginsberg, Interstate Circuit, Reidel*); (3) a growing concern on the part of a number of persons at state interference in what is called "victimless crime," including sexual activity among consenting adults; and (4) a continuing move of the public toward sexual freedom and openness. Federal Judge Irving R. Kaufman, for example, noted:

> If the only reason for a prosecution is to protect an adult against his own moral standards which do harm to no one else, it cannot be tolerated. Private communication seems no less part of freedom than privacy to read one's own books. If not, then the privacy that *Stanley* held inviolable is less robust than we would have thought.[59]

Some legal scholars, says R. G. Decker in the *California Law Review,* find it difficult to understand how "a former Baptist Sunday School teacher could continuously vote to strike down all laws dealing with obscenity."[60] Black's answer might be found in the 1968 CBS interview:

> People . . . write letters and say you're letting my children suffer. There's plenty of argument for the idea that they ought to take care of their children and warn them against things themselves rather than to try and pass a law.[61]

How does one evaluate a judge — especially a judge of such contemporary reknown? It is more safely done by historians. There is not much argument over the greatness of John Marshall or of Oliver Wendell Holmes. Time neutralizes much of the emotion — both pro and con — active judges are bound to evoke. Time tends to even out the peaks and valleys. It is more difficult to attempt to evaluate a judge to whom we are still close. Does one look at the clarity of his written opinions? Study the consequences? Attempt to test his persuasiveness? Conduct a poll among judges and scholars?

If one were to stand Justice Black against these tests in the area of obscenity, one would probably get mixed results. Certainly, he was respected and listened to by judges and philosophers, but he was unable to convince his colleagues on the Supreme Court that he was right about the "absoluteness" of the First Amendment.

Clifford J. Durr, in a memorial tribute to Justice Black, placed Black's years on the bench in perspective:

> Hugo was born and grew to maturity in a frontier community in which horses and mules were not only the principal means of transportation and conveyance, but, behind the plow, a major source of productive energy as well. He lived to see energy measured, not in terms of horsepower, but in terms of megatons of explosive force. He was a grown man when the Wright brothers flew at Kitty Hawk, but he lived to see spaceships exploring the solar system and men walking on the moon. The

remarkable thing about him was not his ability to change with changing times, but the timelessness of the values of justice, freedom, and human dignity which he held so dear and for which he fought so brilliantly during his long life.[62]

But perhaps Anthony Lewis of the *New York Times* relayed earlier the best clue to Hugo Black's impact:

Justice Black's admirers regard him as the most courageous and creative of judges. His critics consider him "lawless," a judge who shapes the law to advance the interest he favors. But no one would question his influence. A Government lawyer put it this way recently:

"The test of his impact on the Supreme Court is to try to envisage it without him. Despite the great issues that have come before the Court, without him these would have been years of complacency."[63]

9 **Black v. contempt**

MICHAEL J. PETRICK

I

If contempt literally means "a despising of the authority, justice or dignity of a court,"[1] American journalists of the early 1970s must have led a galloping movement to heap scorn and disdain upon our judicial system. For in those years, contempt citations issued by judges against members of the news media increased in perhaps unprecedented fashion.

Some observers may muse that this trend actually represents growing scorn by judges for journalists. More likely than not, the trend has little to do with sudden hatred by either party. Rather, the flurry of contempt actions is probably a symptom that both the courts and the media have missed some important historical-legal lessons.

Justice Hugo L. Black provided a valuable lesson through repeated warnings that unless restricted, the laws of contempt can be disastrous to freedom of expression. Black tried to persuade his colleagues on the Supreme Court that certain aspects of the contempt power, as adopted and practiced by the American judiciary, were illegitimate in origin and pernicious in effect. In key decisions, he convinced Court majorities to soften particularly harsh contempt doctrines. He may have won some battles, but did he win the war?

In 1970, attorney Ronald Goldfarb prefaced his extensive study of contempt law with a statement that nearly dismissed contempt as a serious threat

MICHAEL J. PETRICK is associate professor in the College of Journalism at the University of Maryland (College Park). He received the Ph.D. in mass communication from the University of Wisconsin-Madison. His scholarly interests are mass communication law and professional responsibility. He is coauthor (with Steven Chaffee) of *Using the Mass Media: Communication Problems in American Society,* and author of articles related to mass media law.

to the news media. In assessing the situation as it had developed over 150 years, Goldfarb said:

> The contempt power has been almost abandoned in America as a vehicle for controlling press publication about trials—at least where there is no jury. The press will be allowed to criticize judges' decisions, law, and the trial process, immune from punishment for contempt. . . .[W]hile the Supreme Court, like much of the organized bar, has become increasingly critical of press coverage of crime and trial news, it does not appear poised to punish the press for contempt for what it sees as misconduct of this nature.[2]

Goldfarb's optimistic analysis was understandable, in view of two trends that had watered down the use of contempt power against the media. One was a growing realization by both the media and the bar that tensions and disagreements over coverage of trials could be reduced by substantial housecleaning in both camps. Indeed, the Supreme Court in the *Sheppard,*[3] *Estes,*[4] and *Irvin*[5] decisions had applied verbal pressure to trial judges and to the news media to correct abuses that interfered with the administration of justice. By the late 1960s, press/bar groups in several states had hammered out working agreements to reduce conflicts arising out of news coverage of judicial proceedings. It appeared to many observers, including Goldfarb, that a new spirit of restraint by judges, lawyers, and journalists would curb the kinds of disputes that might otherwise lead to contempt citations.

The second trend grew out of the 1941 *Bridges* decision of the Supreme Court,[6] in which Justice Black, in his opinion for the Court, required that citations against the media for out-of-court (or indirect) contempt be subjected to the "clear and present danger" test. Without a showing of such danger, Black stated, persons constitutionally could not be cited for contempt because of what they said or published about a trial or a judge. In the subsequent *Pennekamp*[7] and *Craig*[8] cases, the Court amplified its intent to protect journalists' rights to report and criticize judicial proceedings with minimal fear of contempt citations.

But things seem to have gone awry. Rather than being "almost abandoned," the contempt power has reemerged as a major obstacle to the free flow of information and commentary. Two explanations for this seem plausible. For one thing, some trial judges probably overreacted to the American Bar Association's Reardon Report,[9] which recommended stringent restrictions on out-of-court statements about pending trials.[10] Others apparently misinterpreted the Reardon recommendations as granting broad authority to cite journalists for out-of-court contempt despite the "clear and present danger" requirement set forth in *Bridges.* Although some of these recent judicial abuses of the contempt power have been corrected by appellate courts,[11] its capricious use remains an occupational hazard. Indeed, many contempt convictions are not appealed (although they may well deserve to be). Every unchallenged abuse of the contempt power against a journalist chills First Amendment rights. Its use to control news and criticism about judicial matters could lead to a fettered press submissive to court gag orders for fear of punishment by contempt. The disastrous effect, as Black pointed out in *Bridges*, would be that public discussion of judicial proceedings "would be as effectively discouraged as if a deliberate statutory scheme of censorship had been adopted."[12]

The second reason for the likely rebirth of contempt as a threat to the news media is seen in numerous recent attempts to force journalists to disclose confidentially obtained information or to reveal the identity of news sources in court and grand jury proceedings. At common law, such refusal constitutes direct interference with the process of justice and therefore is punishable by the contempt power. Since 1970, more and more enterprising investigative journalists have used confidential sources to discover and report wrongdoing, often to the embarrassment of police officers and prosecutors. With increasing frequency, such reporters have been brought before grand juries and directed to name their sources or to disclose unpublished information obtained in confidence. Society's stake in protecting and promoting confidential relationships between journalists and news sources has, of course, been recognized in at least 24 states through the passage of so-called "shield laws." But even in those states, appellate courts have shown a disturbing tendency to interpret away the statutory nondisclosure privilege, thus making recalcitrant reporters susceptible to contempt punishment.[13]

In states with no statutory protection, arguments for establishing a common law right of confidentiality have been consistently rejected.[14] Hopes for a judicial ruling that the First Amendment provides journalists with a nondisclosure privilege were dashed in the Supreme Court's 1972 *Branzburg v. Hayes* decision.[15] Some argue that without the protection only an absolute shield law with nationwide applicability could provide, the news media may well have to choose one of two courses: cut back on hard-nosed investigative reporting, or face frequent encounters with the contempt power. It is a disheartening choice.

The law of contempt, particularly as it relates to freedom of expression, is therefore a lively and timely legal issue. Hugo Black helps us understand it.

II

Part of the problem with contempt of court is that it has become an amalgam of offenses, belabored by judges who attempt to categorize and to define its components. Should a particular offense be classified as *direct* or *indirect, civil* or *criminal* contempt? The answers have been inconsistent across time and jurisdictions, and the result has been to blur distinctions among categories.

A contemnor, therefore, often cannot be sure at the time of his offense whether he has committed direct-civil contempt, indirect-criminal contempt, or some other variation. The judicial classification of the offense determines the legal procedures the contemnor is to face and the extent to which he is protected by his constitutional rights. Precedent clearly establishes pro-

ceedings and penalties, but they emerge from the application of unpredict-
able rules. Classification — however confused — is at the heart of a dispute between the judge's contempt power and the accused's rights.

Many American judges have refused to follow the original common law
distinctions among the various kinds of contempt. But by some quirk, most
judges did manage to apply mechanically certain common law rules dealing
with proceedings for, and legal defenses against, contempt. Hugo Black was
not this kind of judge and he tried to change those aspects of contempt law
that he considered illegitimate anachronisms threatening to important liberties.

Black's efforts to revise the laws of contempt all related in some way to
the doctrine of summary judgment, the power of a judge to cite, make a judgment, and punish all in one breath. The rule that a judge could summarily
punish a person for out-of-court (also called indirect, or constructive) contempt drew his ire. That criminal contempt could be punished without the
right to jury trial alarmed him; and the application of the "reasonable
tendency" doctrine to out-of-court contempt cases, thereby inviting judges to
punish according to whim, struck him as tyrannical.

Summariness has long been a whipping-boy for critics of the contempt
power, and deservedly so. Summary judgment, with respect to punishment
for contempt, "refers to the procedure which dispenses with the formality,
delay, and digression that would result from the issuance of process, service of
complaint and answer, holding hearings, taking evidence, listening to
arguments, awaiting briefs, submission of findings, and all that goes with a
conventional court trial."[16] It is, to say the least, an unconventional judicial
proceeding — especially for a legal system that cares about due process — since
the contemnor is both accused and adjudged in a single proceeding by a
single judge.

To call summariness merely unconventional is understatement. Black
claimed that summariness had illegitimate beginnings and oppressive effects.

What legal historians have pieced together as the origin of summary
punishment gives credence to Black's position.[17] Until the fifteenth century
and the days of the Star Chamber, English judges did not use the summary
power unless the accused contemnor admitted his offense. After all, a
criminal pleading guilty does not receive a trial. In all other instances,
contempt — criminal or civil, in-court or out-of-court — was subject to ordinary procedural safeguards, including jury trials on criminal contempt
charges. The Star Chamber changed all that. Star Chamber justice viewed
procedural niceties as unnecessarily burdensome and juries as lawlessly
mischievous. During that period judges — by reason of their legal knowledge
and their loyalties to the Crown — were considered the embodiment of proper
legal procedure. Thus all phases of a contempt proceeding (including accusation, questioning, judging, and sentencing) became the province of the judge.

It would be incorrect to assume that America inherited its doctrines of
summary punishment directly from the Star Chamber. It did not. With the
abolition of the Chamber in 1641, some procedural safeguards were
reinstituted as part of the English common law. Accordingly, summary

punishment was limited only to *direct contempt* offenses—those that took place in the immediate physical presence of the judge. The rationale was that the judge, who had direct firsthand knowledge of the contemptuous act, was in a better position than anyone to administer justice.

Excluding the era of the Star Chamber, then, English common law between 1200 and 1800 legitimized summary punishment in only two kinds of circumstances: where the accused admitted he was guilty of contempt; and where the contempt was committed within the judge's presence. If early American lawmakers wanted to adopt English precedent on the contempt power, they should have included those two restrictions on summariness. But American state courts of the nineteenth century did not so restrict themselves. They chose, instead, to follow a strange mutation of English common law. The mutation was an unjustifiably famous English case, *Rex v. Almon*.[18] That case—though never officially reported and unpublished for 38 years after it was decided—became a precedent adopted by American (as well as English) courts for extending summary judgment to *constructive* contempt. Despite its dubious authenticity, it has been *the* authority for punishment of statements uttered or published outside the courtroom.

The *Almon* case is bizarre in three respects:

(1) The judge who issued the opinion, Sir John Eardley-Wilmot, completely disregarded all the precedent that limited the use of summary contempt procedures; Wilmot did not overrule precedent, he simply ignored it. Without citing a single case as authority, he boldly stated that out-of-court contempt "stands upon the same immemorial usage as supports the whole fabric of the common law," and was as much the law of the land as any other legal process.[19]

(2) Because of a legal technicality, the contempt action against Almon was never completed. Shortly before Wilmot was to deliver his contempt judgment against Almon, an error in the title of the case became apparent: someone named Wilkes mistakenly had been listed as the defendant. Justice Wilmot then asked Almon's attorney, "as a gentleman," to agree to a corrective amendment. But the attorney notified Wilmot that, "as a man of honor," he could not consent, and the case was dropped. Wilmot's opinion tracing summary out-of-court proceedings to "immemorial usage" was never officially delivered in court. Nor has the opinion ever been recorded in official law reports. And although written in 1764 it was not published until 1802, and then by Wilmot's son as part of a collection of his father's "notes."[20] The case, then, lacked the essential stuff that makes precedent; to call Wilmot's opinion purely *dicta* would be to give it more weight than it deserves. Yet precedent it became.

(3) Two eminent judicial figures of eighteenth-century England, Lord Mansfield and Sir William Blackstone, were involved indirectly in the *Almon* affair. Bookseller Almon had published statements criticizing Chief Justice Mansfield to whom Wilmot apparently owed his own judicial office. He therefore considered "criticism of the Lord as bordering on sacrilege."[21] Wilmot was also a friend and consultant of Blackstone's. When Blackstone began writing about contempt of court in his *Commentaries* he conferred

with Wilmot, who had previously written the *Almon* opinion. Blackstone later declared in the *Commentaries* that false statements about pending court activities — even though made out of court — were grounds for contempt. So, said Mansfield, were *true* accounts made without "the proper permission." And so was "anything, in short that demonstrates a gross want of that regard and respect which, when once courts of justice are deprived of, their authority is entirely lost among the people."[22] Moreover, the authority to punish summarily for *all* contempts, Blackstone declared, legitimately stems from "the first principles of judicial establishments."[23] Blackstone, therefore, did more than sanctify the unfounded assertions his friend Wilmot had made in *Almon*. He expanded, through delineation, the types of situations in which courts could proceed summarily to punish out-of-court expression. Blackstone had given his blessing, and American and English courts had only to respond.

Throughout the eighteenth century, and into the nineteenth, the overwhelming judicial response to Blackstone was a resounding "Amen." So the rule allowing summary judgment for constructive contempt became implanted in American law. It soon was so entrenched that courts even skirted legislation limiting summary contempt proceedings to cases of direct contempt. An 1831 federal statute denied federal courts the power to punish for contempt except for "misbehaviors of any person or persons in the presence of said courts, or so near thereto as to obstruct the administration of justice";[24] yet the Supreme Court in 1918 upheld a federal judge who had summarily punished a newspaper publisher for commenting upon a pending court decision.[25] State courts also found ways to avoid legislation that restricted their contempt powers. In general, the Wilmot/Blackstone doctrine prevailed until 1941.

Between 1941 and 1970, the Supreme Court — with Hugo Black as a frequent and vehement spokesman — severely eroded the Wilmot/Blackstone theory of summary judgment by finding that the theory failed to meet constitutional imperatives. The Court largely returned summariness to its limited pre-*Almon* status.

The odious qualities of summary judgment provided the Court with a handy rationale for placing constitutional restrictions on the use of contempt power. In general, the Court has come to the view that judges have no inherent or absolute right to institute summary punishment proceedings. Particularly when summariness runs afoul of certain constitutional rights, use of the contempt power must yield. So far, the Court has listed freedom of the press, due process, and trial by jury as the countervailing constitutional rights.

III

Conflicts between the First Amendment's freedom of the press clause and the power of judges summarily to punish for contempt of court resurrect the bugaboo of classifying contempt as *direct* or *indirect*. As developed through case law, direct contempt "takes place in the very presence of the judge, making all of the elements of the offense matters within his personal knowledge."[26] An indirect contempt is one committed away from the judge's presence, and thus "its demonstration depends on the proof of facts."[27] The distinction can be crucial because the First Amendment places limits on the use of summary punishment for indirect contempt, but not for direct contempt. Thus, a journalist accused of direct contempt for taking photographs in the courtroom during a course of a trial (or for refusing to answer grand jury questions) has no valid First Amendment defense against summary punishment.

Under the old *Almon* doctrine, freedom of the press did not protect against summary proceedings for indirect contempt offenses either. A journalist could be summarily punished without restriction for such things as inaccurately reporting a trial, for editorializing about an uncompleted court proceeding, or for publishing uncomplimentary commentary about a judge.

As late as 1941, the Supreme Court sanctioned the *Almon* doctrine, thus allowing unfettered use of summary judgment in contempt-by-publication cases.[28] The famous 1941 case of *Bridges v. California*[29] has gained fame as the first Supreme Court decision placing First Amendment considerations above the unrestricted power of courts to punish for indirect contempt. The most often cited aspect of the *Bridges* decision — whose 5 to 4 majority opinion was written by Black — was the adoption of the "clear and present danger" test as the applicable doctrine for contempt-by-publication conflicts. That indeed was an important restriction on the contempt power, since it meant judges no longer could constitutionally cite for indirect contempt merely because a news story or editorial might have a "reasonable tendency" to interfere with the administration of justice.

Bridges was important for another reason. It represented the first decision in which a Supreme Court majority questioned the inherent right of courts to summarily punish *any* out-of-court contempts. *Bridges,* in effect, laid the legal groundwork for what was to become a 30-year Court attack on summariness.

The *Bridges* decision involved the constitutionality of contempt citations against labor leader Harry Bridges and the *Los Angeles Times.* Bridges was cited for indirect contempt because he wrote a letter to the Secretary of Labor calling a judge's decision in a labor union case "outrageous." The *Times* was cited for publishing editorials commenting on court cases still in progress; in one of the editorials, the *Times* urged a judge to send two unsentenced defendants to jail because granting them probation would be a "serious mistake."

In his majority opinion, Black held that the contempt citations violated the First Amendment rights of Bridges and the newspaper. Black's rationale, of course, included the statement that punishment for indirect contempt violates the First Amendment unless a "clear and present danger" to justice could be shown.

In relying upon that rationale, Black relied heavily on the view that an inherent, unrestricted right to punish summarily for out-of-court contempt was historically and constitutionally invalid. A purpose of the American Revolution, he claimed, was to change the English common law rule (i.e., the *Almon* doctrine) which granted such unlimited powers to judges.[30] Noting that early state legislation had attempted to restrict severely summary punishment for indirect contempt, he implied that citizens in the early years of the republic had strong desires to protect the press from the contempt power.[31] The Bill of Rights, he argued, deliberately placed restrictions on contempt-by-publication.[32] Previous Supreme Court decisions upholding unrestricted use of contempt proceedings to restrict the press resulted, he said, in an unconstitutional chilling effect on expression:[33]

> It would follow as a practical result of the decisions below that anyone who might wish to give public expression to his views on a pending case involving no matter what problem of public interest, just at the time his audience would be most receptive, would be as effectively discouraged as if a deliberate statutory scheme of censorship had been adopted.

Bridges, then, can be viewed as a two-pronged legal attack on the judicial power to punish summarily. First, by imposing a "clear and present danger" standard, Black's majority limited the type of out-of-court expression that could be constitutionally susceptible to summary contempt proceedings.[34] Second, and perhaps more important, Black managed to pull together the first Court majority willing to challenge the previously hallowed principles of unlimited summariness.

Since *Bridges*, the "clear and present danger" test has been the governing First Amendment doctrine for challenges to indirect contempt citations. The Supreme Court subsequently amplified its application of the test in *Pennekamp v. Florida*,[35] *Craig v. Harney*,[36] and *Wood v. Georgia*.[37] In *Pennekamp*, the Court ruled that editorials and a cartoon criticizing a judicial proceeding did not pose a clear and immediate threat, and that a resulting contempt citation was therefore constitutionally infirm. In *Craig*, admittedly distorted news stories about a pending trial were held protected under the First Amendment for lack of a showing of a serious and imminent danger to the process of justice. And in *Wood*, the Court ruled that criticism of legal proceedings was protected by the First Amendment unless the criticism was clearly designed to impede the course of justice.

It is generally believed that *Bridges* and its progeny have made arbitrary use of indirect contempt citations a negligible threat to the news and opinion media. That belief is valid in terms of constitutional doctrine. Trial courts, however, can display a penchant for ignoring Supreme Court precedent, particularly when the powers of judges are at issue. As suggested early in this chapter, the cause of freedom of expression would seem to require that the media spend the necessary resources to challenge invalid indirect contempt citations, thereby exercising the rights conferred by the *Bridges* legacy.

Having garnered a Supreme Court majority (albeit a slim one) in *Bridges* to narrow the *Almon* doctrine, Black began attacking contempt doctrines generally — particularly summariness — on due process grounds. Four years after *Bridges*, he authored an 8 to 0 decision limiting the power of federal judges to cite for *direct* contempt. The case, *In re Michael,*[38] concerned a witness who gave false testimony before a federal grand jury and was thereupon cited for contempt. Black's opinion held that perjury cannot be constitutionally punished via contempt. Such use of contempt powers is too sweeping, Black wrote, because it would

> permit too great inroads on the procedural safeguards of the Bill of Rights, since contempts are summary in their nature, and leave determination of guilt to a judge rather than a jury.[39]

The 1955 *Murchison* decision extended *Michael* to state proceedings.[40] Murchison, a Detroit policeman, had been a witness in a "John Doe" investigatory proceeding. The judge who conducted the proceeding thought Murchison's testimony was untruthful, so he charged Murchison with perjury and contempt. The Supreme Court, in a 6 to 3 opinion written by Black, decided the judge had violated Murchison's due process rights. Black conceded that direct contempts "can under some circumstances be punished summarily by the trial judge."[41] But, Black noted, the trial judge had based a contempt charge partly on his impression that a witness was uncooperative and "insolent." Judges, Black stated, are supposed to weigh factual *evidence* in making judgments; and since contempt judgments are summary in nature, the factual accuracy of the judge's impressions "could not be tested by adequate cross-examination."[42]

Concern for due process brought a further restriction on use of summary punishment in a 1962 Supreme Court decision, *In re McConnell.*[43] In that case, a trial judge summarily found a lawyer guilty of direct contempt for persistently asking witnesses questions the judge had (erroneously, it turned out) ruled improper. The Supreme Court's 5 to 2 opinion, again written by Black, ruled that attorney McConnell's behavior was properly designed to lay the foundation for a later appeal and therefore was not an obstruction of justice.

Harris v. United States[44] is a more recent example of restricting summariness in favor of due process rights. Harris had refused to answer questions before a federal grand jury, claiming self-incrimination. The presiding judge granted him immunity from prosecution, but Harris still declined to answer and was summarily punished for contempt. In 1965 the Supreme Court (in a 5 to 4 decision written by Justice William O. Douglas and concurred in by Black), held that federal courts may punish summarily for direct contempt only in exceptional circumstances, such as when the offense threatens the court or directly obstructs court proceedings. Refusal to testify before a grand jury, the Court stated, is not such an exceptional circumstance. Further, Douglas wrote, federal courts must provide a separate judicial hearing on contempt charges stemming from nonexceptional situations. Moreover, bringing a recalcitrant grand jury witness before the presiding judge and repeating the questions did not qualify as a separate hearing.

Harris was an abrupt turnabout from the Court's own precedents. Indeed, Douglas's opinion specifically overruled earlier decisions allowing summary punishment for any contemptuous act committed in the presence of a federal judge.

And so direct contempt is no longer punishable summarily merely because it happens to fall under the "direct" category. The Supreme Court's evolving directive seems to be that summary punishment should be meted out only to overcome a serious threat to the court itself or to its current business. Summariness no longer takes automatic constitutional priority over due process rights. That should be some consolation to journalists facing contempt charges for failing to reveal news sources; they are now at least entitled to some procedural safeguards.

Due process could provide a rationale for further curbs on summariness in direct contempt cases, should the Supreme Court decide to expand the trend begun by Black in 1945.

The Sixth Amendment's guarantee of a jury trial to defendants "in all criminal prosecutions" gave Black a third constitutional citadel from which to attack summary punishment. The jury trial issue spurred some of Black's most vehemently eloquent challenges to summariness.

The power to issue summary punishment collides directly with the right to a jury trial in those types of contempt classified as criminal. While case law has always distinguished between a criminal contempt and a civil one, there has never been a neat dividing line. In practice, the distinction usually rests on the purpose behind the punishment imposed. Thus, if a person is punished for contempt in order to rectify a threat to a court's dignity or authority, that contempt is considered criminal.[45] Civil contempt, on the other hand, is punishment for the purpose of enforcing the legal rights of a litigant in a civil lawsuit.[46] Criminal contempt is considered an offense against justice itself and therefore against society.

Although criminal contempt qualified as a "crime" by virtue of its nomenclature and purpose, until 1968 no person cited for the offense could claim a constitutional right to a jury trial. Prior to that the Supreme Court held firm to the *Almon* doctrine that all criminal contempt could be punished summarily.[47]

Black, more than any other Justice, was the Supreme Court's driving force in changing the law of criminal contempt. As a vigorous dissenter in five decisions before 1968, he in effect urged an "absolutist" interpretation of the wording of the Sixth Amendment and of Article III:[48] "All criminal prosecutions" means *all,* including those for criminal contempt.

Black introduced this view in a dissent in the *Sacher* case in 1952.[49] By a 5 to 4 vote, the Court had upheld the power of a federal judge to punish summarily Communist Party defense lawyers for "obstructive tactics" during a Smith Act trial. Black, however, claimed that the contempt proceedings were no more than "criminal prosecutions brought to avenge an alleged public wrong."[50] He called summary judgment in criminal contempt cases "an illegitimate offspring" of the contempt power,[51] and insisted that "a jury is all the more necessary . . . when the alleged offense relates to conduct that has personally affronted a judge."[52]

Sacher foreshadowed Black's oft-quoted 1958 denunciation of summary judgment in *Green v. United States.*[53] In *Green,* Black pulled out all the stops:

> Summary trial of criminal contempt, as now practiced, allows a single functionary of the state, a judge, to lay down the law, to prosecute those who he believes have violated his command (as interpreted by him), to sit "in judgment" on his own charges, and then within the broadest kind of bounds to punish as he sees fit.[54]

Black repeated his view that the Constitution was expressly designed to abolish arbitrary and oppressive government practices, and chided, "Cheap, easy convictions were not the primary concern of those who adopted the Bill of Rights."[55]

He unequivocally called for abandoning *Almon* and overruling Supreme Court precedent which he termed "wrong—wholly wrong."[56] Summary proceedings, he declared, were an "anomaly in the law."[57] And the Wilmot/Blackstone defense of the *Almon* doctrine, Black insisted, "has been wholly discredited by the painstaking research of the eminent authorities. . . ."[58]

He went further, branding summariness "inconsistent with the most rudimentary principles of our system of criminal justice."[59]

Black's stinging words convinced only Justice Douglas and Chief Justice Earl Warren, who joined in the dissent. The majority held firm to precedent and affirmed summary punishment for a man who had jumped bail after being convicted under the Smith Act.

Two years later, Black again had the opportunity to press his attack. But again, he was joined only by Douglas and Warren. The case, *Levine v. United States,*[60] began when Levine refused to answer questions before a federal grand jury after being granted immunity from prosecution; he was then punished summarily by a federal judge in a secret proceeding. The Supreme Court affirmed, but Black compared Levine's ordeal to a Star Chamber inquisition. He said Levine should have had a jury trial: "[I]t is nothing but a fiction to say that by labelling a prosecution for criminal punishment as one for 'contempt' it is changed from that which it actually is."[61]

The issue again confronted the Court, this time more spectacularly, in a 1964 case involving Mississippi Governor Ross Barnett's attempts to stop James Meredith from enrolling at the University of Mississippi. Federal courts had enjoined Barnett from interfering with the racial integration of "Ole Miss," and the governor was prosecuted for disobeying the injunctions. Barnett, preferring to rely on public opinion, demanded a jury trial on the criminal contempt charge; and when the Court of Appeals split 4 to 4 on whether he was so entitled, the question was certified to the Supreme Court. The Court held—this time by a 5 to 4 vote[62]—that a jury trial was not required.[63] Black's dissent in *Barnett* repeated themes expressed earlier in *Sacher, Green,* and *Levine:* that the Constitution required jury trials in criminal contempt cases, that courts had no inherent power to punish summarily, and that summary judgment for criminal contempt was a "judge-invented and judge-maintained" fiction.[64] But there was modicum of hope for Black's position in the *Barnett* majority opinion. In a footnote, Justice Tom Clark hinted that in the future the Court might require jury trials for serious criminal contempt charges. Black called the footnote a "halting but hopeful step" toward what he considered the Constitution's command.[65]

The footnote turned out to be good prophecy. A year after *Barnett,* Clark wrote a majority opinion that clearly indicated the Court was leaning— at least a little—toward Black's position. The case was *Cheff v. Schnackenberg.*[66] Cheff had been charged with criminal contempt of the Seventh Circuit U.S. Court of Appeals and was tried before a special three-judge panel of that court. The judges found him guilty and sentenced him to six months in jail. Cheff had unsuccessfully sought a jury trial, and the Supreme Court granted certiorari to decide whether the judges' panel could constitutionally impose a jail term for criminal contempt without a jury trial.

Although the Court upheld the jail sentence, Clark's majority rationale took a marked turn from previous decisions. *Even if the Court assumed that jury trials were required for serious criminal contempts,* Clark wrote, a six-month jail sentence constituted a "petty offense" and therefore was permissible. Clark was not merely hypothesizing about serious cases. He had plenty of *Almon*-supporting precedent on which to base the majority decision, but used the "petty offense" excuse. The Court clearly was ready to require jury trials in "serious" criminal contempt situations in the future.

Black was not overjoyed, but he did not author his own disagreement. Instead, he joined a Douglas dissent that criticized the evasive "serious" versus "petty" distinction. Douglas noted that contempt sentences had been getting longer in the country and suggested that the federal government viewed all criminal contempts as "serious." He called the majority's six-month formula a "mechanical distinction" and accused the Court of inventing a new "common law crime."[67] Douglas echoed Black's previous conclusion that *all* criminal contempts require a jury trial.

In 1968, the Court flatly admitted that the *Almon*-induced precedent in criminal contempt was wrong. Black in essence had won his point about its illegitimate origins. The occasion was *Bloom v. Illinois,*[68] and for the first time Black voted with the majority in a decision involving punishment for criminal contempt. The case concerned a man who had been cited by an Illinois court for filing a falsely prepared will to probate. He asked for a jury trial, but was turned down and summarily punished. The court imposed a jail sentence of 24 months.

The Supreme Court, with only Justice John Marshall Harlan dissenting, held that "serious" criminal contempts are so much like other "serious" crimes that they require a jury trial. The test for "seriousness," Justice Byron White wrote for the majority, should be the length of sentence imposed. The Court decided that a two-year jail term denoted seriousness.

The implications of *Bloom* were weighty. The Court had struck down a centuries-old doctrine that had been buttressed by several of the Court's own decisions. In White's blunt words, the majority had simply become convinced that criminal contempt "is a crime in every fundamental respect," including the appropriate procedures for its punishment.[69]

Black obviously had a lot to do with the convincing process, but he still had not persuaded his brethren that the word "all" in the Constitution meant "petty" as well as "serious." The Court's reliance on a length-of-sentence formula to determine the right to a jury trial did not eliminate a trial judge's ability to punish summarily for criminal contempt; a judge determined enough to exercise summary judgment need only impose a short jail sentence or a fine.

So *Bloom* left opportunities for evading the new principle it established. This became evident a year later in *Frank v. United States,*[70] in which the Court upheld a summary judgment for criminal contempt because the court had only imposed probation. Writing for a 6 to 3 majority, Justice Thurgood Marshall likened "petty" contempts to misdemeanors which, in criminal law, do not require a jury trial. Black dissented, recapitulating his literal interpretation of the word "all."[71] He reiterated the same theme in a concurring opinion in *Mayberry v. Pennsylvania,* the last criminal contempt decision in which he participated.[72]

IV

Just as he never succeeded in getting his absolutist interpretation of the First Amendment accepted by a Supreme Court majority, Hugo Black failed in completely eliminating summary judgment from the law of criminal contempt. The prospect of eventually attaining the latter would seem to coincide with the possibility of achieving jury trials for all misdemeanors. And treating criminal contempt as any other crime would be a profound revision of the laws of contempt.

If we look at Black-generated changes in contempt law in terms of types of contempt, the impact of those changes on freedom of expression becomes clearer. The indirect and/or criminal varieties of contempt-of-court have always posed the greatest threats to freedom of expression in mass communication.

Black consistently pointed out, and succeeded in forging a majority to agree with him, that both types of contempt power were not inherent or absolute, and that they must bend to more firmly established constitutional rights. As a direct result, punishment for indirect contempt came to require proof of a "clear and present danger" to justice, and severe summary punishments for criminal contempt became unconstitutional.

If attempts to use the contempt power indiscriminately to silence criticism increase, Black's successes in desanctifying the constitutional status of the doctrine of inherent and unrestricted power will become even more crucial.

Black on antitrust as a route of access to newspapers

10

PAUL JESS

To Hugo L. Black the words of the First Amendment, though penultimately important to a free society, were simple. He read the words "Congress shall make no law . . . abridging the freedom of speech, or of the press" as a literal command.[1] The foundation for this reading was Justice Black's firm belief in the libertarian notion that "right" individual and societal conclusions are more likely to be reached out of a multitude of voices than through any sort of authoritarian selection. As he said in the Pentagon Papers case:

> In the First Amendment the Founding Fathers gave the free press the protection it must have to fulfill its essential role in our democracy. The press was to serve the governed, not the governors.[2]

Or in dissent in an earlier case:

> The First Amendment provides the only kind of security system that can preserve a free government—one that leaves the way wide open for people to favor, discuss, advocate, or incite causes and doctrines however obnoxious and antagonistic such views may be to the rest of us.[3]

Professor Jerome A. Barron calls Black's position "romantic" and urges that the First Amendment be reinterpreted to create a "right of access" to the print media.[4]

PAUL JESS is associate professor in the School of Journalism at the University of Kansas. He received the Ph.D. in mass communication from the University of Minnesota. His teaching and research interests lie in press law and in media economics, management, and technology. He is a former reporter, editor-publisher, and printer of midwestern daily and weekly newspapers.

This essay examines a paradox in the views of Justice Black. His "romantic," judicially conservative, even mechanistic reading of the Constitution would almost certainly have caused the late Justice to object to the reinterpretation proposed by Barron. On the other hand, Justice Black's opinions and writings contain suggestions of another path toward a "right of access." Using antitrust law to foster the "multitude of voices" concept unquestionably would have been more acceptable to Black than would the idea of reading the First Amendment as requiring the creation of a right of citizen access to newspapers. Basic antitrust law and an exemption to it—the Newspaper Preservation Act—together provide the tools for a "right of access" Black probably would have endorsed.

I

Probably no proposal in the field of mass communication in the past decade has captured the attention of First Amendment scholars as completely as has Barron's right-of-access concept. Briefly, Barron contends that in modern society significant groups of people are unable to present their ideas to larger society through the established communication channels.

> The avowed emphasis of free speech is still on a freeman's right to "lay what sentiments he pleases before the public." . . . Today ideas reach the millions largely to the extent they are permitted entry into the great metropolitan dailies, news magazines, and broadcasting networks. The soap box is no longer an adequate forum for public discussion. Only the new media of communication can lay sentiments before the public, and it is they rather than government who can most effectively abridge expression by nullifying the opportunity for an idea to win acceptance. As a constitutional theory for the communication of ideas, laissez faire is manifestly irrelevant.[5]

According to Barron, technological advances and concentration of economic power have so changed the nature of communication in American society in the past century that the libertarian concept of the free marketplace of ideas has in effect been nullified.

To Barron, the real threat to the public right to know comes not from government but from the private sector. The owners of the media, in trying to reach the largest audience possible, are motivated primarily by the desire to protect their investments. Barron says owners of the media contend "the first amendment guarantees our freedom to do as we choose with our media." Because freedom of the press has come to be defined by the owners as a private right, "the constitutional imperative of free expression becomes a rationale for repressing competing ideas."[6]

To enable those groups with little or no ability to get their ideas before the general public, Barron proposes reading the First Amendment to require the print media to grant space to responsible holders of divergent views who represent significant sectors of the community. Thus in addition to being a negative force against governmental restraint, the First Amendment would be a positive force as against the total private control of the media.

II

Justice Black's old-fashioned reverence for the First Amendment would not have permitted him to extend its meaning to include a right of access to the media of communication. The words "Congress shall make no law" did not mean Congress shall insure every person a forum. And this was especially true if the forum in question happened to be someone else's private property.

In his book *A Constitutional Faith,* Black dealt with the question this way:

> No matter how urgently a person may wish to exercise his First Amendment guarantees to speak freely, he has no constitutional right to appropriate someone else's property to do so. Our Constitution recognizes and supports the concept of private ownership of property and in the Fifth Amendment provides that "no person shall . . . be deprived of life, liberty or property, without due process of law; nor shall private property be taken for public use without just compensation." The long and short of this problem is that while the First Amendment does guarantee freedom to speak and write, it does not at the same time provide for a speaker or writer to use other people's private property to do so.
>
> [First Amendment] language deals not with supplying people a place to speak, write or assemble, but only with the right to speak, write or assemble.[7]

These words are not surprising. They are, in fact, totally consistent with Justice Black's dissents in, for example, *Brown v. Louisiana*[8] and *Tinker v. Des Moines School District*[9] which so bemuse students who, until they encounter such cases, have pegged Black as a free speech ideologue. The fact that the property in these cases was public rather than private didn't deter Black, at least when the sole function of that public property was for learning or quiet contemplation. For Black, schools and libraries were wholly inappropriate places for demonstrations against social and political ills—no matter how closely those demonstrations were tied to First Amendment rights and no matter how peacefully they were conducted. Such demonstrations are designed to influence, said Black, else why would they be staged? Their purpose is therefore disruptive of the mind. When the locus of such demonstrations is a public place designed for mental activity, the exercise of speech in a form that disrupts or is designed to disrupt or divert mental activity constitutes the "appropriation of someone else's property." Places such as public schools and public libraries were simply not forums for speech. Speech was not accorded secondary or tertiary status in such places—it was accorded no status at all.

In a very real sense, Justice Black's absolute reading of the First Amendment precluded him from expanding the words to give them the positive reading proposed by Barron. But his dogged adherence to the literal command of the First Amendment was not based on absolutism alone. As early as 1945, well before he felt it necessary to adopt an absolutist posture, he specifically rejected the concept of newspapers as quasi-public utilities.[10]

III

In the same case in which Justice Black rejected the notion that newspapers could in some instances be considered common carriers, however, he uttered words that have a distinct "access to the press" ring about them:

> The First Amendment, far from providing an argument against application of the Sherman Act . . . provides powerful reasons to the contrary. [The] Amendment rests on the assumption that the widest possible dissemination of information from diverse and antagonistic sources is essential to the welfare of the public. . . .
>
> It would be strange indeed . . . if the grave concern for freedom of the press which prompted adoption of the First Amendment should be read as a command that the government was without powers to protect that freedom. . . . Surely a command that the government itself shall not impede the free flow of ideas does not afford non-government combinations a refuge if they impose restraints upon that constitutionally guaranteed freedom. Freedom to publish means freedom for all and not for some. . . . Freedom of the press from governmental interference under the First Amendment does not sanction repression of that freedom by private interests.[11]

Thus more than 20 years before Barron propounded his concept of access to the press, Justice Black had not only given his "thumbs down" to that notion, he had suggested another means to the same end—that means being antitrust action.

To Black, the libertarian concept could best be assured through freeing expression of all restraints—government and private. Governmental restraints, of course, were clearly made unconstitutional by the First Amendment. Private restraints of the sort that concern Barron, on the other hand, would be better dealt with as violations of antitrust law. Black approved of the ends sought by Barron, but the means used to achieve the ends were of paramount importance to Black, and Barron's means would have been anathema.

Because means were so important to Black, and because of his penchant for reaching liberal ends by judicially conservative means, he would undoubtedly demand case law and statutory support for achieving the right of access ends he set forth in dicta in *Associated Press*.

IV

Regardless of whether Marshall McLuhan is right in saying the medium is the message, it is certainly clear that the form and function of today's media are so often different as to be almost contradictory. In function the media are message carriers—the conduits of information. In form they are business institutions that require large amounts of capital to oversee and operate. The tensions between these form-function differences lie at the heart of libertarian concern for the elusive concept of the free flow of ideas.

As the institutions, or forms, of the communication media have grown in size and complexity, their management has required the expenditure of increasingly large amounts of time, effort, and money. The result has been relatively less attention being paid to the function of the media.

Although all of the major media exhibit this pattern of institutional growth and consequent diminution of attention to function, the newspaper industry provides the most complex and potentially useful example from the perspective of libertarian theory.

Traditionally the nation's newspapers have owned and operated printing plants. This long-established relationship was begun out of necessity and has continued because the second half of Newton's First Law of Motion (a body at rest tends to remain at rest) seems to apply to human attitudes and behavior as well as to the physical world.

Although they are not usually viewed as such, printing plants owned and operated by newspapers are "captive plants."[12] They play an essential role, but one that is not a part of the primary function of the newspaper. The primary function of the newspaper is to convey information. The primary tasks in fulfilling that function are journalistic. But most of the tasks that are performed daily in the newspaper organization are not journalistic. Rather, they relate to the form or institutional nature of the newspaper organization. Not the least of these nonjournalistic tasks are supplying, operating, and managing the newspaper's captive printing plant.

More than one-half of the payroll of the average daily newspaper goes to production and distribution workers. By contrast, less than one-quarter goes to editorial and advertising employees together. If editorial employees only are considered, about 15 percent of the daily newspaper payroll is journalistic. Two-thirds of a medium-sized daily newspaper's total expenses results from production. In newspapers with 100,000 or more circulation, administrative expenses approximate the editorial payroll. Given the relative expense patterns in the daily newspaper, it is understandable that most of the administrative attention of the newspaper organization is directed at nonjournalistic activity. To expect the institution to behave otherwise would be naive.[13]

The implications of this form-function dichotomy go beyond the problem of diversion of institutional attention, worrisome though that problem may be. The development of the newspaper as an institution of formidable economic stature has had a profound and harmful impact on the libertarian ideal as well. The establishment of the newspaper's captive printing plant as the normal mode of operation has combined, over the years, with the increasing economic power of the more successful newspaper organizations to reduce the number of competing newspaper voices available to each marketplace. Moreover, these same forces have combined to discourage the establishment or reestablishment of local newspaper competition.

The relationship between newspapers and printing plants is an understandable one, and one that probably was not consciously developed as a means of stifling competition. The growing economic concentration of newspapers is probably a result of natural economic forces at work in our system. Nevertheless, the combination of these two factors has created in the industry a condition that is susceptible to antitrust action. The case law and statutory foundation Justice Black would have demanded can be developed to attack that susceptibility.

Although it is fashionable among critics of ownership concentration in the media to view the Newspaper Preservation Act with a mixture of disdain and horror, it is also possible to view that legislation as a step in the direction of increasing the number of voices in the marketplace of ideas. Julius Rosenwald, the late retail magnate-philanthropist, is reputed to have once remarked, "The secret of business success is when you have a lemon, make lemonade." If, as its critics contend, the Newspaper Preservation Act is a lemon, perhaps the Rosenwald formula can be applied to turn it into something both palatable and nourishing.

The joint operating agreement permitted under the Newspaper Preservation Act should not be viewed as an unmitigated evil. The jointly operated plant — if it is an entity separate from each of the joint partners — forces the participants to recognize that their businesses are composed of discrete segments. No longer is it easy to confuse function and form or to be administratively mesmerized by the economic realities of the latter. The newspaper becomes less an economic institution and more a functional tool of communication. Those activities related to business, circulation, or production are separated from those that are journalistic. The nonjournalistic activities are, of course, performed and paid for — but they are contracted rather than overseen. The operation of the newspaper is cured of the institutional schizophrenia that otherwise inhibits all of its activities.

If newspaper printing plants were thus separated from the journalistic functions — if they were made independent rather than captive — the benefits that would accrue to the journalistic aspects of the newspaper would be enormous. If the separation of printing plants from journalistic activities that is now "permitted" through the Newspaper Preservation Act were to be made mandatory, all of the nation's newspapers would reap those benefits now reserved to a few.

Mandatory divestiture of captive printing plants by daily newspapers would require no massive reinterpretation of the nation's basic antitrust law. The bridging cases, or stepping stones, have already been decided by the Supreme Court. With some help from Congress, the Court has, since about the end of World War II, treated antitrust violations in such a way that a sound legal argument can be made against ownership of printing plants by monopoly newspapers.

It should be remembered that although the Sherman and Clayton Acts, the core of antitrust law, do not outlaw concentration or bigness per se, they were both enacted because of the fear of the unfettered concentration of economic power. The Acts proscribe monopoly and restraint of trade, and the definitions of illegality are couched in terms of conduct. Early antitrust law enforcement, therefore, was predicated on conduct. The assumption was that if predatory conduct could be eliminated, the model of perfect competition would descend upon the marketplace. Unfortunately, this focus on behavior tended to obscure structural cause and effect and to inhibit inquiry into such matters.

It eventually became evident that no matter how tightly conduct was confined, the evils of monopoly remained firmly entrenched. So long as the market structure that spawned the monopolistic practice remained, punishing conduct was not effective.

Not only is conduct now less important in the overall determination of antitrust violation than was once the case, the very interpretation of what constitutes illegal conduct has changed. Practices that were once prohibited only if they could be proved to be part of a master plan to monopolize are now forbidden if they alter or interfere with the structural makeup of the market. The Court even suggested, in *Lorain Journal Co. v. United States,*[14] and *United States v. Griffith,*[15] that behavior that is perfectly legitimate under competitive circumstances may be illegal when practiced by a firm with monopoly power.

Before the Celler-Kefauver amendment to Clayton 7 in 1950, the only barrier to entry the Court considered violative of the Clayton Act was size. If the accused firm was enough larger than its competitors to exercise market control pressures successfully, it was guilty of erecting barriers to entry. Even then there had to be a showing of intent to monopolize. Now, however, business practices that erect barriers to entry are held violative even in the absence of intent to monopolize or restrain trade. As the Court said in *Griffith:*

> It is . . . not always necessary to find a specific intent to restrain trade or to build a monopoly in order to find that the antitrust laws have been violated. It is sufficient that a restraint of trade or monopoly results as a consequence of a defendant's conduct or business arrangements.[16]

More serious even than practices that erect barriers to entry into the marketplace are those that are said to close the market to competition entirely. The growth of the concept of market foreclosure began with the judicial recognition in 1945 by Circuit Court Judge Learned Hand that "the antitrust laws are as much violated by the prevention of competition as by its destruction."[17] In a progression of cases during the next three years the Supreme

Court followed Judge Hand's lead and held that the mere existence of foreclosure power, coupled with intent, was illegal,[18] that foreclosing a substantial market was illegal per se,[19] and that "the use of monopoly power, however legally acquired, to foreclose competition . . . is unlawful."[20]

The practice of owning or controlling those operations that either precede or follow one's primary business is called vertical integration. Beginning in 1949, the Court coalesced vertical integration and market foreclosure. In that year the Court ruled that an exclusive-dealing contract amounted to vertical integration that foreclosed the market to competition and was therefore illegal.[21] By 1962 the Court was able to find that vertical integration accomplished by means of merger was illegal in a market whose trend was toward oligopoly.[22] Such a merger, said the Court, would foreclose the market to competitors.

Vertical integration, the Court has found, forecloses access to a segment of the market because competitors can no longer buy the needed product or service from the integrated firm. Nor can potential competitors, standing at the edge of the market, deal with the captured firm. If the integrated firm has no competitors it has monopoly or horizontal power as well as vertical power. This combination creates a leverage for the strengthening and extension of horizontal power to a greater extent than does the exercise of horizontal power alone. Vertical integration which involves a monopolist therefore becomes a means of protecting the advantages of monopoly by raising barriers to entry to the point of foreclosure.

All of the steps but one have been taken toward declaring captive printing plants anticompetitive. That last step is to determine that vertical integration by internal growth is monopolizing. The Court has held that a local newspaper market is a suitable market for antitrust purposes.[23] Monopoly power is generally inferred from the share of the market controlled by the defendant firm. A daily newspaper with no local daily competition therefore has monopoly power in its market.

Two things are needed to make separation of monopoly newspapers from their printing plants consistent with the philosophies of Justice Black. First, the ownership of captive plants needs to be shown to have the effect of furthering monopoly power. Second, legislative action consistent with antitrust law is needed to provide a model for the separation because such divestiture is a matter of statutory rather than constitutional interpretation.

Although the proscriptions of antitrust law have never been applied to a case of vertical integration by internal growth, the bridging cases to permit that reading have been decided. In *Brown Shoe, supra.,* the Court held that vertical integration is anticompetitive and subject to regulation when found in markets where the trend is toward oligopoly. In *Griffith, supra.,* the Court ruled that monopoly power, however unintentionally or lawfully acquired, is illegal if it restrains trade through the foreclosure of the market to competition. In *Standard Stations, supra.,* the Court required that the Sherman, Clayton, and Federal Trade Commission Acts be read jointly as a national-policy antitrust unit. This amalgamation permits a broader application of the market foreclosure concept than was possible when the Acts were read separately. In *Federal Trade Commisssion v. Motion Picture Advertising Services Co.*, the Court said:

> It is, we think, plain . . . that a device which has sewed up a market so tightly for the benefit of a few falls within the prohibition of the Sherman Act and is therefore an "unfair method of competition" within the meaning of section 5(a) of the Federal Trade Commission Act.[24]

Vertical integration through internal growth as manifested in a newspaper's ownership of captive printing facilities prevents competitors from entering the market as anything but fully integrated enterprises. This would appear to be market foreclosure and presumptively an anticompetitive device.

The Newspaper Preservation Act would appear to provide the appropriate legislative model for divestiture of captive printing plants. The stated intent of that Act was to restore and maintain competition in the vital newspaper business. The means to achieve that end consisted of the separation of production and editorial functions of newspapers. Those ends and means can both be applied to divestiture in monopoly newspaper markets throughout the nation rather than in a few scattered cities with competing dailies.

V

Although the question of divestiture of printing plants from newspapers has never come before the Court, it is clear that Justice Black did not feel that the First Amendment protected the business of newspapering from governmental regulation. As he said in 1945:

> Publishers are engaged in business for profit exactly as are other businessmen who sell food, steel, aluminum, or anything else people need or want. . . . All are alike covered by the Sherman Act. The fact that the publisher handles news while others handle food does not . . . afford the publisher a peculiar constitutional sanctuary in which he can with impunity violate laws regulating his business practices.[25]

Black was not insistent that a business practice be specifically outlawed before it could be held violative of the nation's antitrust laws. He, too, was concerned about foreclosure of the market to potential competitors. As he said about exclusive-dealing contracts, which foreclosed the news market in *Associated Press:*

> The net effect [of the exclusive contracts] is seriously to limit the opportunity of any new paper to enter these cities. Trade restraints of this character . . . tend to block the initiative which brings newcomers into

a field of business and to frustrate the free enterprise system which it was
the purpose of the Sherman Act to protect.[26]

Justice Black would probably have accepted the notion that captive
printing plants represented a form of vertical integration that fostered
monopoly and market foreclosure. As to the application of the Newspaper
Preservation Act as a means to alleviate that monopoly, the reaction of Black
is somewhat more difficult to predict. Inasmuch as he voted with the majority
in *Citizen Publishing, supra.,* we know that he did not approve of joint
operating agreements between newspapers because such agreements foreclosed the market to potential competitors. It is entirely possible that he could
have been persuaded that the stated intent of the Newspaper Preservation Act
was more important than the legalization of joint agreements. Under such circumstances, it would not have been difficult for him to view the divestiture of
printing plants as a means to that end — a means entirely consistent with both
antitrust law and the dictates of libertarian theory.

11   Had Black ruled in *Branzburg* . . .

A. DAVID GORDON

I

The American legal history of journalist's privilege—the right to protect confidential sources or information—has been marked by confusion stretching back over 100 years. The lack of clarity unfortunately was not resolved by the first Supreme Court decision dealing directly with this topic in June of 1972. That *Branzburg v. Hayes*[1] decision denied First Amendment protection for journalists' confidential sources and information in grand jury proceedings. But subsequent lower court decisions, involving other types of proceedings as well, have both denied and granted an evidentiary privilege for journalists. If anything, the developments of the first five years following *Branzburg* have muddied the legal waters further. The initial reaction within the media to push hard for shield statutes in place of the protection denied by the Supreme Court has given way to considerable differences of opinion as to whether confidentiality can best be safeguarded by statute or by reliance on the courts in the absence of legislative action.[2]

On the other side of the question are those who argue that journalists have little or no need to protect the confidentiality of their sources or information against disclosure in legal proceedings. At the heart of this issue is

A. DAVID GORDON is associate professor of journalism and urban affairs at Northwestern University. He holds a Ph.D. in mass communications from the University of Wisconsin. His major interests are in media-society relationships and communications law, with particular emphasis on journalists' confidential sources. His recent research concerns newspaper policies on election coverage and endorsements, and he has previously written several articles on the reporter's privilege and other journalism law topics. He has also been active in Northwestern University's urban affairs field studies programs, and is currently serving as master of the university's community studies residential college.

the tension between the free flow of information to the public and the need of the judicial system for "every man's evidence" in order to allow the courts to decide cases on the basis of a complete record of testimony, in fairness to all parties.[3] Recently, and especially since 1968, this tension has at times developed into an open conflict between law enforcement agencies and their conception of what is best for society and journalists who express their belief that some values should take precedence over total efficiency in either the law enforcement or the judicial administration processes. One of those values, the supporters of journalist's privilege argue, is an electorate informed on all matters of importance. And they claim protection of confidential sources or information is an important part of ensuring an adequate flow of information to that electorate.

To those who desire First Amendment protection to resolve this confidentiality problem, it is indeed unfortunate that the Supreme Court took up the question only after Justice Hugo Black retired. With him on the Court, it seems safe to say, the *Branzburg* decision would have gone 5 to 4 in *favor* of journalist's privilege, rather than against it by the same margin. Justice Black never had the opportunity to write a full-fledged opinion on the subject (though he did have — and didn't take — the opportunity to dissent from the Court's refusal to grant certiorari in three earlier privilege cases). But although no privilege case came before the Court while he sat on it, Justice Black's general approach to freedom of the press cases anticipated both the minority position in *Branzburg* and how the issue has frequently been resolved by lower courts, particularly in civil proceedings, since *Branzburg*. Justice Black's general philosophy on this portion of the First Amendment and on the need for an informed electorate also gives clear guidance as to how and why a different Supreme Court *could* resolve the grand jury type of privilege case differently in the future.

The crux of the legal argument in *Branzburg* was a balancing of law enforcement needs, as represented by the grand jury procedure, against the values of press freedom as protected by the First Amendment. For the majority, as expressed in Justice Byron White's plurality opinion, legitimate law enforcement requirements would always take precedence over protection for newsgathering activities. For Justice Potter Stewart, in his dissent, some sort of balance between competing needs must be struck. And for Justice William O. Douglas, in a separate dissent, the First Amendment must predominate.[4]

Justice Douglas, long associated with Justice Black in an absolutist approach to the First Amendment, may well have been speaking for his late colleague in arguing that newsgathering should take precedence over the grand jury process. During his tenure on the Court, Justice Black objected strongly to striking any balance that weighed against freedom of speech and the press. In *Bridges v. California*,[5] for example, he held for the majority that activities that led to contempt citations against the *Los Angeles Times* did not constitute such a grave danger to the judicial process as to require abridgement of press freedom. While those activities — editorial comment and news stories on pending cases — differed from the nondisclosure of sources or information, the general principle remains constant in both types of cases: does freedom of the press extend its protection to activities that may interfere with the administration of justice, and if so, how far?

Justice Black, in *Bridges,* said the First Amendment provided such protection in the absence of a "clear and present danger." In the circumstances of that case he found freedom of the press more valuable than the totally unimpeded functioning of the judiciary. He argued that:

> the unqualified prohibitions laid down by the framers [of the Constitution] were intended to give to liberty of the press as to the other liberties, the broadest scope that could be countenanced in an orderly society.[6]

His argument was for liberty defined within the context of an orderly society, and he believed that a truly orderly society must be reached through specific considerations and values — among them freedom of the press.

Rather than looking first to the professed needs of the government, Justice Black consistently looked to the needs of the individual.[7] His opinion in the 1971 *Pentagon Papers* case put this philosophy succinctly and can serve as a rebuttal to efforts in the *Branzburg* case to balance freedom of the press with criminal justice procedures: "The word 'security' is a broad, vague generality whose contours should not be invoked to abrogate the fundamental law embodied in the First Amendment."[8] Substitute "law enforcement" for "security," and you have perhaps an approximation of what Justice Black might have said in *Branzburg,* had he still been on the Court. But he carried the argument further in the *Pentagon Papers* opinion when he wrote that there is no real security unless the security system makes a casualty of *informed* representative government. He said that defending the nation from external danger — and, arguably, the society from internal disorders as well — cannot take precedence over developing a society worth defending. Quoting from a 1937 opinion by Chief Justice Hughes, he argued that the greater the importance of safeguarding against incitements to violent change,

> the more imperative is the need to preserve inviolate the constitutional rights of free speech, free press and free assembly, in order to maintain the opportunity for free political discussion. . . .[9]

Only in that way can government truly stay responsive to the people and change take place peacefully.

Journalist's privilege, of course, cannot be justified merely for convenience. The privilege, rather, is needed to help provide a free flow of information to the public, on the basis of which, presumably, voters make their ultimate decisions on matters of public policy. Watergate is a recent and sensational example of important information unearthed by the news media with the help of confidential sources.[10] But other recent illustrations of the need for confidential sources abound, many of them involving groups outside the mainstream of society. The drug culture and the Black Panthers, the news

sources involved in the trio of cases that comprised *Branzburg,* are ready examples. Unless members of such groups can and do trust reporters to protect
their identities and some of the background information they provide, they
simply won't talk to reporters. And if they don't, many stories about non-
Establishment thoughts and dissatisfactions will remain unwritten until overt
actions erupt, shocking or outraging a public caught unwarned and un-
prepared. To determine the importance of the issue in the society of the 1970s
is unquestionably not a matter of simply counting the number of stories that
rely on confidential sources or information. Rather, the important question is
the quality of the stories based on confidentiality. As several observers have
noted, the stories that will likely suffer most from a decrease in confidentiality
will be in-depth analyses of complex issues,[11] and as society grows more complex and difficult to understand, this type of interpretive reporting is what we
can least afford to lose.

Justice Black's philosophy of a free press was well put in his 1966 opinion
for eight members of the Court, holding that an Alabama law prohibiting
editorials on election day violated the provisions of the First Amendment:

> The Constitution specifically selected the press . . . to play an impor-
> tant role in the discussion of public affairs. . . . Suppression of the
> right of the press to praise or criticize governmental agents and to *clamor
> and contend for or against change,* which is all that this editorial did,
> muzzles one of the very agencies the Framers of our Constitution
> thoughtfully and deliberately selected to *improve our society* and keep it
> free.[12]

With such freedom to gather and provide information for their audiences, the
news media can indeed help create an informed citizenry capable at least oc-
casionally of cutting through the complexities of life in the latter third of the
twentieth century and of making rational decisions about where it wants that
life to head.

To use the news media as instruments for such democratic decision making, and to safeguard those media under the First Amendment, involves risks,
as Justice Black was well aware. But to him, the result was well worth the
gamble. Note, for example, the general concern he expressed for free discussion in 1960:

> Our First Amendment was a bold effort . . . to establish a country with
> no legal restrictions of any kind upon the subjects people could in-
> vestigate, discuss, and deny. The Framers knew, better perhaps than we
> do today, the risks they were taking. They knew that free speech might be
> the friend of change and revolution. But they also knew that it is always
> the deadliest enemy of tyranny. With this knowledge they still believed
> that the ultimate happiness and security of a nation lies in its ability to
> explore, to change, to grow and ceaselessly to adapt itself to new
> knowledge born of inquiry free from any kind of governmental control
> over the mind and spirit of man.[13]

It is this concern for the benefits of an unfettered press in this country that would likely have led Justice Black to extend First Amendment protection to journalist's privilege, even in the face of grand juries' need for evidence. But with him off the Court, the reluctance to recognize evidentiary privilege for journalists, which was a constant theme in American judicial history, found the five votes necessary for reaffirmation — in *Branzburg* — at the Supreme Court level.

II

Prior to 1958, claims of journalist's privilege were almost always grounded in the common law and, in reported cases, were uniformly denied. In the 110 years following the first reported American case in 1848,[14] some 22 privilege cases found their way into the law reports, and 21 of those held against the claim of journalist's privilege. The single exception was a 1915 case[15] in which the Supreme Court acceded to a plea against self-incrimination under the Fifth Amendment and agreed to let an editor and a reporter from the *New York Tribune* keep their sources confidential. That decision, however, is an aberration in the history of privilege, and added more to the confusion than to the development of legal precedent.

During this same time span, there were more than 30 unreported journalist's privilege cases, and as early as 1920 the privilege was recognized informally.[16] Since then, in at least a dozen instances up to 1958, six involving legislative bodies, demands for confidential sources were dropped for a wide variety of reasons and without any punishment meted out to the journalists involved. Thus the common law precedent on the subject was built upon those situations where courts or legislatures insisted on learning a source's identity, and ignored those cases where the journalist's position was allowed to prevail.

Demands for disclosure of confidential sources were based on everything from the interests of society as a whole to petty and self-centered ends. The circumstances in which the demands were made ranged from criminal investigations and prosecutions to suits against third parties, and even to libel suits against the media themselves. Perhaps the only real constant in the American history of privilege is the almost uniform refusal of journalists to disclose their confidential sources, regardless of either judicial pressure or the legal consequences. Often that refusal was grounded simply in their ethics. On many occasions, the refusal was elaborated with arguments about societal benefits, which sounded strangely like those made in support of the demand to reveal the sources. And this is the crux of the whole controversy — the differing perspectives on whether or not society is best served by allowing confidentiality, and if so, to what degree?

Certainly the current tension between the free flow of information to the public and the needs of an orderly system of law enforcement and judicial administration is not at all new and in fact seems to be cyclical. The recent rash of cases and incidents is certainly not unprecedented. Between 1930 and

1940, at least 22 privilege cases cropped up outside the law reports, many of them coming early in the decade and several of them constituting blatant harassment of reporters or editors, albeit for differing reasons. Two 1934 Kentucky cases serve as extreme examples of situations where no possible societal benefits could result from harassing journalists to reveal their confidential sources.

In the first situation, a *Louisville Courier-Journal* editorial page editor was matched against a vindictive state legislative committee attempting to discover whether a state representative wrote a letter to the editor sharply criticizing the legislature. This "affront" to legislative dignity included a stinging parody of the 23rd Psalm, written from the viewpoint of a legislative proposal:

> The Floor Leader is my shepherd. I shall not want (unless it pleases him). He maketh me lie down in the committees; . . . he restoreth my soul (if fifty-one members want it); . . . Thou preparest to table me in the presence of other factions; thou anointest my head with amendments; my cup is turned over. Surely politics and corruption shall follow me all the days of my life, and I shall dwell in the house of the politician forever.[17]

The editor, Vance Armentrout, insisted he was honor bound to keep the source's name secret, especially in view of a guarantee of anonymity published daily at the top of the letters column. And despite House action fining him $25 for his contemptuous defiance, Armentrout never paid the fine and never revealed the name.[18]

The second case involved two young reporters on the *Danville* (Ky.) *Advocate* who were tipped to the upcoming hanging in effigy of a state legislator. The tipster's identity was demanded of them as part of an investigation into the incident by the local Police Court, ostensibly to preserve the peace and prevent future breaches of it. The two reporters steadfastly refused to reveal the tipster's name during the two-week investigation. The case finally ended when two participants in the "hanging" admitted their complicity and were fined $10 apiece. In the meantime, the two reporters had gone through 11 separate contempt trials, served 45 hours each in jail, and paid a total of $22 in fines and costs.[19]

Aside from the frivolous nature of these two cases, they illustrate two important aspects of the privilege controversy. One is that threats of punishment usually don't work—journalists have almost always taken the attitude that a promise of confidentiality must be honored even at the cost of going to jail. And second, as shown by the small fines in both cases, punishment for refusal to break a confidence has frequently been much lighter than sentences for other forms of contempt. This latter point leaves one wondering whether the whole issue is really as crucial to judicial administration as some legalists have maintained.

As in these cases, the usual journalist's privilege situation involves a reporter refusing to violate confidences and being sentenced for contempt. Even if the punishment is minimal, as it often has been, the journalist bears the burden of a confrontation society apparently cannot resolve any other way. It would seem that if the information being sought were really vital to the proceeding at hand, journalists would be asked again and again to reveal it and would be cited for contempt each time they refused. Yet, this simply hasn't happened. In virtually every case, reported or unreported, the person has served the jail sentence or paid the fine and the matter has been dropped.[20] It seems very much as if the sentences are partly an effort to "save face" for the legal system; perhaps repeated efforts have rarely been made to secure the information because prosecutors or judges are afraid the public might not stand for them. If this interpretation is correct, renewed efforts to deal with the impasse are needed, so journalists don't bear the sole burden of resolving conflicting interests within society.

Another argument against compulsory disclosure of confidential material, voiced by the news media and others, is that the information sought is either readily available elsewhere or not really significant to the proceeding at hand. Perhaps the best illustration of the latter point was a 1961 case in Duluth, Minnesota, which was one of the very few known instances in which a journalist actually gave in to demands to reveal confidential material. The case arose — as do so many privilege matters — from a news story reported to the public, with the journalist brought into the situation solely as a third party who perhaps had some information that *might* be of value to one party or the other in the litigation. This case involved a Great Lakes shipping strike; the newsman was editor of the Duluth labor newspaper, and he said later he revealed his confidential source primarily to avoid focusing attention away from the labor issues involved in the strike and, instead, onto his refusal to testify.[21] How well he succeeded is proven by the fact that in more than 30 pages of recorded proceedings following the newsman's disclosure there is *no* reference whatever to the source for his story.[22] In fact, the presiding judge said 10 years later that the name of the source was "a very incidental· thing" and "had nothing to do with the merits of the case," as it turned out.[23]

Three years earlier, in the 1958 *Garland v. Torre* case, the First Amendment argument was raised for the first time as a basis for journalist's privilege. Since then, the constitutional protection argument has become the one used most frequently to justify safeguarding of confidential sources and information, but until late 1970 success was just as elusive under this approach as under the common law argument. In that 12-year span, nine other privilege cases reached the law reports, all of them holding against the journalist and five of them citing *Torre* directly. But those citations of *Torre* misread it almost universally on the applicability of the First Amendment to journalist's privilege. In *Torre,* the court said only that "the concept that it is the duty of a witness to testify in a court of law has roots *fully as deep* in our history as does the guarantee of a free press."[24] Under this balancing approach to determining where society's interests lie, the court held that the privilege claim had to give way in the particular circumstances of *Torre,* where the identity of the confidential source "went to the heart of the plaintiff's claim."[25]

Torre was perhaps a poor initial case in which to raise First Amendment questions, since it involved issues that most people considered of less than major importance for society. Some observers at the time expressed dissatisfaction with fighting a First Amendment battle over what was labeled a "gossip column."[26] Others recognized that despite the relatively trivial societal interest in a radio-television column dealing with whether Judy Garland was overweight and depressed—that she was allegedly over the hill rather than over the rainbow, as a student punster once put it—the precedent set in the case would be far-reaching and "difficult to combat regardless of the varying merits of future cases."[27] In the ensuing 12 years, court decisions seemed to imply a relationship between the First Amendment and journalist's privilege but then held against any privilege almost automatically. These court decisions often cited *Torre* without making any apparent effort to balance the interests involved in the later case, and especially without taking into account the differing fact situations and the possibility that the information in the subsequent cases might be either less crucial to the legal dispute, or of more import to society.[28]

The privilege decisions between 1958 and 1972 were all resolved in lower courts although *Torre* and two other cases resulted in unsuccessful petitions to the U.S. Supreme Court for writs of certiorari. In two of those three cases, Justice Douglas dissented from the Court's refusal to grant certiorari.[29] Justice Black did not dissent from the Court's refusal to hear these cases, at least on the record. And the record seems to indicate that he was not publicly concerned with the journalist's privilege issue during this period of time.[30] Justice Black was on the Court when it decided to hear the trio of cases later decided under the *Branzburg* title,[31] but no clues exist on his position at that time, and he left the Court the following fall, well before oral arguments were heard in these cases. But although Justice Black wrote no privilege opinions, his other First Amendment opinions provide a solid indication of what he would have written given the opportunity. Those other opinions, not coincidentally, provide the major strands for a fabric of precedent the Supreme Court might well have used to build a strong First Amendment framework for journalist's privilege had it chosen to read some of its prior decisions more thoroughly.

III

Justice Black's treatment of First Amendment rights early in his Supreme Court career, in *Bridges,* has been discussed above.[32] His use of the "clear and present danger" formula was a kind of balancing approach, but one that unquestionably gave priority to First Amendment values in contrast to competing societal interests. This opinion took the Court toward the preferred position Justice Black later gave to the first Amendment—or at least to the first two-thirds of it. The later Court opinions in free speech and press cases, many of them by Justice Black, lend considerable support to the argument in favor of journalist's privilege as an integral part of press freedom, to a degree greater than the Supreme Court acknowledged in *Branzburg*. Some of this material, admittedly, is *dicta*, but some represents holdings in related areas where parallels to privilege can easily be drawn.

In a number of decisions, the Court has held that freedom of the press covers the public distribution of newspapers, handbills, leaflets, and other types of literature.[33] In one such case, Justice Black said: "To act as good citizens they [the people] must be informed. In order to enable them to be properly informed their information must not be censored."[34] In another area, the Supreme Court ruled that forced disclosure of an organization's membership list would impinge on the group members' freedom of association, and that disclosure was not required in the absence of a showing that the list was important to the issues under litigation.[35]

In still another area, the Supreme Court has also provided guidelines that could be used to point the way to First Amendment protection for a journalist's confidential sources. In the 1960 decision in *Talley v. California*,[36] a five-justice majority held, through Justice Black, that a Los Angeles ordinance requiring the identification of the sponsors on handbills was a violation of the freedoms of speech and the press. Justice Black reviewed a long series of prior cases dealing with the distribution of literature and noted that various kinds of anonymous publications "have played an important role in the progress of mankind."[37] He added that requiring identification of the author or sponsor of material undoubtedly "would tend to restrict freedom to distribute information and thereby freedom of expression,"[38] and drew a parallel to the pair of cases that protected membership lists from disclosure. In those cases, as well as in *Talley*, Justice Black said, "identification and fear of reprisal might deter perfectly peaceful discussions of public matters of importance."[39]

This decision only provided a parallel for the principle of privilege. But this parallel becomes much more important when it is noted that two of the earliest privilege cases—both of them key precedents in the early development of the common law denying evidentiary privilege for journalists—were not really efforts to protect confidential sources, but rather were libel suits in which the defendants asserted unsuccessfully a right to protect the identity of the offending article's author.[40] In subsequent cases, these two precedents were cited several times as if they were identical to the later situations, which actually involved confidential sources rather than anonymous publication. Several of those later cases also became key precedents in the unbroken common law holdings against journalist's privilege—just one more instance of the confusion that has surrounded the legal developments on this issue. In light of the *Talley* decision, then, perhaps even that common law precedent should be reexamined, since *Talley* strongly supported a general First Amendment right of anonymous publication, albeit not in a libel situation.

In any event, *Talley* provides general support for the conclusion that the

First Amendment at times protects identities the government in its wisdom would like disclosed. It does so, as Justice Black said, on the assumption that such protection will enhance the flow of information to the public and thereby raise the level of public discussion about public affairs. That rationale received even more direct support in the series of cases that greatly restricted libel law between 1964 and 1974, in the interests of promoting exactly such informed public discussion. Although the Supreme Court was unwilling to reach Justice Black's conclusion that libel laws should be abolished, its statements on libel moved forcefully in the direction of encouraging public awareness, from *New York Times Co. v. Sullivan*[41] in 1964 until *Gertz v. Welch*[42] in 1974 — the latter some 2½ years after Justice Black had left the Court. Quoting an early twentieth-century Kansas case, the Supreme Court said in 1964 that it was vital to society that voters discuss the character and qualifications of candidates for office. The great advantages of such discussions

> more than counterbalance the inconvenience of private persons whose conduct may be involved, and occasional injury to the reputations of individuals must yield to the public welfare, although at times such injury may be great.[43]

To enable the media to carry out this function of facilitating public discussion, the Court adopted its "actual malice" rule for public officials, requiring them to prove that the publisher either knew his material was false, or published in reckless disregard of whether it was false.[44]

Justice Black wrote a concurring opinion in *Sullivan* in which — together with Justice Douglas — he argued for an absolute, unconditional First Amendment privilege to publish criticism of official conduct. He said that the

> freedom to discuss public affairs and public officials is unquestionably, as the Court today holds, the kind of speech the First Amendment was primarily designed to keep within the area of free discussion. To punish the exercise of this right to discuss public affairs or to penalize it through libel judgments is to abridge or shut off discussion of the very kind most needed.[45]

This willingness to limit private rights in favor of First Amendment freedoms was carried further by the Supreme Court in subsequent cases, particularly in *Time, Inc. v. Hill*.[46] There, in extending the "public official–public figure" rule of *Sullivan* and its successor libel cases into the privacy area, the Court rejected an invasion of privacy claim because it failed to show that the material in the story at issue was included with "knowing or reckless falsity." This holding led two lawyers advocating First Amendment protection for journalist's privilege to write, in 1969:

> Thus, in *Time, Inc. v. Hill,* the family suffered injury to its reputation but was denied recovery in a civil suit because of the danger to the

free flow of news. Analogously, the injury to a litigant in a civil action caused by his inability to force a newsman to identify his confidential source is justified by the superior interest in the dissemination of news.[47]

Justice Black took the opportunity in *Hill* to reiterate what he had said in earlier concurring opinions dealing with the *Sullivan* doctrine. In a brief concurring opinion, he repeated the need for freedom of speech and press unfettered by laws allowing what he viewed as harassment via libel or privacy suits. He had special words of criticism for the substitution of such phrases as "reckless disregard of the truth" for the clear and unequivocal wording he saw in the First Amendment.[48] Justice Black based this literalist approach on what he believed was "the clearly expressed purpose of the Founders to guarantee the press a favored spot in our free society."[49] He saved his strongest words for the "recently popularized weighing and balancing formula," which he called "that Constitution-ignoring-and-destroying technique,"[50] thus moving well beyond his (somewhat weighted) balancing formula of *Bridges,* at least in civil cases involving the First Amendment.

Four years later, in *Rosenbloom v. Metromedia,*[51] the Court extended the category of plaintiff who had to prove actual malice to include everyone involved in issues of public interest or general concern, a position foreshadowed back in 1966 in a concurring opinion by Justice Douglas in which Justice Black also joined.[52] In *Rosenbloom,* which was to be his final word from the Court on libel doctrines, Justice Black wrote a brief concurrence restating the themes of his opinions since 1964, and concluded:

> I agree of course that First Amendment protection extends to "all discussion and communication involving matters of public or general concern, without regard to whether the persons involved are famous or anonymous."[53]

The *Sullivan* doctrine has also been extended into areas beyond libel and privacy. Criteria based on the "actual malice" standard are being used to protect freedom of speech on new frontiers. For example, the dismissal of a high school teacher in Illinois for criticizing the school board and superintendent was overturned because he was held to be discussing "questions of legitimate public interest," and no proof was offered of false statements made knowingly or recklessly.[54] This broadening protection of First Amendment rights, against competing rights of both private individuals and governmental bodies, seems a compelling reason to consider seriously a more meaningful First Amendment protection for journalist's privilege. Another concurring opinion, this one by Justices Black and Douglas in *Bates v. Little Rock,* gives explicit support to such protection even where government is a party in the case. They wrote that

> First Amendment rights are beyond abridgement either by legislation that directly restrains their exercise or by suppression or impairment through harassment, humiliation, or exposure.[55]

More directly parallel to the journalist's privilege area, though, is Justice Black's position in the internal security cases of the 1950s. Starting in 1951, fears of internal subversion led the Supreme Court—over the strong objections of Justices Black and Douglas—to give away First Amendment rights of speech in favor of protecting the national security. But as Cold War fears diminished, the pendulum began swinging back to Justice Black's side of the philosophical fence by late in the decade. In a 1957 opinion, concurring in part and dissenting in part, Justice Black faced the security-speech dilemma with his usual clarity:

> The First Amendment provides the only kind of security system that can preserve a free government—one that leaves the way wide open for people to favor, discuss, advocate, or incite causes and doctrines however obnoxious and antagonistic such views may be to the rest of us.[56]

If this is true where internal security is concerned—and this approach was strengthened in a 1969 decision greatly limiting state criminal syndicalism statutes[57]—then it ought to be just as true in regard to law enforcement. That process, too, is not an absolute, as witness the Fifth Amendment provision against self-incrimination, or the flexible rule governing the disclosure of the identity of government informers.[58]

Rather than setting up even the law enforcement process as an absolute value, before which journalist's privilege must always give way, it would be better to look at the public interest in general in resolving this conflict of values. And the fact that this broader public interest "is used to deny the privilege at common law in most jurisdictions and grant it by statute in a strong minority"[59] is reason enough to define the conflict within a broader scale of values than either media or bar have shown at all times.

Justice Black put this whole issue into perspective in a 1968 television interview, when asked about the law enforcement problems posed by the Supreme Court's decisions protecting defendants' rights and the constitutional provisions on which they were based:

> They practically all relate to the way cases shall be tried. And practically all of them make it more difficult to convict people of crime. What about guaranteeing a man a right to a lawyer? Of course that makes it more difficult to convict him. What about saying he shall not be compelled to be a witness against himself? That makes it more difficult to convict him. What about the "no search—[no] unreasonable search or seizure shall be made?" That makes it more difficult. . . . They were, every one, intended to make it more difficult, before the doors of a prison closed on a man because of his trial.[60]

The Supreme Court decisions noted here might well have been considered more carefully by the Supreme Court in deciding *Branzburg,* and should be given close scrutiny for their philosophical support of an informed public, when the next journalist's privilege case is accepted for review. Certainly, if the Court decides to extend First Amendment coverage more thoroughly to newsman's privilege, it can do so by replowing old constitutional ground rather than by breaking entirely new legal furrows.

IV

Although the Supreme Court in *Branzburg* rejected a blanket First Amendment protection for journalists' confidential relationships, the decision is in fact relatively limited, at least until it is fleshed out by subsequent Court decisions. Speaking for the Court, Justice White extended First Amendment protection to news gathering,[61] and this was a significant advance. In previous cases, various lower courts had specifically held against such protection for the gathering of news while extending it to news dissemination[62] — a position that at the least overlooked the logical difficulty of disseminating what you are not free to gather. But after this step toward more protection for journalists, the Court held that "there is no First Amendment privilege to refuse to answer the relevant and material questions asked during a good-faith grand jury investigation."[63] Justice White used the *Sullivan* and subsequent libel decisions to bolster his point that "the press is not free to publish with impunity everything and anything it desires to publish."[64] The only mention of one of Justice Black's opinions, in the plurality opinion or in Justice Powell's concurrence, was from a considerably different context — the quotation from *Associated Press v. United States* that "freedom of the press from governmental interference under the First Amendment does not sanction repression of that freedom by private interests."[65] That was quoted in an attempt to establish that media agreements to withhold information do not have First Amendment sanction for overriding all competing societal interests. The White opinion held that the government had met the burden of showing "compelling" or "paramount" state interests, thus allowing the indirect burden to be placed on First Amendment rights.[66]

In addition to Justice White's extension of First Amendment protection to news gathering, *Branzburg* held out some possible reassurance to journalists in the crucial Powell concurring opinion. This opinion noted that state and federal authorities should not feel free to utilize the media as part of the government investigative process, and that "no harassment of newsmen will be tolerated."[67] Justice Powell said that if the information sought is only remotely related to the focus of an investigation or if it is requested without any legitimate law enforcement need being served, a newsman will be able to secure a protective order to maintain a confidential relationship. He added:

> The asserted claim to privilege should be judged on its facts by the striking of a proper balance between freedom of the press and the obligation of all citizens to give relevant testimony with respect to criminal conduct. The balance of these vital constitutional and societal interests on a case-by-case basis accords with the tried and traditional way of adjudicating such questions.[68]

This approach, which refuses to subordinate law enforcement interests in any way, falls far short of what Justice Black saw as the proper weight to be given the First Amendment in conflicts with other constitutional provisions or societal interests. Nevertheless, on paper it is a significant step toward achieving at least equality for journalist's privilege when it conflicts with law enforcement. Unfortunately, the step may well exist only on paper, since the first test of the harassment argument brought no protection for the privilege.

In the *Lightman* case, which stretched out through 1972 and 1973, a strong claim was made that the information was demanded at least in part to harass the reporter and his paper.[69] Nonetheless, the Maryland courts required the newsman to answer the questions put to him, and the Supreme Court refused to review the case, without comment even from Justice Powell. Lightman subsequently became only the fifth reporter to reveal part of his confidential material, when he purged himself of contempt by telling the grand jury the name of the resort community "pipe shop" where he had been offered marijuana, but—perhaps in a compromise—he was not asked to identify the clerk who offered it to him.[70]

Justice Stewart's dissent in *Branzburg* called the majority's denial of First Amendment protection a "crabbed view of the First Amendment [which] reflects a disturbing insensitivity to the critical role of an independent press in our society."[71] This dissent—by the same jurist who wrote the *Torre* opinion while on the Court of Appeals—made it explicit that interpreters of *Torre* were wrong when they used it to justify a ban on First Amendment protection for journalist's privilege in all situations.[72] Justice Stewart, joined by Justices Brennan and Marshall, argued for a "proper balance between the public interest in the efficient administration of justice and the First Amendment guarantee of the fullest flow of information," and came down hard for providing "special safeguards" for First Amendment rights.[73] In fleeting passages, the Stewart dissent was reminiscent of Justice Black's reasoning in support of an unfettered press, even though Justice Stewart's conclusion fell short of the absolute journalists' privilege that Justice Black would likely have espoused and that was expressed here by Justice Douglas's dissent. Justice Stewart wrote:

> The reporter's constitutional right to a confidential relationship with his source stems from the broad societal interest in a full and free flow of information to the public. It is this basic concern that underlies the Constitution's protection of a free press. . . .
> Thus we cannot escape the conclusion that when neither the reporter nor his source can rely on the shield of confidentiality against unrestrained use of the grand jury's subpoena power, valuable information will not be published and the public dialogue will inevitably be impoverished.[74]

The Stewart dissent, indeed, referred to opinions by Justice Black a number of times, primarily in the context of the need for an "enlightened choice by an informed citizenry"[75] if the democratic ideal is to work well.

Justice Black's opinion in *Talley v. California*, in particular, seemed to have an impact on Justice Stewart here, and was cited three times in the section of the dissent dealing with the need for a free flow of information and ideas to the public (along with an extensive quote from *Talley* in a footnote there).[76] Perhaps surprisingly, the Stewart dissent did not refer to *Bridges v. California*, although it developed a formula quite reminiscent of Justice Black's approach in *Bridges*. In setting up a standard to determine where the First Amendment must give way to the information needs of the grand jury in particular and the law enforcement process in general, this formula placed considerably more emphasis on the need for an unfettered press than did the *Branzburg* majority. Justice Stewart suggested that, before a reporter must reveal confidential material to a grand jury,

> the government must (1) show that there is probable cause to believe that the newsman has information that is clearly relevant to a specific probable violation of the law; (2) demonstrate that the information sought cannot be obtained by alternative means less destructive of First Amendment rights; and (3) demonstrate a compelling and overriding interest in the information.[77]

This three-part test of the necessity for any infringement on First Amendment rights, even by the law enforcement process, was derived from a number of prior Court decisions, including *Sweezy v. New Hampshire*. In that 1957 case, involving a legislative subpoena, Chief Justice Earl Warren—in an opinion for the Court, including Justice Black, wrote that:

> It is particularly important that the exercise of the power of compulsory process be carefully circumscribed when the investigative process tends to impinge upon such highly sensitive areas as freedom of speech or press, freedom of political association, and freedom of communication of ideas.[78]

The Stewart formula, of course, is far from absolute in the protection it would afford to journalist's privilege. But most proponents of evidentiary privilege for journalists agree that at some point, freedom of the press should give way to the orderly functioning of the judicial process. The argument, at the moment, is over where to draw that line, and how much interference with the judicial process must be permitted in the name of First Amendment freedoms. This would require a case-by-case approach in the journalist's privilege area, a prospect that scared neither Justice Powell in his concurrence nor Justice Stewart in his dissent, and an approach that has in fact been taken by lower courts in many privilege cases subsequent to *Branzburg*. Justice Stewart, in fact, indicated that the delicate, case-by-case judgments required by his formula should pose no real problems:

> That, after all, is the function of courts of law. Better such judgments, however difficult, than the simplistic and stultifying absolutism adopted

by the Court in denying any force to the First Amendment in these cases.[79]

V

In his *Branzburg* dissent, Justice Douglas emphatically separated himself from those who would agree that at some point, journalist's privilege should give way to law enforcement needs. He argued that no "compelling need" could possibly be proven in this case, and, in words reminiscent of Justice Black, criticized the *New York Times* brief because it

> takes the amazing position that First Amendment rights are to be balanced against other needs or conveniences of the government. My belief is that all of the "balancing" was done by those who wrote the Bill of Rights.[80]

Justice Douglas saw the issue in absolute terms and "repudiated the timid, watered-down, emasculated versions of the First Amendment" advanced in arguments by both the government and the *New York Times*.[81] He criticized the "infamy" of the "clear and present danger" test[82] and said that his view was close to that of Alexander Meiklejohn, whose writings also had a major impact on the views of Justice Black. "The right to know is crucial to the governing powers of the people, to paraphrase Alexander Meiklejohn," Justice Douglas wrote. "Knowledge is essential to informed decisions."[83] Surprisingly, Justice Douglas quoted from Justice Black's opinions only once in his *Branzburg* dissent — a reference to the concurring opinion in the *Pentagon Papers* which immediately followed the Meiklejohn paraphrase quoted above: "The press was to serve the governed, not the governors. . . . The press was protected so that it could bare the secrets of government and inform the people."[84]

Justice Stewart also referred to Meiklejohn's writings as support for his concern about information being available to ensure an enlightened citizenry.[85] Such support for broad access to news, as a First Amendment right essential to a free society, is available throughout Meiklejohn's writings. Justice Black's absolutist interpretation of the speech and press clauses of the First Amendment owed much to Meiklejohn, a debt he acknowledged among other places in a footnote to his flat statement in *Sullivan* that "an unconditional right to say what one pleases about public affairs is what I consider to be the minimum guarantee of the First Amendment."[86]

Meiklejohn strongly supported the freedoms of speech and press in order "to give to every voting member of the body politic the fullest possible participation in the understanding of those problems with which the citizens of a self-governing society must deal."[87] He said the search for truth in such a society cannot be balanced against other interests, on equal terms. Rather, he said, the attempt to know and to understand has a unique status, a unique authority, to which all other activities are subordinated. . . . Political self-government comes into being only insofar as the common judgment, the available intelligence, of the community takes control over interests, only insofar as its authority over them is recognized and effective.[88]

In support of this position, Meiklejohn postulated two distinct categories of speech, guaranteed to different extents by two different amendments in the Bill of Rights.[89] He sharply criticized the "clear and present danger" doctrine of Justice Holmes, on the grounds that it had led to the annulment rather than to the interpretation of the First Amendment.[90] Meiklejohn argued, by contrast, that in the areas of public discussion and public policy, there is an unabridgeable *freedom* of speech guaranteed by the First Amendment. But, he said, there is also a civil *liberty* of speech pertaining to discussion of private policy, protected by the Fifth Amendment and limitable by the government provided due process guarantees are observed. Meiklejohn saw a fundamentally important distinction between these two concepts of protected speech, based on the two roles filled by free citizens:

As the makers of the laws, they have duties and responsibilities which require an absolute freedom. As the subjects of the laws, they have possessions and rights, to which belongs a relative freedom.[91]

To Meiklejohn, the key to this First Amendment–Fifth Amendment dichotomy was whether speech (assumedly including the press) is concerned with the public interest or merely with a private interest. He said that as long as a person's

active words are those of participation in public discussion and public decision of matters of public policy, the freedom of those words may not be abridged. That freedom is the basic postulate of a society which is governed by the votes of its citizens.[92]

Such public discussion, together with the other vital First Amendment rights, were placed "beyond the reach of legislative limitation, beyond even the due process of law."[93] In later works, Meiklejohn expounded this position in broader terms. He said that the "revolutionary intent of the First Amendment is, then, to deny to all subordinate agencies authority to abridge the freedom of the electoral power of the people."[94] Political freedom, according to Meiklejohn, is the absolute societal value, "while self-preservation is a conditional and relative consequence of it."[95] The sanctity of the freedoms protected by the First Amendment, particularly those of speech and press, are thus necessary to promote the conditions required for maintaining true political freedom within a rational democratic system.

This, in essence, is what Justice Black said in a public interview in 1962, when questioned about the need to preserve the country's security, even perhaps at the expense of some First Amendment freedoms.

My answer to the statement that this Government should preserve itself is yes. The method I would adopt is different, however, from that of some other people. I think it can be preserved only by leaving people with the utmost freedom to think and to hope and to talk and to dream if they want to dream. I do not think this Government must look to force, stifling the minds and aspirations of the people. Yes, I believe in self-preservation, but I would preserve it as the Founders said, by leaving people free.[96]

A further development of Meiklejohn's approach, specifically in regard to the news media, categorized the dichotomy as "freedom of information" on the one hand—corresponding to Meiklejohn's "public rights" protected absolutely by the First Amendment—and "freedom of expression" on the other—corresponding to Meiklejohn's Fifth Amendment "private rights" protected against abridgement without due process.[97] In this approach, freedom of information was viewed "as a basis for political freedom and the democratic process."[98] This dichotomy is very reminiscent of the argument used unsuccessfully shortly after *Torre,* in the *Goodfader* decision, where the Hawaii Supreme Court refused to distinguish between news of governmental affairs in that case and the news of entertainment personalities in *Torre.*[99] This distinction, however, was not needed in *Branzburg,* since all three cases there involved information on topics of importance to an informed electorate. And certainly, when the government's subpoena power is used to elicit journalists' information for use in the law enforcement process, the information in question is very likely to fall into the "public rights" portion of the Meiklejohn equation.

VI

Part of the uncertainty about the meaning of the *Branzburg* decision is that it applied specifically to journalists appearing before grand juries but said nothing about other circumstances. What will happen in other fact situations is still open to argument and conjecture, though lower courts are increasingly providing some precedents. Later in 1972, two lower federal courts granted a First Amendment privilege to a journalist who refused to identify the realtor whose pseudonym appeared on an article about alleged Chicago block-busting practices. The journalist was—as usual—involved as a third party, this time in a civil case. Early in 1973, the Supreme Court let that grant of privilege stand by refusing certiorari,[100] an action that for the present supports the existence of some forms of journalist's privilege based on the First Amendment. This is particularly true since the federal Court of Appeals decision in the case called *Branzburg* a "limited principle," and used it as one precedent in granting the privilege where a grand jury was not involved. This holding emphasized "a paramount public interest in the maintenance of a vigorous, aggressive and independent press," and stressed that in civil cases "courts must recognize that the public interest in non-disclosure of journalists' confidential news sources will often be weightier than the private interest in compelled disclosure."[101]

A number of other lower courts since *Branzburg* have also allowed newsmen to refuse to testify about confidential sources of information, on various grounds. In several instances, courts held that information sought in criminal proceedings was not material enough to require disclosure of confidential matters.[102] An even stronger First Amendment protection against disclosure has been granted in a number of other civil suits, including one growing out of the Watergate situation where materiality and lack of alternative sources were not established to the court's satisfaction. That decision was held to be consistent with *Branzburg*, especially since the importance of the case "transcends anything yet encountered in the annals of American judicial history."[103]

Even in libel cases where the news medium is a party, the question of First Amendment protection from compulsory disclosure has been decided both ways since *Branzburg*.[104] But a number of lower courts, in both civil and criminal cases, have denied claims of privilege, on the grounds that some interest other than the First Amendment was overriding in the particular circumstances of each case.[105] The lengthy jail stays of William Farr and Peter Bridge and the shorter jail stays for other journalists who upheld the principle of nondisclosure are sure evidence that the First Amendment does not protect confidentiality under all circumstances.[106]

A reasonable guess as to the present status of journalists' privilege under the First Amendment is that journalists may withhold confidential sources of information as third parties in civil cases unless the material is crucial to the case; that where journalists are directly involved in civil cases, the test of materiality may well be somewhat less stringent; and that there is no privilege before grand juries operating in good faith. The question of what protection journalists have in criminal trials remains unsettled, though there is some indication that demands by defendants for immaterial information will not override claims of First Amendment protection. Resolution of the remaining uncertainty may well await the next privilege case the Supreme Court accepts for review: if it is a strong one from the standpoint of maintaining confidentiality, it could result in more extensive First Amendment protection for the privilege, even in the absence of any change in the *Branzburg* precedent regarding grand juries. If it is a weak case, the present ban on privilege before grand juries could well be broadened.

Given the uncertainty of First Amendment protection for confidential sources and information, the other route that could provide such protection is that of statute. Indeed, in the *Branzburg* decision the Supreme Court invited state or federal legislative action as the remedy for privilege problems.[107] But the legislative approach poses two major difficulties: the inflexibility of most statutory language, and the difficulty of insuring that the protection will in fact extend as far as intended. Once written into statutory form, language is hard to adapt to unforeseen conditions and new developments within society. For instance, any law that attempts to define who is a journalist would need an omniscient drafter if it is to take into account new media forms technology and other developments may well bring about.

The differing wordings of the 26 state shield laws in existence at the end of 1975 have caused considerable confusion over exactly who is covered under what circumstances. For example, the Arkansas shield law (*Arkansas Statutes Annotated,* Section 43-917, 1964) allows the journalist's privilege to be divested if it is shown that the material was presented "in bad faith, with malice, and not in the interest of the public welfare." Moreover, the statute covers confidential sources, but not material, and makes no attempt to define its terms. By contrast, the more recent New York statute (Chapter 615, Section 79-h, Laws of 1970) defines the eight terms it uses, and covers the confidentiality of "any news or the source of any such news." Even laws that purport to provide an absolute privilege run the danger of being interpreted out of effective existence. Until the *Branzburg* case the Kentucky shield law was thought to be absolute regarding sources of information. But then the state's highest court ruled that "confidential sources" in Kentucky did not include people observed in the act of breaking the law, even if the observations were possible only because of a confidential journalist-source relationship.[108] This decision totally ignored the difference between observations that are possible in public and those that take place in private and are observable only upon invitation from a confidential source. Despite its logical weakness, that is the current interpretation of the language of the Kentucky shield law.

Similarly, the *Lightman* decision provided a breach in what had been assumed to be Maryland's all-encompassing protection for news sources. In California, William Farr went to jail in 1972 and again in 1976 in part because the state's shield law originally did not cover ex-reporters and he was asked for his confidential source while he was temporarily out of the newspaper field. The California courts also held in the *Farr* and *Rosato* cases that shield legislation would not apply—under the separation of powers doctrine—in situations where a court was acting to protect the enforcement of its own proper orders. Building on this latter holding, the New Mexico Supreme Court in 1976 raised an even broader threat to shield laws when it ruled them invalid in that state's judicial proceedings under the separation of powers doctrine.[109]

Laws deliberately worded to provide exceptions to a grant of privilege are even more suspect in terms of protecting journalists. Most of the bills proposed on both the state and federal levels in the wake of *Branzburg*— including the New Mexico statute—have been less than absolute in their coverage, and many have been sharply criticized for that reason. Even the strongest proposals generally leave some room for an occasional breach for some overriding concern, notwithstanding the experience that shows that such statutory loopholes will likely be interpreted to strip away the protection more often than anticipated.

Such an approach is bound to cause massive confusion, particularly if varying state shield laws operate in the same arena with a limited First Amendment privilege allowing an undefined amount of protection. Neither journalists nor lawyers may know exactly who is protected by what kinds of privilege in which circumstances. The situation is vaguely reminiscent of Justice Black's 1967 warning in regard to libel in which he urged the Supreme Court not to set itself up as the arbiter of what becomes so abusive as to be unconstitutional. Rather, he wrote, absolute freedom to discuss public affairs should be allowed, without the threat of press harassment through libel suits. Otherwise, he said,

> we are rapidly but surely getting ourselves in the dilemma we found ourselves in when we were compelled to overrule the ill-starred case of *Betts v. Brady,* 316 U.S. 455, 62, S. Ct. 1252, 86 L. ed. 1595, in order that the state courts of the country might be able to determine with some degree of certainty when an indigent person was entitled to the benefit of a lawyer.[110]

Justice Black's strong philosophical defense of an unfettered press developed despite his personal feelings about the way in which the nation's papers treated him after his appointment to the Supreme Court. One observer wrote in 1961:

> A certain bitterness toward newspapers shows to this day, because of the part they played in what he considered a disingenuous attack. But his total commitment to freedom of the press as a doctrine has not been affected by this distaste for newspapers in real life.[111]

No more convincing argument can be made in response to the position that granting freedom of the press in extreme degrees will lead to some abuses of that freedom. It will, and, as Justice Black indicated so many times, the abuses and the inconveniences must be taken along with the advantages, which far outweigh them.[112]

Among those inconveniences, at times, will be the law enforcement process and judicial administration in general, if journalists are allowed any kind of an evidentiary privilege. And unless one wishes to provide an absolute freedom of the press in all possible situations, it is crucial to define how conflicts between competing societal interests can be resolved. What limits, minimal or otherwise, must be placed on journalist's evidentiary privilege under the First Amendment to prevent it from infringing on overall societal needs? Is it simply a question of public versus private news, as outlined in Meiklejohn's theory?[113] Should journalist's privilege end where libel is involved?[114] What about refusals to disclose a confidential source where that source has apparently violated the law, as in the *Branzburg* fact situation?[115] What about sources who have violated a grand jury oath of secrecy? Should the circumstances of each instance have an effect on any such violations of grand jurors' oaths?

Perhaps overriding all of these questions in some people's minds is the need to define who is a journalist, a necessity under a First Amendment approach just as much as it is under a shield statute. Similarly necessary are solutions to all the other definitional problems that would plague attempts to write a shield law flexible enough to cover differing circumstances but tight enough to be capable of consistent interpretation. But to answer all of these questions in concrete detail in advance of specific fact situations would be to fall into the same trap of inflexibility that lurks behind the statutory approach.

One observer would resolve the dilemma in terms of national security and the importance of the information to prevent a miscarriage of justice. Don H. Reuben, attorney for a number of Chicago media, said that no newsman would want to "live with the accusation of suppressing critical facts in a public inquiry."[116] Reuben was speaking specifically of unpublished information for which subpoenas have been issued, but his points are equally applicable to the broader confidential source question. He said that

> when the national security is involved, and a court so finds, or there is a clear and present danger that without the press responding justice will not be done, the press has to answer a reasonable subpoena and should want to do so.[117]

That position, obviously, falls short of an absolute privilege, but it goes a great deal further than the Supreme Court has yet gone. It is doubtful that even Justice Black, in his later years, would have argued for an absolute privilege in any and all situations, or for all kinds of stories, given his concern for the line between speech and conduct, and the ability of government to control the latter on a nondiscriminatory basis.[118] But it is certain that, for Justice Black, any breaches in the wall protecting journalist's privilege would have to be carefully circumscribed to prevent any greater erosion than might originally have been intended or desired.

With this in mind, and hopefully in the spirit with which Justice Black might have approached the problem, a set of 11 underlying postulates can be formulated to construct a strongly libertarian but not quite absolute framework for determining the extent of journalist's privilege. These are as follows:

1. "Journalist" must be defined very broadly. Any attempt to limit the definition to types of activity meeting judicial approval at any given moment would be to open the door to arbitrary censorship. As the *Buchanan* decision warned, any constitutional basis for journalist's privilege requires its extension to "disreputable" or "underground" papers and others whose credentials may be in momentary disfavor.[119] Thus, any person working in a news or editorial capacity for a publication, wire service, or syndicate of general circulation — including free lance reporters or photographers employed in that capacity — or for a broadcasting station licensed or regulated by the Federal Communications Commission, should be defined as a journalist. The privilege must also cover former journalists who are asked about confidential material which they received while so employed.

2. "Source" should also be defined broadly, to avoid any possibility of misinterpretation, as in the *Branzburg* decision at the state level.[120]

3. Attempts to define "news" have the same drawbacks as efforts to define "journalist." Perhaps the decision in an unreported 1925 case, that news is anything determined worthy of a place in a paper, is the best guideline to follow.[121]

4. Efforts to define "news of public value" or some similar classification run into even more subjective or ideological roadblocks of the kind that Justice Black continually warned against, especially in light of values that change with time and circumstances. Here, however, Meiklejohn's dichotomy could prove invaluable. In the area of his unabridgeable First Amendment freedom of speech—concerning public interests—the journalist's right to confidentiality should be absolute, unless the journalist chooses to waive it. In other areas—those concerned with Meiklejohn's civil liberty of speech, covering private interests unrelated to society's overall welfare—the privilege could be less than absolute, and might be weighed against certain competing interests. Under this approach, the courts would have to serve as arbiters of whether a particular matter fell into the public-interest area, or whether it was related to something less central than political freedom and the functioning of democratic society. To some degree, this would require a case-by-case approach to privilege, but that should not be a valid deterrent since courts are already taking this approach in such related areas as contempt by publication and the government-informer privilege.[122] The problems would come in the gray areas near the borderline of the public-interest area. If the contrast were between, for example, the governmental affairs that were at the heart of the *Goodfader* case and the entertainment news that formed the basis of the *Torre* case, the determination would not be difficult. But when the issue was news of the activity of some small group now outside society's mainstream but potentially able to affect it, then the choice theoretically might be more difficult. Some of these theoretical problems, however, are likely to disappear if the other criteria outlined here are also applied.

5. The general postulate that news of public interest should confer greater protection for confidentiality than news of private interest must be complemented by a strong presumption *in favor* of First Amendment protection for journalist's privilege wherever that privilege is less than absolute. The shield of confidentiality should be stripped away only as a last resort, when information is so crucial that an important proceeding would be subverted without it, and it cannot possibly be obtained in any other way. This, of course, would apply only in Meiklejohn's "private interests" area. Otherwise, the privilege would be absolute.

6. The privilege should apply to all media, not just the print media. Although almost all past battles have involved representatives of print media, the issue is one of equal importance to electronic journalists, as witness the affidavits from CBS newsmen in connection with the 1970 federal shield law proposal and the *Caldwell* proceedings.[123]

7. The privilege should apply before all governmental agencies that

have the power to compel testimony, whether these are arms of the judicial, legislative, or administrative branches of government, and regardless of the level of government involved.

8. Media should not be able to take advantage of evidentiary privilege unfairly in libel suits. If a libel defense is based on a claim of a reliable source, that should become a matter for jury determination, and the identity of the source should be revealed. If a journalist does not wish to reveal a confidential source, other defenses to the libel charge must be used.[124]

9. The question of illegal actions by the confidential source cannot be answered definitively in the abstract. While such actions should perhaps mitigate against the right to confidentiality, the rule cannot be absolute. In some situations, especially where the alleged illegal act is not a major felony, it may be far overshadowed by the importance of the information made available to the public (actually and potentially) through the cloak of confidentiality. In such cases, courts should remain free to use their discretion.

10. In weighing carefully the importance of the source's name to the proceeding, the availability of the desired information from other sources should be crucial. So should the question of whether the absence of the source's name, and the information gained thereby, would cripple the legal proceeding or whether it would merely inconvenience it. For example, in *Torre*, the information sought "went to the heart of the plaintiff's case,"[125] and Miss Garland's suits were eventually dropped without disclosure.[126] By contrast, in the next case in which the Supreme Court refused certiorari, the Colorado Supreme Court imprisoned a reporter for 30 days for refusal to disclose a confidential source as part of a disbarment proceeding. The source's name (and, specifically, whether that source was the lawyer involved in the proceeding) was apparently not necessary to the court, since the lawyer involved was eventually disbarred even without it.[127]

11. The importance of the proceeding to society must also be weighed in any consideration of privilege claims. The police court inquiry or the attempt to vindicate legislative dignity, in the two 1934 Kentucky cases noted earlier,[128] should not weigh as heavily as a situation where murder or other felonies might be involved. Yet, in the past, little or no judicial distinction has been made between these different types of cases.

This less-than-absolute approach to journalist's privilege puts tremendous power in the hands of the judiciary, although no more so than on First Amendment issues in general. While the track record of judges until very recently has not been encouraging in this regard, the willingness of many lower courts to grant the privilege following *Branzburg* makes the outlook somewhat more promising. And if there were available clear guidelines that placed a heavy presumption in favor of journalist's privilege, the likelihood of adequate protection in all instances would be greatly increased. Certainly if the media cannot rely on the judiciary for a fair assessment of what is a legal as well as an ethical issue, then the problems run much deeper than the single area of journalist's privilege. And, of course, the same type of interpretive power would reside in the judiciary in the case of any shield statute except one that somehow was absolute and ironclad in its conferral of evidentiary privilege.

What must be remembered is that the actual number of cases where confidential materials have been demanded from journalists is quite small, and by themselves represent only a small problem.[129] What does matter, though, in the words of Justices Black and Douglas, is the "chilling effect" of such cases on the broader flow of information between sensitive sources and other journalists.[130] It is those situations that will be harmed by the few incidents in which journalists are actually cited and punished for contempt. And it is this wider effect that was so often the focal point of Justice Black's concern for an unfettered press in this country. Writing of Justice Black shortly after he had left the Court, Justice Douglas said that for his late colleague,

> there was no constitutional authority for judges to decide that some speech or some publications ran against the grain of public approval. The original design of the Constitution was to keep the lines of communication and ideas open, the hope being that, in time, experience would help produce a mature people. . . .
>
> His central theme was certainly the First Amendment. The market place of ideas was to him a political reality. He took Jefferson and Madison literally and he felt deeply and sincerely that the real secret of our security and success was the maintenance of a Society of the Dialogue.[131]

Wallace Mendelson put it somewhat differently in his comparison of Justices Black and Frankfurter: "Democracy, then, is the *unfettered exchange of ideas* with public control of *action* in accordance with those thoughts which win acceptance in the marketplace of reason."[132]

Any marketplace of ideas and reason presupposes the existence of conflicting "truths" out of which an informed society can come. And those various truths must, of course, include the non-Establishment points of view that are bound to reach public attention through violence or confrontation tactics if not through the mass media — and that, as the *Branzburg* and *Caldwell* cases illustrate, are more likely to come via the media if confidential journalist-source relationships are available to help air them even if they run "against the grain of public approval."

Neither the mass media nor judicial administration are ends in themselves, although in the clash over privilege some partisans on both sides have seemingly forgotten that point. What does remain an overall goal is the welfare of the society as a whole, and this is likely to be harmed if the amount of available information is reduced appreciably by the hesitancy of anonymous sources to risk revelation. If the citizens of a democracy cannot obtain adequate information on which to base intelligent choices about their government and society, democratic theory loses its major underpinning. As society becomes increasingly complex, the need for adequate information is intensified and the roles of the media should become even more important, both as information purveyors and as forums for differing points of view. Access to the media, both direct (letters to the editor, for example, as in the *Armentrout* case) and indirect, will be lessened if sources fail to trust journalists, and every such diminution will reduce the diversity of opinion and the amount of information available to the public.

The preferred position various Supreme Court decisions have given to the mass media under the First Amendment is a recognition of the role they play in providing necessary information to the electorate. Justice Black saw this clearly, but the position is hardly novel with him. Zechariah Chafee saw this as a partnership between government and the press, with the latter furnishing the information and ideas that are indispensable for a sound public opinion, and with government responsible for transforming that sound public opinion into action.[133] In short, the goal—as the Hutchins Commission stated over a quarter of a century ago—is to provide enough information to raise the level of public discussion and disagreement from the plane of violence to the plane of rational debate.[134]

For too long now, many lawyers and judges have failed to recognize the importance of confidentiality in achieving this goal, which they usually profess to favor. There is more than a touch of irony in Justice Blackmun's vote against journalist's privilege in *Branzburg*, contrasted with his acceptance of the sanctity of confidentiality between doctor and patient in the abortion cases decided in 1973.[135] But then, Justice Blackmun once served as house counsel for the Mayo Clinic, and had a firsthand understanding of the doctor-patient relationship that he lacked regarding the journalist-source relationship.

The *Branzburg* decision, despite its essentially negative implications, was a tentative first step away from the old attitude of the bench and bar that routinely denied journalist's privilege in most circumstances, merely to follow existing precedent. That old precedent is changing, but it needs to change more quickly. As the author of the unsuccessful 1949 shield law in New York wrote that year:

> Those lawyers, district attorneys and bar associations who are hesitant about granting the privilege, fail to recognize that law is a malleable thing, that is must meet changing conditions or be changed. The fact is that in our complex society, government has become so vast, so intricate, so remote in its internal administration, that our average citizen has neither the time nor experience to check on his public officials, and must usually rely on a free press for an audit of official activities. Therefore we must strengthen the hand of the free press so that it will not be hampered in its search for news—even at the expense of violating some of the cherished legal dogmas about privileged communications.[136]

In the years since that passage was written, the need to protect the journalist's privilege has become even more crucial to society as a whole. The Supreme Court has recognized similar problems in the areas of libel, privacy, anonymous publication, freedom of association, and freedom of speech, among others, often in vibrant opinions by Justice Black. It is time now to extend similar First Amendment protection to journalists' confidential material in all situations—and perhaps contrary to the spirit of Justice Black, subject to the usual judicial review of First Amendment rights, although with a very strong presumption in favor of the privilege.[137] This would take the burden off the shoulders and consciences of individual journalists. It would also provide some flexibility for those judges—for example, the trial judge in the *Torre* case[138]—who have said that the behavior of journalists protecting confidential sources has not been personally offensive to them, but nonetheless has required punishment under existing law. Constitutional protection for confidential sources would benefit society by enlarging the flow of information to the public, especially in Meiklejohn's public-interest area—including the law enforcement and judicial administration processes—while still retaining enough flexibility to prevent major abuses of the privilege.

The key in the law enforcement area may well come from Justice Black's opinions—going all the way back to *Bridges* where he wrote of giving liberty of the press "the broadest scope that could be countenanced *in an orderly society.*"[139] The Wisconsin Supreme Court in 1971 took note of this phrase but concluded that the society in which an Army math research center could be bombed, killing a graduate student, was not orderly. Thus, the fundamental freedom to walk unafraid into public buildings had to take precedence over the claims of the editor of an alternative paper to the confidentiality of his sources.[140] But—as has usually been the case—where the society remains orderly, where there is no immediate or real threat to human life, confidentiality of sources and information should be absolutely protected by the First Amendment even in the law enforcement area—if one believes, with Justice Black, that there is little point in "saving" a society where public discourse is fettered.

On a pragmatic level, too, the practice of confidentiality deserves greater protection than it has received, at least if the thinking of the American Bar Association Section of Criminal Law carries any weight. In a 1968 publication dealing with the need to plan carefully the judicial procedures to be followed in cases of widespread civil disorders, this group said:

> Representatives of the media should be consulted and asked to participate in making emergency plans. The media have frequently proven willing to share and safeguard confidences when they understand the reason for proposed actions. . . . Often the media have contacts within the community which are not available to public officials and can provide valuable insight to community feelings and reactions which can be of distinct assistance in planning for emergencies.[141]

This, too, is part of the general process of law enforcement. And this compelling statement of societal benefit realized from the confidential relationship of journalist and source makes an absolutist reading of *Branzburg* in the law enforcement area a bit like trying to eat one's cake and have it, too.

While few people in the media or outside it would argue for an absolutely inviolable right to protect confidential sources and information, most would agree on the need to move at least some distance beyond *Branzburg*, notwithstanding some favorable lower court decisions since then. Although the argument remains unsettled as to how best to do this, it is time to look once again to the legacy of Hugo Black and extend this evidentiary privilege to journalists under the protection of the First Amendment.

Expression and conduct in the opinions of Justice Black

12

EVERETTE E. DENNIS, NEIL A. LAVICK, J. EDWARD GERALD

For most of his thirty-four years on the Supreme Court Justice Hugo L. Black was known for the force and consistency of his near-absolutist views on First Amendment freedoms. Yet, near the end of his life, some critics suggested that Justice Black's basic constitutional views had changed.[1] In several social protest cases he found himself in the company of his more conservative colleagues, which to some represented "a dramatic reversal of a champion of free speech."[2] Black acknowledged this criticism in the Carpentier Lectures at Columbia University in 1968. Taking note of "current comments that I have changed my views with the implication that I am now deciding constitutional issues differently from the way I would have several years ago," he offered this

EVERETTE E. DENNIS is associate professor of journalism and mass communication at the University of Minnesota from which he received the Ph.D. He is the author of *The Media Society, Evidence about Mass Communication in America,* and coauthor of *New Strategies for Public Affairs Reporting* and *Other Voices, the New Journalism in America,* as well as editor of *The Magic Writing Machine.* A frequent contributor to law reviews and scholarly journals in mass communication, his interests include mass communication and society, communications law, popular culture, and contemporary reporting.

J. EDWARD GERALD is professor, School of Journalism and Mass Communication, University of Minnesota (emeritus). He is author of *The Press and the Constitution, the British Press under Government Economic Controls,* and *The Social Responsibility of the Press,* as well as journal articles on topics of special interest in constitutional rights and liberties, the press as a social institution (including economics of the mass media), and interpretative reporting.

NEIL A. LAVICK will receive a degree in law from Syracuse University in 1978 where he is managing editor of the Syracuse Journal of International Law and Commerce. He holds the M.A. degree in mass communication from the University of Minnesota and has been a public relations director for a Minneapolis firm. His publications and research interests have been in the areas of public relations and public international law.

strong retort: "I can say categorically that I have not changed my basic constitutional philosophy in the last forty years."[3]

Central to the mounting criticism of Justice Black in his last days on the Court was the argument that many of his opinions represented an abandonment of his commitment to liberalism. Some of the critics even went so far as to suggest that Black had moved from the liberal position once represented by such Justices as Frank Murphy and John Rutledge to a stance more sympathetic to Justice Felix Frankfurter who, because of his deference to state and local legislative policy, had been viewed as conservative. However, political labels and categories applied to Justice Black reflect the notions of critics and are not always an adequate base for analysis.

It is more useful to examine the general thrust of the critics' proposition in terms of the distinction Justice Black made between action and expression in free speech and press cases. This paper examines Justice Black's opinions in a number of cases commonly regarded as departures from his earlier views. Before considering the specific cases, it is important to recall the dramatic historical, political, and social developments that occurred during Black's tenure on the Court.

In 1937 Black became Franklin D. Roosevelt's first appointee to the Supreme Court. Then a U.S. Senator from Alabama, Black joined a Court that was notably hostile to the New Deal. In the years that followed he advanced an activist-libertarian philosophy favorable to labor and the civil liberties. In spite of a world war, foreign involvements in Korea and Vietnam, McCarthyism and the Cold War, he resisted the "pressures, passions and fears" of the times.[4] Firm in his belief in free speech and free press as he defined them, Black "contributed to the elevation of the individual and his place in the democratic process,"[5] in the view of Irving Dilliard. Yet Justice Black remained open to reasonable arguments for change. As Raymond Decker observed:

> Thus, although on the surface Justice Black appeared to be an uncompromising philosophical absolutist, he could readily accept change on the level of legal philosophy if accomplished through legally consistent procedures.[6]

Black wrote, "life itself is change and one who fails to recognize this must indeed be narrow-minded."[7] By change, Black did not mean a fundamental alteration in constitutional principles but an open-minded application of those principles in light of changing circumstances. Thus how the facts in each case interrelated became the controlling mechanism by which Black decided whether a case was basically a matter of expression or one of action. As he wrote in *Brown v. Louisiana*:

> The First Amendment, I think, protects speech, writings, and expression of views in any manner in which they can be legitimately and validly communicated. But I have never believed that it gives any person or group of persons the constitutional right to go wherever they want,

whenever they please, without regard to the rights of private or public property. . . . It does not guarantee to any person the right to use someone else's property, even that owned by government and dedicated to other purposes, as a stage to express dissident ideas.[8]

He reiterated the distinction between conduct and speech in the Carpentier Lectures: "Punishment for an overt, illegal act is one thing, but punishment of a person because he says something, believes something or associates with others who believe the same thing is forbidden by the express language of the First Amendment."[9] Further he drew a closer constitutional distinction:

It is not difficult to understand why the Founders believed that the peace and tranquility of society absolutely compel . . . the distinction between constitutionally protected freedom of religion, speech and press, and unconstitutionally protected conduct and picketing and street marching. It marks the difference between arguing for changes in the governing rules of society and in engaging in conduct designed to break and defy valid regulatory laws.[10]

In part the view that Justice Black abandoned his libertarian views in joining with conservative Justices on several free expression cases assumes that his was an unqualified absolutism. A civil libertarian making that assumption would expect Black to be in his corner on every and all issues. In a sense, and on certain speech issues, notably libel and obscenity, Black was an absolutist. As he put it:

I think I have made clear my belief that the Constitution guarantees absolute freedom of speech, and I have not flinched in applying the First Amendment to protect ideas I abhor. I have also continuously voted within the court to strike down all obscenity and libel laws as unconstitutional. In giving absolute protection to free speech, however, I have always been careful to draw a line between speech and conduct.[11]

In so distinguishing, Black seemed to identify and apply consistent standards. As extracted from a reading of his opinions in selected freedom of expression cases, it appears that Black used what Thomas I. Emerson called— and considered unacceptable—the two-level theory "that undertakes to distinguish in assembly cases between 'pure speech' and 'speech plus,' the latter receiving a lesser degree of protection under the First Amendment."[12] Clearly in any case dealing with freedom of expression, the communication content received absolute protection. This included published criticism of the government and areas such as libel and obscenity. There was, Mr. Justice Black reasoned, no right of government to control thought. However, the conduct attendant on the expression did not enjoy the same protection.

Even though he abhorred "balancing" of rights, particularly when he did not agree with the outcome, Black applied a modified balancing test to distinguish between pure speech and speech plus. He wrote:

I said, in *Barenblatt v. United States*, 360 U.S. 109 (1959), "even . . . laws governing conduct . . . must be tested by a balancing process, if they indirectly affect ideas." A good example of what I am talking about here is the case of *Schneider v. Irvington*, 308 U.S. 147 (1939), which involved ordinances prohibiting the distribution of hand-bills in order to prevent littering. The Supreme Court forbade application of such ordinances when they affected the distribution of literature designed to spread ideas. There were other ways, we said, to protect the city from littering which would not sacrifice the right of the people to be informed. But let me make absolutely clear that this kind of balancing should be used only where a law is aimed at conduct and indirectly affects speech; a law directly aimed at curtailing speech and political persuasion can, in my opinion, never be saved through a balancing process.[13]

Justice Black reiterated his preference for the two-level theory in a dissent in *Mishkin v. New York:*

I think the Founders of our Nation in adopting the First Amendment meant precisely that the Federal Government should pass "no law" regulating speech and press but should confine its legislation to the regulation of conduct. So too, that policy of the First Amendment made applicable to the States by the Fourteenth, leaves the States vast power to regulate conduct but no power at all, in my opinion, to make the expression of views a crime.[14]

In his view of the First Amendment, speech and press enjoyed a preferred position while claims made under the rights of assembly and petition were examined in the context of appropriateness. Once he had determined whether the issue in a case under consideration was in the realm of speech plus or of conduct, Justice Black applied his standards of appropriateness which he defined in terms of time, place, and circumstances. These standards are seen in several of the cases critics described as deviations in the Black philosophy. These alleged deviations are in three general areas: labor picketing, demonstrations and civil rights, and symbolic speech.

I

It was in the labor picketing line of cases that the two-level theory clearly emerged. To many critics it appeared that Justice Black's dissent in *Amalgamated Food Employees Union v. Logan Valley Plaza, Inc.*, was inconsistent with his views in earlier labor picketing opinions. In that case the Court struck down use of "no trespassing" laws to stop union members from picketing in a supermarket parcel pickup zone to protest the fact that the labor force was nonunion. But Black disagreed resolutely, saying:

> To hold that store owners are compelled by law to supply picketing areas for pickets to drive store customers away is to create a court-made law wholly disregarding the constitutional basis on which private ownership of property rests in this country. And of course picketing, that is patrolling, is not free speech and not protected as such. . . . These pickets do have a constitutional right to speak about Weis' [the owner] refusal to hire union labor, but they do not have a constitutional right to compel Weis to furnish them a place to do so on its property.[15]

Here Black argued that the picketing was unlawful *conduct* rather than *pure speech* and applied his standard of appropriateness of place. As he would later write in *A Constitutional Faith*, "there is no First Amendment right for people to picket on the private premises of another to try to convert the owner or others to the views of the pickets."[16]

Perhaps it was because Black had taken issue with labor pickets that critics thought he had retreated from libertarianism. After all, they might have reasoned, didn't Justice Black join with the majority in *Thornhill v. Alabama*, 310 U.S. 88 (1940), the landmark case that struck down Alabama's law against picketing? The Alabama law voided by the Court in that case was found so broad and vague as to pose a "pervasive threat" to freedom of discussion.

A year after *Thornhill*, in *Milk Wagon Drivers Union v. Meadowmoor Dairies, Inc.*, the Court upheld an injunction against labor picketing, saying that the pickets were "enmeshed with contemporaneously violent conduct which is concededly outlawed."[17] Justice Black disagreed, suggesting that the injunction against the unionists was again overbroad. The violence cited had taken place five years before the case was decided by the Illinois Supreme Court and seven years before the U.S. Supreme Court opinion. In that dissent Black maintained that "a state has the power to adopt laws of general application to provide that the streets shall be used for the purpose for which they primarily exist [travel], and because the preservation of peace and order is one of the first duties of government."[18] But he took issue with the Court, saying, along with Justice Douglas, that he could find no evidence to connect the pickets here injured with "any act of violence."[19]

While Black's stance in *Thornhill* and *Milk Wagon Drivers* might be viewed as prolabor, he at no time granted absolute rights of speech to labor pickets. He hinged his opinion on the overbreadth and vagueness of the law and injunction, which he found to be the true constitutional issue.

This is not inconsistent with the 1968 *Amalgamated Food Employees* case. However, a precedent with a rationale closer to the *Amalgamated* case was *Marsh v. Alabama*. That case dealt with a member of the Jehovah's Witness faith who distributed religious literature on the streets of a company-owned town. When she distributed literature, she was arrested and convicted under an Alabama state law that forbade entering or remaining on the premises of another after being warned not to do so. Justice Black voted to reverse the conviction. In doing so he asked and answered this question:

"Under what circumstances can private property be treated as though it were public?" The answer the *Marsh* case gives is when that property has taken on *all* the attributes of a town, i.e., "residential buildings, streets, a system of sewers, a sewage disposal plant and a 'business block' on which business places are situated."[20]

Consistent in these cases is the distinction Black drew between expression and conduct. Thus in *Giboney v. Empire Storage and Ice Co.*, he denounced pickets found to be in violation of Missouri's antitrust and boycott laws as outside free speech protection. He wrote: "It rarely has been suggested that the constitutional freedom for speech and press extends its immunity to speech or writing used as an integral part of conduct in violation of a valid criminal statute. We reject that contention now."[21] There is little aberrance in Black's posture in *Amalgamated Food Employees* in light of this line of cases.

II

During the 1940s the Supreme Court handled a heavy load of labor union cases, but by the 1950s it was increasingly turning attention to political and social issues, notably civil rights. An expanding economy and greater personal affluence seemed to spawn a more liberally oriented, tolerant America. The demise of McCarthyism and the decision against school segregation in *Brown v. Topeka Board of Education*, 347 U.S. 483 (1954), set the stage for more First Amendment rulings in the 1960s. When equal rights agitation expanded into protests of the Vietnam conflict, the Court was deluged with cases that gave new scope for use of the two-level theory.

Justice Black continued to draw a distinction between expression and conduct in the demonstration and civil rights cases. In *Brown v. Louisiana* five black youths staged a peaceful sit-in at a public library to protest against segregation policies. The youths were convicted under the state's breach of peace statute. The Supreme Court, in an opinion by Justice Abe Fortas, reversed, indicating that "the statute was deliberately and purposely applied solely to terminate the reasonable, orderly, and limited exercise of the right to protest the unconstitutional segregation of a public facility."[22]

Dissenting, Black viewed the sit-ins as unprotected conduct. There is a difference, he said, between protests that occur in the streets and protests that occur in public buildings:

> The problems of state regulation of the streets on the one hand, and public buildings on the other, are quite obviously separate and distinct. Public buildings such as libraries, schoolhouses, fire departments, court-houses, and executive mansions are maintained to perform certain specific and vital functions. Order and tranquility of a sort entirely unknown to the public streets are essential to their normal operation. . . . It is incomprehensible to me that a State must measure disturbances in its libraries and on the streets with identical standards.[23]

Concentrating on the speech-plus nature of the case, Black felt that the library, which requires order and tranquility for its normal operation, is an inappropriate place for the sit-in. Recognizing that this was not an aberration in Black's philosophy, one legal scholar wrote, "During 1962-66, despite his sit-in opinions, it was hard to discern any real mellowing in Black's decades-long commitment to freedom of speech."[24]

A different problem arose in *Adderley v. Florida,* 385 U.S. 39 (1966), when students demonstrated in front of a jailhouse to protest the arrest of fellow students demonstrating against local racial segregation. When they refused to vacate the premises, they were arrested for violating a Florida trespass law. The Supreme Court upheld the lower court and Justice Black wrote the opinion for the majority. In language strikingly similar to that of his dissent in *Brown v. Louisiana,* he wrote:

> The State, no less than a private owner of property, has the power to preserve the property under its control for the use to which it is lawfully dedicated. For this reason there is no merit to the petitioners' argument that they had a constitutional right to stay on the property, over the jail custodian's objections, because "this area chosen for the peaceful civil rights demonstration was not only 'reasonable' but also particularly appropriate. . . ." Such an argument has as its major unarticulated premise the assumption that people who want to propagandize protests or views have a constitutional right to do so whenever and however and wherever they please.[25]

Here again Black reiterated his basic position that speech cannot in all circumstances avoid restraint. When expression is bound up with conduct, speech as action must be evaluated in light of its appropriateness. In this case, speech-plus cannot be protected because it interferes with the smooth functioning of the jailhouse.

Both *Brown* and *Adderley* are in line with *Cox v. Louisiana* (No. 24), 379 U.S. 536 (1965), and (No. 49), 379 U.S. 559 (1965). In No. 24, demonstrators were convicted for disturbing the peace and obstructing public passages; No. 49 concerned picketing before a courthouse. The Supreme Court overturned both convictions. Black concurred in No. 24 and dissented in No. 49. Holding that there was no "constitutional right to engage in the conduct of picketing or patrolling, whether on publicly owned streets or on privately owned property,"[26] Black nonetheless found the Louisiana breach of the peace statute unconstitutionally broad and vague. He wrote:

> [The] statute [has] given policemen an unlimited power to order people off the streets, [whenever they personally decide] that views being expressed on the street are provoking or might provoke a breach of the peace. Such a statute does not provide for government by clearly defined laws, but rather for government by the moment-to-moment opinions of a policeman on the beat.[27]

But Black would not go so far as to allow picketing near a courthouse. On this aspect of the case he asserted:

> This statute, like the federal one which it closely resembles, was enacted to protect courts and court officials from the intimidation and dangers that inhere in large gatherings at the courthouse doors and jail doors to protest arrest and to influence court officials in performing their duties. The very purpose of a court system is to adjudicate controversies, both criminal and civil, in the calmness and solemnity of the courtroom according to legal procedures. Justice cannot be rightly administered, nor are the lives and safety of prisoners secure, where throngs of people clamor against the processes of justice right outside the courthouse or jailhouse doors. The streets are not now and never have been the proper place to administer justice.[28]

Another case in this line is *Coates v. Cincinnati,* in which the Court in an opinion by Justice Potter Stewart declared unconstitutional a city ordinance making it a criminal offense for three or more persons to assemble on any sidewalk and there conduct themselves in a manner annoying to passersby. Black dissented as did Chief Justice Warren Burger and Justices Harry Blackmun and Byron White, but in a separate opinion he cited procedural grounds, saying that he would "vacate the judgment and remand the case with instructions that the trial court give both parties an opportunity to supplement the record so that we may determine whether the conduct actually punished is the kind of conduct which it is within the power of the State to punish."[29]

III

If some students of Justice Black were puzzled by his behavior in the labor and civil rights cases mentioned, their fears were intensified by his vote in *Cohen v. California,* 403 U.S. 15 (1971). Casting a dissenting vote with the Supreme Court's first two Nixon appointees, Chief Justice Burger and Associate Justice Blackmun, Black stood with them against extending First Amendment protection to this instance of symbolic speech.

The term "symbolic speech" is relatively new to the language of the Court. Symbolic speech, which grew in part out of protests over the Vietnam war, included activities ranging from burning draft cards to pouring blood on selective service records. Thomas I. Emerson has termed it "new forms of communication that would reach a wider audience than was possible through ordinary procedures."[30] The Supreme Court itself has been reluctant to advance a specific definition, although a note in the *Columbia Law Review* suggests the following criteria:

> First, the conduct should be assertive in nature. This will generally mean that the conduct is a departure from the actor's normal activities

(i.e. it is not a natural preference of personal appearance) and cannot adequately be explained unless a desire to communicate is presumed. Second, the actor must have reason to expect that his audience will recognize his conduct as communication. Third, communicative value does not depend on whether the idea sought to be expressed can be verbalized. The symbolism or medium may be an idea in itself.[31]

In the *Cohen* case a war protester wore a jacket emblazoned with the words "Fuck the Draft" in a Los Angeles courthouse corridor. His conviction under a disturbing-the-peace statute was overturned by the Supreme Court. In a majority opinion Justice John Marshall Harlan said, "The conviction quite clearly rests upon the asserted offensiveness of the *words* Cohen used to convey his message to the public. The only 'conduct' which the state ought to punish is the fact of communication."[32]

Although he did not himself write an opinion in the case, Justice Black joined with Chief Justice Burger in a dissenting opinion written by Justice Blackmun. "*Cohen*'s absurd and immature antic," Justice Blackmun said, "was mainly conduct and little speech."[33]

In two earlier symbolic speech cases, *Tinker v. Des Moines School District* and *Street v. New York*, 394 U.S. 576 (1969), Black took similar stances. In *Tinker* two high school students wearing black armbands protesting the Vietnam war in violation of administrative order to the contrary had been suspended from school. Failing to find that the armbands caused "substantial interference" with the work of the school, the Court in an opinion of Justice Fortas found for the students. The armbands were declared to be permissible freedom of expression. The majority opinion hinged on a lack of evidence that the expression disrupted the school's operation or collided "with the rights of other students to be secure and to be let alone."[34]

Justice Black sharply dissented. Relying again on his notions of appropriateness, he seemed to abhor the thought of protests inside a school building. In Black's concept of an orderly society, this was strikingly inappropriate. He wrote:

> While I have always believed that under the First and Fourteenth Amendments neither the State nor the Federal Government has any authority to regulate or censor the content of speech, I have never believed that any person has a right to give speeches or engage in demonstrations where he pleases and when he pleases. This Court has already rejected such a notion [referring to *Cox v. Louisiana*].[35]

In interpreting the facts of the case, Black took issue with the majority:

> I think the record overwhelmingly shows that the armbands did exactly what the elected school officials and principals foresaw they would, that is, took the students' minds off their classwork and diverted them to thoughts about the highly emotional subject of the Vietnam war.[36]

Focusing on the appropriateness (time, place, circumstance) standard, Black wrote:

> The truth is that a teacher of kindergarten, grammar school, or high school pupils no more carries into a school with him a complete right to freedom of speech and expression than an anti-Catholic or anti-Semite carries with him a complete freedom of speech and religion into a Catholic church or Jewish synagogue. Nor does a person carry with him into the United States Senate or House, or into the Supreme Court, or any other court, a complete constitutional right to go into those places contrary to their rules and speak his mind on any subject he pleases. It is a myth to say that any person has a constitutional right to say what he pleases, where he pleases, and when he pleases. Our court has decided precisely the opposite.[37]

In the *Street* case, Black was again in the minority. The majority had ruled that the flag mutilation statute was unconstitutionally applied to a man who burned a flag in the street as a gesture of despair upon the death of Dr. Martin Luther King. The law, as applied, "permit him [the appellant] to be punished for merely speaking defiant or contemptuous words about the American flag,"[38] wrote Justice Harlan in the majority opinion. Justice Black repeated his consistent differentiation of speech and action. To him flag-burning, regardless of the words that accompanied it, was action. In his dissent he wrote:

> It passes my belief that anything in the Federal Constitution bars a State from making the deliberate burning of the American Flag an offense. It is immaterial to me that words are spoken in connection with the burning. It is the *burning* of the flag that the State has set its face against.[39]

Thus the reasoning enunciated by Black in *Tinker* and *Street* is in line with his earlier views in *Cox, Brown,* and *Adderley* which he also regarded as issues of conduct rather than pure expression. Justice Black could not countenance protests at schoolhouses, libraries, or jailhouses. Such activity, he maintained, would disrupt the orderly processes of government.[40]

IV

Justice Black's consistency in the cases cited in this paper demonstrate why he has been "a disappointment for those who like to pigeonhole justices."[41] Those who wanted to see Black as a doctrinaire liberal should not have been misled because he repeatedly made his philosophy on speech-action cases clear. In a 1962 dialogue with Professor Edmond Cahn of New York University, Black was asked, "would it be constitutional to prosecute someone who falsely shouted 'fire' in a theater?" He responded:

> If a person creates disorder in a theater, they would get him there not
> because of *what* he hollered but because he *hollered*. They would get him
> not because of any views he had but because they thought he did not have
> any views that they wanted to hear there. That is the way I answer: not
> because of what he shouted but because he shouted.[42]

In an article that utilized both traditional legal research methods and
empirical analysis, Professor S. Sidney Ulmer of the University of Kentucky
observed that any assessment of Black is necessarily complex. He wrote:

> We cannot assert, as some might like, that Hugo Black was unsuccessful
> in developing early in his career on the Court a philosophical orientation
> sufficient to enable him to decide consistently all cases coming before
> him in the period 1937–1971. One cannot refute Black's belief, expressed
> in 1937, that he would continue to be the same man after going to the
> Court as before, nor, from the perspective of traditional analysis, his
> claim that he had not changed his philosophy regarding the Constitution
> for forty years. The inability flows from three factors: (1) a lengthy serv-
> ice on the Court resulting in voluminous writings from which statements
> and arguments to support diverse viewpoints can be culled, (2) the always
> available argument that cases are unique and must be decided on their
> unique facts, and (3) the fact that Black was never a doctrinaire liberal of
> the Murphy stripe—as his opinions, votes and remarks in conference
> make clear. Thus, in regard to the third factor, he had greater flexibility
> within his constitutional philosophy to take positions unfavorable to civil
> liberty than those who assume the doctrinaire liberal model are wont to
> recognize.[43]

Justice Black was consistent both in drawing the distinction between
pure speech and speech-plus and in applying standards of time, place, and
circumstance to conduct.

To suggest that Justice Black was aberrant in opinions in which he sided
with more conservative colleagues is to misunderstand his view of assembly
and petition in the context of the First Amendment. To suggest that Justice
Black abandoned his activist position and to support such a claim by citing a
few speech-plus cases is inadequate proof. During the years when Black was
writing the labor, civil rights, and symbolic speech opinions, he also advanced
absolutist opinions in libel and obscenity cases. And similarly, it was in one of
the last opinions of his career, *New York Times v. United States* and *United
States v. Washington Post,* that he wrote:

> Both the history and language of the First Amendment support the view
> that the press must be left free to publish news, whatever the source,
> without censorship, injunctions, or prior restraints.[44]

The doubts of some legal scholars and journalists aside, Justice Black's
extraordinary contribution to the understanding and interpretation of the
First Amendment is logically intact. He was resolute in his opinions and consistent in stating his principles.

Bibliography

Writings by Justice Black

BLACK, HUGO L., A CONSTITUTIONAL FAITH, New York: Alfred A. Knopf (1969). The Justice's Carpentier lectures at Columbia University.
_____. "The Bill of Rights," James Madison Lecture at New York University, Feb. 17, 1960, 35 N.Y.U.L. REV. 865 (1960).
_____. "SINCERELY YOUR FRIEND," LETTERS OF MR. JUSTICE HUGO L. BLACK TO JEROME A. COOPER, University, Ala.: University of Alabama Press (1973).
Cahn, Edmond, *Justice Black and First Amendment "Absolutes": A Public Interview,* 37 N.Y.U.L. REV. 549 (1962).
"CBS News Special, Mr. Justice Black and the Bill of Rights." Transcript of interview broadcast Dec. 3, 1968, with reporters Eric Sevareid and Martin Agronsky.
DILLIARD, IRVING, ONE MAN'S STAND FOR FREEDOM, MR. JUSTICE BLACK AND THE BILL OF RIGHTS, New York: Alfred A. Knopf (1963). An essay by Dilliard and selections from Black's opinions on Bill of Rights cases.

Biographical materials

BLACK, HUGO, JR., MY FATHER: A REMEMBRANCE, New York: Random House (1975).
DAVIS, HAZEL (BLACK), UNCLE HUGO, AN INTIMATE PORTRAIT OF MR. JUSTICE BLACK, Amarillo, Tex.: privately printed (1965).
Douglas, William O., "Mr. Justice Black," THE PROGRESSIVE, November, 1971.
Durr, Clifford J., *Hugo L. Black: A Personal Appraisal,* 6 GEORGIA L. REV. 1 (1971).
HAMILTON, VIRGINIA VAN DER VEER, HUGO BLACK: THE ALABAMA YEARS, Baton Rouge: Louisiana State University Press (1972).
United States. 92nd Congress, First Session, 1971, *Memorial Addresses and Other Tributes in the Congress of the United States on the Life and Contributions of Hugo LaFayette Black,* Washington, D.C.: U.S. Government Printing Office (1972).
United States. Supreme Court, *In Memoriam of the Honorable Hugo LaFayette Black, Proceedings of the Bar and Officers of the Supreme Court of the United States, Proceedings before the Supreme Court of the United States.* Washington, D.C., April 18, 1972, The Court.

Analysis of Justice Black's work

BALL, HOWARD, THE VISION AND DREAM OF HUGO L. BLACK, AN EXAMINATION OF JUDICIAL PHILOSOPHY, University, Ala.: University of Alabama Press (1975).
Decker, Raymond C., *Justice Hugo L. Black: The Balancer of Absolutes,* 59 CALIF. L. REV. 1335 (1971).
DUNNE, GERALD T., HUGO BLACK AND THE JUDICIAL REVOLUTION, New York: Simon & Schuster (1977).
FRANK, JOHN P., MR. JUSTICE BLACK, THE MAN AND HIS OPINIONS, New York: Knopf (1949).
Freund, Paul A., *Mr. Justice Black and the Judicial Function,* 14 U.C.L.A. L. REV. 476 (1967).
Kalven, Harry, Jr., *Upon Rereading Mr. Justice Black on the First Amendment,* 14A U.C.L.A. L. REV. 398 (1966–67).
Lewis, Anthony, "Justice Black at 75: Still the Dissenter," N.Y. Times Magazine, 26 Feb. 1961, in LEVY, LEONARD, ed., THE SUPREME COURT UNDER EARL WARREN, New York: Quadrangle Books (1972).
McBride, Patrick M., *Mr. Justice Black and His Qualified Absolutes,* 2 LOYOLA L. REV. 37 (1969).

172

MEADOR, DANIEL J., MR. JUSTICE BLACK AND HIS BOOKS, Charlottesville: University Press of Virginia (1974).

MENDELSON, WALLACE, JUSTICES BLACK AND FRANKFURTER, CONFLICT IN THE COURT, 2d ed., Chicago: University of Chicago Press (1966).

Reich, Charles A., *Mr. Justice Black and the Living Constitution*, 76 HARV. L. REV. 673 (1962-63).

STRICKLAND, STEPHEN P., ed., HUGO BLACK AND THE SUPREME COURT: A SYMPOSIUM, Indianapolis: Bobbs-Merrill (1967).

WILLIAMS, CHARLOTTE, HUGO L. BLACK, A STUDY OF THE JUDICIAL PROCESS, Baltimore: Johns Hopkins University Press (1950).

Notes

Chapter 1

1. Supreme Court Tribute to Justice Black, 92 S. Ct. 5, 11 (1971).
2. 312 U.S. 287 (1941).
3. New York Times v. United States, 403 U.S. 713, 716 (1971).
4. Cahn, Edmond, *Justice Black and First Amendment "Absolutes": A Public Interview,* 37 N.Y.U.L. REV. 549, 554 (1962).
5. BLACK, HUGO, JR., MY FATHER: A REMEMBRANCE, New York: Random House (1975), vii-viii.
6. See May 23, 1938, at 26.
7. BLACK, HUGO, JR., note 5 *supra,* at 183-84.
8. Snowiss, Sylvia, *The Legacy of Justice Black,* 1973 SUPREME COURT REVIEW 187.
9. *Id.* at 227.
10. Barnett, Vincent M., Jr., *Mr. Justice Black and the Supreme Court,* 8 U. CHI. L. REV. 20, 41 (1940).
11. Snowiss, note 8 *supra,* at 227.
12. Note 4 *supra,* at 549.
13. Note 1 *supra,* at 5.

Chapter 2

1. N.Y. Times, 26 Nov. 1971, p. 23, cols. 2-3.
2. On Communist affiliation and labor union leadership, see his dissent in American Communications Assn. v. Douds, 339 U.S. 382, 445, (1950); United States v. Brown, 381 U.S. 437 (1965); on Communist affiliation and public school employment, see his dissent in Adler v. Board of Education, 342 U.S. 485, 496 (1952); Keyishian v. Board of Regents, 385 U.S. 589 (1967); on loyalty oaths, see his concurrence in Wieman v. Updegraff, 344 U.S. 183, 192 (1952); Baggett v. Bullitt, 377 U.S. 360 (1964); Elfbrandt v. Russell, 384 U.S. 11 (1966); on membership in subversive organizations and admission to the bar, see his dissent in Konigsberg v. State Bar, 366 U.S. 36, 56 (1961); Baird v. State Bar of Arizona, 401 U.S. 1 (1971).
3. On libel, see New York Times Co. v. Sullivan, 376 U.S. 254, 293 (1964); Rosenbloom v. Metromedia, 403 U.S. 29 (1971); on obscenity, see Smith v. California, 361 U.S. 147, 155 (1959); Rudrup v. New York, 386 U.S. 767 (1967).
4. Miranda v. Arizona, 384 U.S. 436 (1966).
5. Gallègos v. Nebraska, 342 U.S. 55, 73 (1951).
6. 345 U.S. 22, 36 (1953).
7. 390 U.S. 39 (1968).
8. 378 U.S. 5 (1964).
9. 322 U.S. 487, 494 (1944).
10. See Schmerber v. California, 384 U.S. 757, 773 (1966); United States v. Wade, 388 U.S. 218, 243-46 (1967); Gilbert v. California, 388 U.S. 263, 277 (1967).
11. 351 U.S. 12 (1956).
12. 372 U.S. 335 (1963).
13. 316 U.S. 455, 474 (1942).
14. *Compare* Bloom v. Illinois, 391 U.S. 194 (1968), and Mayberry v. Pennsylvania, 400 U.S. 455 (1971), *with* Justice Black's dissent in Sacher v. United States, 343 U.S. 1, 14 (1952).

15. 328 U.S. 649, 566 (1946).
16. 369 U.S. 186 (1962).
17. See Wesberry v. Sanders, 376 U.S. 1 (1964); and Reynolds v. Sims, 377 U.S. 533 (1964).
18. See, *e.g.*, Brown v. Louisiana, 383 U.S. 131, 151 (1966); Tinker v. Des Moines School District, 393 U.S. 503, 515 (1969); Cohen v. California, 403 U.S. 15 (1971).
19. See, *e.g.*, Spinelli v. United States, 393 U.S. 410, 429 (1969); Coolidge v. New Hampshire, 403 U.S. 443, 493 (1971).
20. See Berger v. New York, 388 U.S. 41, 70 (1967); Katz v. United States, 389 U.S. 347, 364 (1967).
21. See Kaufman v. United States, 394 U.S. 217, 231 (1969); Harris v. Nelson, 394 U.S. 286, 301 (1969); Wade v. Wilson, 396 U.S. 282, 287 (1970).
22. See, *e.g.*, Harper v. Virginia Board of Elections, 383 U.S. 663, 670 (1966); Goldberg v. Kelly, 397 U.S. 254, 271 (1970); Boddie v. Connecticut, 401 U.S. 371, 389 (1971); James v. Valtierra, 402 U.S. 137 (1971).
23. See *e.g.*, Baird v. State Bar of Arizona, 401 U.S. 1 (1971); New York Times v. United States, 403 U.S. 713, 714 (1971); California v. Byers, 402 U.S. 424, 459 (1971).
24. See, particularly, Turner v. United States, 396 U.S. 398, 425 (1970).
25. Douglas, *Mr. Justice Black: A Foreword,* 65 YALE L. J. 449, 450 (1956).
26. Kurland, *Hugo Lafayette Black: In Memoriam,* 20 J. PUB. L. 359, 360-61 (1971).
27. Black, *The Bill of Rights,* 35 N.Y.U.L. REV. 865, 881 (1960).
28. Milk Wagon Drivers v. Meadowmoor Dairies, 312 U.S. 287, 301 (1941).
29. Adamson v. California, 332 U.S. 46, 71 (1947).
30. Feldman v. United States, 322 U.S. 487, 501-02 (1944). See also Black, note 27 *supra,* at 880; Bartkus v. Illinois, 359 U.S. 121, 150 (1959).
31. Black acknowledged that the language of the Eighth Amendment, another essential supplement to the First Amendment, is imprecise in that it bans *excessive* fines and *unusual* punishments. Black, note 27 *supra,* at 871-72. During his tenure, there was little Eighth Amendment litigation and thus little opportunity to see how he would interpret the Amendment in particular situations. For his opinion that the Eighth Amendment does not bar capital punishment, see McGautha v. California, 402 U.S. 183, 226 (1971). See also Mishkin v. New York, 383 U.S. 502, 517 (1966).
32. Goldberg v. Kelly, 397 U.S. 254, 276-77 (1970).
33. Black treated the "impartial jury" provision of the Sixth Amendment as an imprecise clause, and denied it absolute enforcement. See text *infra,* at notes 116-23.
34. Black's treatment of the Equal Protection Clause defies easy summation. See text *infra,* at notes 151-76.
35. Rochin v. California, 342 U.S. 165, 176 (1952). See also Berger v. New York, 388 U.S. 41, 74-75 (1967).
36. Foster v. California, 394 U.S. 440, 448-49 (1969); *In re* Winship, 397 U.S. 358, 377 (1970); Boddie v. Connecticut, 401 U.S. 371, 394 (1971).
37. *In re* Winship, 397 U.S. 358, 384-85 (1970).
38. Griswold v. Connecticut, 381 U.S. 479, 510-18 (1965); Sniadach v. Family Finance Corp., 395 U.S. 337, 345 (1969).
39. Rochin v. California, 342 U.S. 165, 177 (1952); Turner v. United States, 396 U.S. 398, 425 (1970).
40. On the Fourth Amendment, see Harris v. United States, 331 U.S. 145 (1947); Wolf v. Colorado, 338 U.S. 25 (1949); Ker v. California, 374 U.S. 23 (1963); on due process, see Griswold v. Connecticut, 381 U.S. 479, 507 (1965); Sheppard v. Maxwell, 384 U.S. 333 (1966) (Black's departure from the libertarian position here became evident only after the success of the selective incorporation notions); on equal protection, see Kotch v. Pilot Commissioners, 330 U.S. 552 (1947); Goesaert v. Cleary, 335 U.S. 464 (1948). The charges of inconsistency in his First Amendment adjudication raise more complicated questions. See text *infra,* at notes 195-233.
41. Carlson v. Landon, 342 U.S. 524, 555-56 (1952); Barenblatt v. United States, 360 U.S. 109, 144-46 (1959); Konigsberg v. State Bar, 366 U.S. 36, 78 (1961); Communist Party v. Subversive Activities Control Board, 367 U.S. 1, 168-69 (1961).
42. Griswold v. Connecticut, 381 U.S. 479, 522 (1965). See also Harper v. Virginia Board of Elections, 383 U.S. 663, 675-80 (1966); Berger v. New York, 388 U.S. 41, 87 (1967); Boddie v. Connecticut, 401 U.S. 371, 394 (1971).
43. Adamson v. California, 332 U.S. 46, 89 (1947); Braden v. United States, 365 U.S. 431, 444-45 (1961). See also Turner v. United States, 396 U.S. 398, 425-26 (1970).
44. The most thorough examination and criticism of Black's historical argument is found in Fairman, *Does the Fourteenth Amendment Incorporate the Bill of Rights? The Original*

Understanding, 2 STAN. L. REV. 5 (1949). Among those clearly sympathetic to Black's constitutional views, see LEVY, LEGACY OF SUPPRESSION (1960); Meiklejohn, *The First Amendment Is an Absolute,* 1961 SUPREME COURT REVIEW 245, 263-64.

45. The clearest statement of this position is Rostow, *The Democratic Character of Judicial Review,* 66 HARV. L. REV. 193, 194-203 (1952).

46. See McKay, *The Preference for Freedom,* 34 N.Y.U.L. REV. 1182 (1959); Frantz, *Is the First Amendment Law?—A Reply to Professor Mendelson,* 51 CALIF. L. REV. 729, 738-44, 753-54 (1963).

47. See Justice Murphy's dissent, joined by Justice Rutledge, in Adamson v. California, 332 U.S. 46, 123 (1947); Douglas, Murphy, and Rutledge, dissenting in Wolf v. Colorado, 338 U.S. 25, 40, 41, 47 (1949). The consequences of this divergence were not visible as long as incorporation and First Amendment problems—two areas where Justice Black's literalism served the same ends as those served by activism—dominated the Court's work.

48. See Justice Harlan's challenge to Justice Black on this score. Griswold v. Connecticut, 381 U.S. 479, 501 (1965). See also the discussion of the declaratory theory of law by Justices Clark and Black in Linkletter v. Walker, 381 U.S. 618, 622-29, 643 (1965); and Justice Black in DeBacker v. Brainard, 396 U.S. 28, 34 (1969).

49. BLACK, A CONSTITUTIONAL FAITH 41 (1969).

50. 332 U.S. at 90-92. The internal quotation is from a Black opinion, F.P.C. v. Pipeline Co., 315 U.S. 575, 601, n.4 (1942).

51. Wechsler, *Toward Neutral Principles of Constitutional Law,* 73 HARV. L. REV. 1 (1959).

52. See Pollak, *Racial Discrimination and Judicial Integrity: A Reply to Professor Wechsler,* 108 U. PA. L. REV. 1 (1959); Henkin, *Some Reflections on Current Constitutional Controversies,* 109 U. PA. L. REV. 637, 652-55 (1961); Rostow, *American Legal Realism and the Sense of the Profession,* 34 ROCKY MT. L. REV. 123, 135-46 (1962).

53. On the bench this shift is most visible in the work of Justice Douglas. He has urged the judiciary to respond to evolving needs, openly eschewing the restraint that original intent might provide. Harper v. Virginia Board of Elections, 383 U.S. 663, 669-70 (1966); Oregon v. Mitchell, 400 U.S. 112, 139-40 (1970). See also Reitman v. Mulkey, 387 U.S. 369, 381 (1967); Walz v. Tax Commission, 397 U.S. 664, 700-06 (1970); Younger v. Harris, 401 U.S. 37, 58 (1971). He makes no serious attempt to distinguish judicial decision-making from legislative decision-making. Off the bench, this position is most clearly stated in Miller & Howell, *The Myth of Neutrality in Constitutional Adjudication,* 27 U. CHI. L. REV. 661 (1960).

54. See Mueller & Schwartz, *The Principle of Neutral Principles,* 7 U.C.L.A. L. REV. 571 (1960).

55. Katzenbach v. Morgan, 384 U.S. 641, 665-71 (1966); Oregon v. Mitchell, 400 U.S. 112, 204-09 (1970).

56. Board of Education v. Barnette, 319 U.S. 624, 646 (1943).

57. Dennis v. United States, 341 U.S. 494, 517 (1951).

58. Mackey v. United States, 401 U.S. 667, 677-81 (1971).

59. See, *e.g.,* Kaufman v. United States, 394 U.S. 217, 242-43 (1969); Shapiro v. Thompson, 394 U.S. 618, 655 (1969); In re Stolar, 401 U.S. 23, 34 (1971).

60. Griswold v. Connecticut, 381 U.S. 479, 501 (1965). See also Oregon v. Mitchell, 400 U.S. 112, 152 (1970); Sniadach v. Family Finance Corp., 395 U.S. 337, 342-43 (1969).

61. Griswold v. Connecticut, 381 U.S. 479, 507 (1965); Harper v. Virginia Board of Elections, 383 U.S. 663, 677 (1966). See also In re Winship, 397 U.S. 358, 385-86 (1970).

62. Sheppard v. Maxwell, 384 U.S. 333 (1966); Katz v. United States, 389 U.S. 347, 364 (1967); Sibron v. New York, 392 U.S. 40, 79 (1968); Hunter v. Erickson, 393 U.S. 385, 396 (1969); Boddie v. Connecticut, 401 U.S. 371, 389 (1971); In re Winship, 397 U.S. 358, 377 (1970). Chief Justice Burger and Mr. Justice Stewart also dissented in *Winship.* Their dissents, however, rested on disagreement with In re Gault, 387 U.S. 1 (1967). Neither joined Black's dissent. For a similar assessment of Justice Black's conception of the judiciary see Freund, *Mr. Justice Black and the Judicial Function,* 14 U.C.L.A. L. REV. 467 (1967).

63. Chambers v. Florida, 309 U.S. 227, 238 (1940). For similar statements, see Feldman v. United States, 322 U.S. 487, 500-01 (1944); Bartkus v. Illinois, 359 U.S. 121, 163 (1959).

64. Justice Black's equation of welfare with charity was also contrary to the implications of his earlier work. Goldberg v. Kelly, 397 U.S. 254, 275 (1970).

65. FRANK, MR. JUSTICE BLACK: THE MAN AND HIS OPINIONS (1949), especially chap. 4; STRICKLAND, ed., HUGO BLACK AND THE SUPREME COURT: A SYMPOSIUM 279-80 n. 11 (1967). For a statement of Justice Black's commitment to the competitive mechanism, see Northern Pacific Railway v. United States, 356 U.S. 1, 4 (1958).

66. See the defense of the thirty-hour work bill made by Justice Black when he was a senator in

1933. 77 Cong. Rec. 115, 1126–27 (1933). His argument centered on the interdependence of employer and employee and on the need to reduce the work week as a consequence of the increased productivity of modern machinery. He stressed the desirability of stripping away the "spirit of avarice" that unfortunately attaches itself to the spirit of commerce, in order to "preserve for the people the beneficent advantages that a fair trade and commerce can afford a nation."

67. Feldman v. United States, 322 U.S. 487, 501 (1944); Adamson v. California, 332 U.S. 46, 88–89 (1947); Black, note 27 *supra*, at 880; Communist Party v. Subversive Activities Control Board, 367 U.S. 1, 149–63, 167–69 (1961).

68. See, *e.g.*, Konigsberg v. State Bar, 366 U.S. 36, 78 (1961); Black, note 49 *supra*, at 63, 65–66. In defending the thirty-hour work bill, Senator Black spoke of the rights of ownership of property "honestly acquired and fairly used," and the rights of workers to enjoy "health, happiness, and security justly theirs in proportion to their industry, frugality, energy, and honesty." 77 Cong. Rec., at 1115. See also, text *infra*, at notes 241–43.

69. Black, note 49 *supra*, at 65–66.

70. See *In re* Winship, 397 U.S. 358 (1970).

71. See Sheppard v. Maxwell, 384 U.S. 333 (1966).

72. Kurland, note 26 *supra*, at 362.

73. Quoted in Black, *Reminiscences*, 18 Ala. L. Rev. 8 (1965).

Chapter 3

1. New York Times v. United States, 402 U.S. 713 (1971).

2. CBS television special on the Pentagon Papers case, July 2, 1971, confirmed by letter to Teeter from CBS correspondent Daniel Schorr, Aug. 12, 1972; "Excerpts of Arguments Before Supreme Court," Washington Post, 27 June 1971.

3. The First Amendment says: "Congress shall make no law respecting an establishment of religion, or prohibiting the free exercise thereof; or abridging the freedom of speech, or of the press; or the right of the people peaceably to assemble, and to petition the Government for a redress of grievances."

4. Cahn, Edmond, *Justice Black and First Amendment "Absolutes": A Public Interview*, 37 N.Y.U.L. Rev. 549, 553 (1962).

5. *Ibid.*

6. Black, Hugo L., *The Bill of Rights*, 35 N.Y.U.L. Rev. 865, 867 (1960).

7. The best work to date is Miller, Charles, The Supreme Court and The Uses of History, Cambridge, Mass.: The Belknap Press (1969). See also five articles, all titled *Use by the United States Supreme Court of Extrinsic Aids in Constitutional Construction*, Calif. L. Rev., Vols. 26 and 27 (1937–1939).

8. Wofford, John G., *The Blinding Light: The Uses of History in Constitutional Interpretation*, 31 U. Chi. L. Rev. 502, 533 (1964).

9. Kelly, Alfred H., *Clio and the Court: An Illicit Love Affair*, 1965 Supreme Court Review 122.

10. See, *e.g.*, note 4 *supra*, at 550–55. For a backhanded compliment to Black's historical scholarship, see Kelly, *id.* at 134.

11. See, *e.g.*, Fairman, Charles, *Does the Fourteenth Amendment Incorporate the Bill of Rights? The Original Understanding*, 2 Stan. L. Rev. 5, 78–81, 139 (1949); Kelly, *id.* at 132–34; Murphy, Paul, *Time to Reclaim: The Current Challenge of American Constitutional History*, 69 Amer. Hist. Rev. 64–65 (1963).

12. 332 U.S. 46, 59–68 (1948).

13. *Id.* at 68–123.

14. Engel v. Vitale, 370 U.S. 421 (1962).

15. Murphy, note 11 *supra*.

16. Quoted in Beale, Howard K., Charles A. Beard, Lexington, Ky.: University of Kentucky Press (1954), 144.

17. Bailey, Thomas A., *The Mythmakers of American History*, 55 J. Amer. Hist. 19 (1968).

18. Gottschalk, Louis, Understanding History, New York: Alfred A. Knopf (1959), 46.

19. *Id.* at 26–29, 44–49; see also Nevins, Allan, The Gateway to History, New York: Anchor Books, Doubleday & Co., rev. ed. (1962), 189–225; Barzun, Jacques, and Graff, Henry, The Modern Researcher, New York: Harcourt, Brace (1957), 88–114.

20. Gottschalk, note 18 *supra*, at 46.

21. Fischer, David Hackett, Historians' Fallacies, New York: Harper & Row (1970), ix.

22. Quoted in Bailey, note 17 *supra*, at 11.

23. Quoted in MILLER, note 7 *supra,* at 200.
24. *Id.* at 96.
25. 362 U.S. 60, 64-65 (1960).
26. Nelson, Harold L., *Seditious Libel in Colonial America,* 3 AMER. J. LEGAL HIST. 160, 172 (1959).
27. Bailey, note 17 *supra,* at 10.
28. Black, note 6 *supra.*
29. 366 U.S. 36, 61 (1960).
30. BLACK, HUGO L., A CONSTITUTIONAL FAITH, New York: Alfred A. Knopf (1969), 3-4, 6, 9.
31. *Compare* Beard, Charles A., *Written History as an Act of Faith,* 39 AMER. HIST. REV. 226 (1934).
32. KAPLAN, ABRAHAM, THE CONDUCT OF INQUIRY, San Francisco: Chandler Publishing Co. (1964), 28. Even respected Justice Brennan has been caught with his history down. See, *e.g.,* Roth v. United States, 354 U.S. 476, 484, where Brennan treated the history of blasphemy as being identical with the history of obscenity.
33. 367 U.S. 1, 137-69 (1960); see also MILLER, note 7 *supra,* at 91.
34. *Id.* at 159-61 (1960).
35. *Id.* at 155-56.
36. *Id.* at 159-60.
37. MILLER, note 7 *supra,* at 93-94.
38. FISKE, JOHN, THE CRITICAL PERIOD IN AMERICAN HISTORY, Boston: Houghton-Mifflin (1888).
39. Books by historians who persisted in seeing the Revolutionary generation as consisting of mortals include, *e.g.:* JENSEN, MERRILL, THE NEW NATION: A HISTORY OF THE UNITED STATES DURING THE CONFEDERATION, 1781-1789, New York: Alfred A. Knopf (1958), and THE ARTICLES OF CONFEDERATION, Madison, Wis.: University of Wisconsin Press, 3rd printing (1959); BEARD, CHARLES A., AN ECONOMIC INTERPRETATION OF THE CONSTITUTION, New York: Macmillan (1913); and LEVY, LEONARD, FREEDOM OF SPEECH AND PRESS IN EARLY AMERICAN HISTORY: LEGACY OF SUPPRESSION, New York: Harper & Row (1963).
40. BLACK, note 30 *supra,* at 6; *compare* FISKE, note 38 *supra.*
41. See JENSEN, MERRILL, ed., THE DOCUMENTARY HISTORY OF THE RATIFICATION OF THE CONSTITUTION, Vol. II, Pennsylvania, Madison, Wis.: State Historical Society of Wisconsin (1976), 128-31.
42. MADISON, JAMES, JOURNAL OF THE FEDERAL CONVENTION, Chicago: Albert Scott and Co. (1893), 85.
43. BLACK, note 30 *supra,* at 65-66.
44. Quoted in BALL, HOWARD, THE VISION AND THE DREAM OF JUSTICE HUGO L. BLACK, University, Ala.: University of Alabama Press (1975), 2.
45. JENSEN, note 39 *supra,* at 3-4, quoting FARRAND, MAX, ed., THE RECORDS OF THE FEDERAL CONVENTION OF 1787, 3 vols., New Haven (1911), I: 26-27.
46. *Id.* at 4, quoting FARRAND, *id.* at 299.
47. Cahn, note 4 *supra,* at 548.
48. Dissenting opinion in Milk Wagon Drivers Union v. Meadowmoor Dairies, 312 U.S. 287, 301, n. 4 (1941).
49. FORD, PAUL L. ed., THE WORKS OF THOMAS JEFFERSON, New York: G. P. Putnam's Sons, 12 vols. (1904-1905), in Vol. 9, at 451-52.
50. NELSON, HAROLD L., and TEETER, DWIGHT L., JR., LAW OF MASS COMMUNICATIONS, 2nd ed., Mineola, N.Y.: Foundation Press (1973), 7, quoting 4 BLACKSTONE, COMMENTARIES 151-52.
51. BRANT, IRVING, THE BILL OF RIGHTS: ITS ORIGIN AND MEANING, New York: Mentor Books (1967), 76.
52. See, *e.g.,* MAIN, JACKSON T., THE ANTIFEDERALISTS: CRITICS OF THE CONSTITUTION, 1781-1788, Chapel Hill: University of North Carolina Press (1961), especially at 158-62; WOOD, GORDON S., THE CREATION OF THE AMERICAN REPUBLIC, 1776-1787, Chapel Hill: University of North Carolina Press (1969), 536-43.
53. LEVY, note 39 *supra,* at xxi-xxii.
54. *Id.* at 3-4, quoting Roche, John P., *American Liberty: An Examination of the "Tradition" of Freedom,* in KONVITZ, MILTON R., and ROSSITER, CLINTON, eds., ASPECTS OF LIBERTY, Ithaca, N.Y.: Cornell University Press (1958), 130.
55. MILLER, note 7 *supra,* at 176.
56. *Ibid.*
57. *Ibid.,* quoting Dumbauld.
58. *Ibid.,* quoting Dumbauld.

59. HURST, JAMES WILLARD, THE GROWTH OF AMERICAN LAW: THE LAW MAKERS, Boston: Little, Brown & Co. (1950), 203.
60. Lewis, Anthony, "The Light and the Dark," International Herald Tribune, 22–23 April 1972, at 6.

Chapter 4

1. The lecture, entitled "The Bill of Rights," was delivered at the New York University School of Law on February 17, 1960. It is published in 35 N.Y.U.L. REV. 865 (1960).
2. The First Amendment reads as follows: "Congress shall make no law respecting an establishment of religion, or prohibiting the free exercise thereof; or abridging the freedom of speech, or of the press; or the right of the people peaceably to assemble, and to petition the Government for a redress of grievances."

Chapter 6

1. EMERSON, THOMAS I., THE SYSTEM OF FREEDOM OF EXPRESSION, New York: Vintage Books (1970), 535.
2. Cahn, Edmond, *Justice Black and First Amendment "Absolutes": A Public Interview*, 37 N.Y.U.L. REV. 549, 557 (1962).
3. 343 U.S. 250, 275 (1952).
4. 376 U.S. 254, 297 (1964).
5. EMERSON, note 1 *supra*, especially at 517–18, 543, 547; but also: many sources cited in these notes, plus personal interviews with half a dozen former law clerks for Justice Black and other Justices. No attempt is made here to discuss the more technical details of libel law, lower court decisions, defenses, etc. The purpose is to discuss Black and the major issues and decisions that came to the Court during his time.
6. EMERSON, note 1 *supra*, at 518.
7. Broadcasting is for all practical purposes considered under libel law as a mass medium (often recorded, filmed, taped, read from written scripts) to the extent that slander was originally never meant to cover.
8. KONVITZ, MILTON, FUNDAMENTAL LIBERTIES OF A FREE PEOPLE, Ithaca, N.Y.: Cornell University Press (1957), 136.
9. EMERSON, Note 1 *supra*, especially at 517 and 528. Also: Time, Inc. v. Hill, 385 U.S. 374 (1967) and Cantrell v. Forest City Publishing Co., 419 U.S. 245 (1974).
10. Former Chief Justice Earl Warren in Kalven, Harry, Jr., *Upon Rereading Mr. Justice Black on the First Amendment*, 14A U.C.L.A. L. REV. 398 (1967).
11. Reich, Charles A., *Mr. Justice Black and the Living Constitution*, 76 HARV. L. REV. 673, 701 (1962–1963).
12. McNulty, John K., review of HUGO BLACK AND THE SUPREME COURT: A SYMPOSIUM (1967), STRICKLAND, STEPHEN P., ed., in 56 CALIF. L. REV. 1185 (1967).
13. KONVITZ, note 8 *supra*, at 276.
14. Reich, note 11 *supra*, at 751.
15. *Id.* at 724–25.
16. Cahn interview, note 2 *supra*, at 562.
17. Kalven, note 10 *supra*.
18. *Id.* at 432.
19. KONVITZ, note 8 *supra*, at 127.
20. Cahn, note 2 *supra*, at 552.
21. Justice Black, *e.g.*, dissented in Ginzburg v. Goldwater, 396 U.S. 1049, 1052 (1970): "[E]ven if I believed in a balancing process to determine scope of the First Amendment, which I do not. . . ." He then went on to apply balancing principles. Similar phrasing can be found in cases such as Beauharnais v. Illinois, note 3 *supra*, at 275. See also EMERSON, note 1 *supra*, at 395.
22. Stressed in Ginzburg v. Goldwater, *id.*, at 1049, 1051, and in New York Times Co. v. Sullivan, 376 U.S. 250, 295 (1964).
23. Gertz v. Robert Welch, Inc., 418 U.S. 323 (1974). Black might also have been bothered by the fact that the Court decided Gertz was a private citizen. And, of course, the same might

well have held true for Time, Inc. v. Firestone, 424 U.S. 448 (1976). Such projections of how a Justice might have thought or voted are always risky. But in these cases (giving "private citizen" status), Black's writing and voting patterns would have left his position safely projected, or reasonably so.

24. See Reich, note 11 *supra*, at 704, among others. Also based on personal interviews with former law clerks at the U.S. Supreme Court.
25. *Id.* at 673, 680.
26. Cahn, note 2 *supra*, at 558–59.
27. *Id.* at 557, 560–61.
28. *Id.* at 553–54.
29. See Reich, especially, note 11 *supra*, and *passim*, 673–754. Also based on personal interviews with former U.S. Supreme Court law clerks.
30. *Id.* at 718.
31. Kalven, note 10 *supra*, at 429, and Freund, Paul A., *Mr. Justice Black and the Judicial Function*, 14 U.C.L.A. L. REV. 397, 473 (1967).
32. EMERSON, note 1 *supra*, at 529.
33. Note 21 *supra*, at 1053.
34. Note 4 *supra*, at 293. Although the best way to analyze the Justice's views would be to review all legal briefs and Court records of oral arguments, the evidence is here overwhelming: six specific references to the dollar amount involved meant the issue was much on Justice Black's mind in the 1964 case. There is also evidence, although less certain, that his views about excessive dollar amounts in libel cases would not have left him totally unhappy with part of the Gertz v. Robert Welch, Inc. 418 U.S. 323 (1974), decision limiting punitive damages to only situations where actual malice (reckless disregard for the truth or knowingly publishing false information) could be proved.
35. Based on Freund, note 31 *supra*, and *passim*, and a synthesis from personal interviews with former law clerks and writings about the Justice.
36. As phrased by KONVITZ, note 8 *supra*, at 136.
37. Kalven, note 10 *supra*, at 430. Also: Beauharnais v. Illinois, 343 U.S. 250, 267–75, compared with Black's other opinions in this area. Also: Justice Black's writings in GREY, DAVID L., in THE SUPREME COURT AND THE NEWS MEDIA, Evanston: Northwestern University Press (1968).
38. Kalven, *id.* at 440, 437.
39. Reich, note 11 *supra*, at 695, 700, plus personal interviews.
40. *Ibid.*, and *passim*, plus interviews.
41. Estes v. Texas, 381 U.S. 532 (1965); Sheppard v. Maxwell, 384 U.S. 333 (1966).
42. See other chapters in this book, especially Chapter 12 on speech-plus issues. Also based on McNulty, note 12 *supra*, at 1181, and interviews.
43. Beauharnais v. Illinois, 343 U.S. 250, 270 (1952).
44. *Id.* at 273–74.
45. *Id.* at 274.
46. *Id.* at 275.
47. 376 U.S. 254, 297 (1964).
48. *Id.* at 294.
49. *Id.* at 297.
50. Based primarily on interviews with former U.S. Supreme Court law clerks.
51. Note 49 *supra*, at 293.
52. *Ibid.*
53. 385 U.S. 374, 398 (1967).
54. 379 U.S. 64, 80 (1964).
55. Rosenblatt v. Baer, 383 U.S. 75, 95 (1966).
56. *Ibid.* and Ginzburg v. Goldwater, 396 U.S. 1049, 1052 (1970).
57. Ginzburg v. Goldwater, *id.* at 1050.
58. *Id.* at 1051–52.
59. Curtis Publishing Co. v. Butts and Associated Press v. Walker, 388 U.S. 130 (1967).
60. *Id.*, with Black concurring and dissenting, at 172.
61. *Id.* at 171.
62. *Ibid.*
63. *Ibid.*
64. Based largely on analysis of the Justice's writings, plus interviews with former law clerks. Best estimate of his personal slowdown is 1967 or 1968, although some talk even of 1966 while others prefer 1969 or 1970 with his Ginzburg v. Goldwater dissent in early 1970 as one of his last major statements.

65. 390 U.S. 727 (1968).
66. Rosenbloom v. Metromedia, 403 U.S. 29, 57 (1971).
67. Rosenbloom, *ibid.*
68. *Ibid.*
69. HACHTEN, WILLIAM, THE SUPREME COURT ON FREEDOM OF THE PRESS, Ames: Iowa State University Press (1960), 139, and *passim.* And see, especially, interpretations from EMERSON, note 1 *supra,* at 529-30.
70. Kalven, note 10 *supra,* at 444.
71. EMERSON, note 1 *supra,* at 529-30, and HACHTEN, note 73 *supra,* and *passim,* plus the personal interviews with former Supreme Court law clerks.
72. Beauharnais v. Illinois, 343 U.S. 250, especially *passim,* 267-75 (1952).
73. Curtis Publishing Co. v. Butts, 388 U.S. 130, 171 (1967); Ginzburg v. Goldwater, 396 U.S. 1049, 1051-52 (1970).
74. Rosenblatt v. Baer, 383 U.S. 75, 95 (1966); Rosenbloom v. Metromedia, 403 U.S. 29, 57 (1971).
75. Ginzburg v. Goldwater, 396 U.S. 1049, 1052 (1970).
76. *Id.* at 1051-52.
77. EMERSON, note 1 *supra,* at 539.
78. *Id.* at 535, especially, plus also the *Gertz* case, note 23 *supra.*
79. *Id.* at 533.

Chapter 7

1. BLACK, HUGO L., A CONSTITUTIONAL FAITH, New York: Alfred A. Knopf (1969), 9-10.
2. In Tinker v. Des Moines School District, 393 U.S. 503 (1969), Black dissents angrily from the Court's decision to find wearing of black armbands by school children in protest of the Vietnam war protected speech.
3. Cox v. Louisiana, 379 U.S. 536 (1965). In some respects this seems to have been a watershed case for Black. In his dissent he strongly objected to picketing, patrolling, or parading in or near a courthouse.
4. Bivens v. Six Unknown Named Agents of Fed. Bur. of Narc., 403 U.S. 388 (1970). In *Bivens* the Court upheld an action for damages resulting from a warrantless entry of a suspect's apartment and his arrest without probable cause. Black dissented on the grounds that there was no statutory justification for such a suit and in doing so he derogated the Fourth Amendment issue in the case. In *Harris,* a case also turning on the question of probable cause, Black voted with the majority reversing a lower court judgment for the defendant. Harlan, joined by Douglas, Brennan, and Marshall, dissented.
5. Griswold v. Connecticut, 381 U.S. 479 (1965). The Court does not tell us what kinds of activity are included in privacy, what guarantees of the Bill of Rights are *primarily* responsible for its protection, or what kinds of governmental and social interests justify limitations on privacy.
6. Ferguson v. Skrupa, 372 U.S. 726, 730 (1963).
7. Black had expressed similar ideas in his famous doctrinal dissent in Adamson v. People of State of California, 332 U.S. 46, 90-92 (1947): "But to pass upon the constitutionality of statutes by looking to the particular standards enumerated in the Bill of Rights and other parts of the Constitution is one thing; to invalidate statutes because of application of 'natural law' deemed to be above and undefined by the Constitution is another. In the one instance, courts proceeding within clearly marked constitutional boundaries seek to execute policies written into the Constitution; in the other they roam at will in the limitless area of their own beliefs as to reasonableness and actually select policies, a responsibility which the Constitution entrusts to the legislative representatives of the people."
8. Meyer v. Nebraska, 262 U.S. 390, 399 (1923).
9. 388 U.S. 41 (1967).
10. Olmstead v. United States, 277 U.S. 438 (1928). This case is notable for Justice Brandeis's exhaustive and powerful dissent, in which he said in part: "Clauses guaranteeing to the individual protection against specific abuses of power must have a similar capacity of adaption to a changing world. . . . [A] principle to be vital must be capable of wider application than the mischief which gave it birth. They [the framers] recognized the significance of man's spiritual nature, of his feelings and of his intellect. They knew that only a part of the pain, pleasure and satisfaction of life are to be found in material things. They sought to protect Americans in their beliefs, their thoughts, their emotions and their sensations. They

conferred, as against Government, the right to be let alone—the most comprehensive of rights and the right most valued by civilized men."

11. Note 9 *supra*.
12. 389 U.S. 347 (1967).
13. 338 U.S. 25 (1949). In Weeks v. United States, 232 U.S. 383 (1914) the Court had adopted the rule that papers illegally seized by federal officials could not be received in evidence in federal trials.
14. 367 U.S. 643 (1961).
15. Boyd v. United States, 116 U.S. 616 (1886).
16. For examples of the application of Civil Rights legislation, see Heart of Atlanta Motel, Inc. v. United States, 379 U.S. 241 (1964), and Katzenbach v. McClung, 379 U.S. 294 (1964).
17. Rochin v. People of California, 342 U.S. 165 (1952).
18. Jane Roe v. Wade, 410 U.S. 113 (1973).
19. Skinner v. Oklahoma, 316 U.S. 535 (1942).
20. Loving v. Virginia, 388 U.S. 1 (1967).
21. Eisenstadt v. Baird, 405 U.S. 438 (1971).
22. Pierce v. Society of Sisters, 268 U.S. 510 (1925).
23. 343 U.S. 451 (1952).
24. Others have found privacy protected in the Fifth Amendment's Due Process Clause. Beaney, William, *e.g.*, *The Constitutional Right to Privacy*, 1962 SUPREME COURT REVIEW 212, 232, would extract privacy from the confusion of the Fourth Amendment and view it as a liberty protected by the Fifth Amendment. This is also Justice Burton's position in his opinion for the majority in *Pollak*. The Fourteenth Amendment would govern state infringements.
25. 394 U.S. 557 (1969).
26. 357 U.S. 116 (1958).
27. Time, Inc. v. Hill, 385 U.S. 374 (1967).
28. PEMBER, DON R., PRIVACY AND THE PRESS, Seattle: University of Washington Press (1972).
29. Dennis v. United States, 341 U.S. 494 (1951).
30. Pound, Roscoe, *Survey of Social Interests*, 57 HARV. L. REV. 2 (1943).
31. EMERSON, THOMAS I., THE SYSTEM OF FREEDOM OF EXPRESSION, New York: Vintage Books (1970), 550.
32. WESTIN, ALAN, PRIVACY AND FREEDOM, New York: Atheneum (1968); MILLER, ARTHUR R., THE ASSAULT ON PRIVACY, Ann Arbor: University of Michigan Press (1971).
33. In Rosenbloom v. Metromedia, 403 U.S. 29 (1971), Justices Brennan and Blackmun, Chief Justice Burger, Justice White, and the late Justice Black were prepared to broaden the concept of "public interest" to apply to libel as well as privacy. More recently, a British Parliamentary Committee report, *Privacy* (Kenneth Younger, chairman), London: Her Majesty's Stationary Office (1972), 47, distinguishes between news "of" public interest (that which satisfies curiosity or a desire to be entertained) and news "in" the public interest (presumably that which the public needs to know). The latter but not the former would overcome privacy claims.
34. HURST, JAMES WILLARD, LAW AND CONDITIONS OF FREEDOM, Madison: University of Wisconsin Press (1956), 8.
35. New York Times Co. v. Sullivan, 376 U.S. 245 (1964).
36. Note 26 *supra*.
37. Kalven, Harry, Jr., *The Reasonable Man and the First Amendment*, 1967 SUPREME COURT REVIEW 284.
38. "Privacy and the Law: Symposium," *University of Illinois Forum*, 1971: 2, at 164. But see Cantrell v. Forest City Publishing Co., 419 U.S. 245 (1974).
39. WESTIN, note 3 *supra*, at 337.
40. Olmstead v. United States, 277 U.S. 438 (1928).
41. Warren, Samuel D., and Brandeis, Louis D., *The Right of Privacy*, 4 HARV. L. REV. 193 (1890).
42. Boyd v. United States, 116 U.S. 616 (1886).
43. Prosser, Dean, *Privacy*, 48 CALIF. L. REV. 383 (1960).
44. Kovacs v. Cooper, 336 U.S. 77 (1949); Breard v. Alexandria, 341 U.S. 622 (1951).
45. WESTIN, Note 31 *supra*, at 342.
46. NAACP v. Alabama, 357 U.S. 449 (1958).
47. Watkins v. United States, 354 U.S. 178 (1957).
48. Sweezy v. New Hampshire, 354 U.S. 234 (1957).
49. Baird v. State Bar of Arizona, 401 U.S. 1 (1970).
50. Talley v. California, 362 U.S. 60 (1960).
51. Massiah v. United States, 377 U.S. 20 (1964).
52. Frank v. State of Maryland, 359 U.S. 360 (1959).

53. Escobedo v. Illinois, 378 U.S. 478 (1964); Miranda v. Arizona, 384 U.S. 436 (1966).
54. American Communication Ass'n., CIO v. Douds, 339 U.S. 382 (1950); Adler v. Board of Education, 342 U.S. 485 (1952); Torcaso v. Watkins, 367 U.S. 488 (1961).
55. Lopez v. United States, 373 U.S. 427 (1963). See also Terry v. Ohio, 392 U.S. 1 (1968).
56. 403 U.S. 388 (1970).
57. 403 U.S. 443 (1970).
58. United States v. White, 401 U.S. 745 (1970).
59. Associated Press *et al.* v. United States, 326 U.S. 1 (1945).
60. WESTIN, note 31 *supra,* at 7.
61. *Id.* at 42.
62. "Privacy and the Law: Symposium," note 37 *supra,* at 154–67.
63. Laird v. Tatum, 408 U.S. 1 (1971).
64. WILLIAMS, CHARLOTTE, HUGO L. BLACK, A STUDY IN THE JUDICIAL PROCESS, Baltimore: The Johns Hopkins Press (1950).
65. Freund, Paul A., *Mr. Justice Black and the Judicial Function,* 14 U.C.L.A. L. REV. 397, 468–69 (1967).
66. Harper v. Virginia Board of Elections, 383 U.S. 663 (1966).
67. Freund, Paul A., *Privacy: One Concept Or Many,* in PENNOCK, J. ROLAND, and CHAPMAN, JOHN W., eds. PRIVACY, New York: Atherton Press (1971), 188.
68. Union Pacific Ry. Co. v. Botsford, 141 U.S. 250, 252 (1891).
69. STRICKLAND, STEPHEN P., ed., HUGO BLACK AND THE SUPREME COURT: A SYMPOSIUM, Indianapolis: Bobbs-Merrill (1967), xii.
70. Poe v. Ullman, 367 U.S. 497, 543 (1961).
71. National Mutual Ins. Co. v. Tidewater Transfer Co., Inc., 337 U.S. 582, 646 (1948).
72. 316 U.S. 129 (1942).
73. Abel v. United States, 362 U.S. 217 (1960).
74. Note 69 *supra.*
75. Freund, *Privacy: One Concept Or Many,* note 66 *supra,* at 195.
76. EMERSON, note 30 *supra,* at 562.

Chapter 8

1. Cited by Kalven, Harry, Jr., in *Metaphysics of the Law of Obscenity,* 1960 SUPREME COURT REVIEW 44.
2. United States v. Reidel, 402 U.S. 351, 380 (1971).
3. Smith v. California, 361 U.S. 147 (1959), Justice Black concurring.
4. ERNST, MORRIS L., and SCHWARTZ, ALAN U., CENSORSHIP: THE SEARCH FOR THE OBSCENE, New York: Macmillan (1964), 190.
5. Cahn, Edmond, *Justice Black and First Amendment "Absolutes": A Public Interview,* 37 N.Y.U.L. REV. 549, 561 (1962).
6. GREY, DAVID L., THE SUPREME COURT AND THE NEWS MEDIA, Evanston: Northwestern University Press (1968), 54.
7. Frank, John P., *Hugo L. Black,* THE NEW REPUBLIC, Oct. 9, 1971, at 16.
8. McBride, Patrick, *Mr. Justice Black and his Qualified Absolutes,* 2 LOYOLA L. REV. 37, 56 (1969).
9. Ash, Michael, *The Growth of Justice Black's Philosophy on Freedom of Speech: 1962–1966,* 1967 WISC. L. REV. 840.
10. *Id.* at 854.
11. 354 U.S. 476 (1957).
12. *Id.* at 489.
13. 361 U.S. 147 (1959).
14. 370 U.S. 478 (1962).
15. Memoirs v. Massachusetts, 383 U.S. 413 (1966).
16. 383 U.S. 502 (1966).
17. 383 U.S. 463 (1966).
18. Note 16 *supra,* at 517.
19. Note 17 *supra,* at 481.
20. *Roth,* note 11 *supra,* at 495.
21. Kalven, Harry, Jr., *Upon Rereading Mr. Justice Black on the First Amendment,* 14A U.C.L.A. L. REV. 428, 447 (1967).

22. Note 17 *supra*, at 495.
23. 386 U.S. 767 (1967).
24. 390 U.S. 629 (1968).
25. 394 U.S. 557 (1969).
26. *Id.* at 565.
27. 402 U.S. 351 (1971).
28. 402 U.S. 363 (1971).
29. Teeter, Dwight, Jr., and Pember, Don R., *Obscenity, 1971: The Rejuvenation of State Power and the Return to Roth,* 17 VILLANOVA L. REV. 211 (1971).
30. Note 28 *supra*, at 383.
31. Mutual Film Corp. v. Ohio, 236 U.S. 230 (1915).
32. United States v. Paramount Pictures, Inc., 334 U.S. 131 (1948).
33. Joseph Burstyn, Inc. v. Wilson, 343 U.S. 495 (1952).
34. Kingsley International Pictures Corp. v. Regents, 360 U.S. 684 (1959).
35. 365 U.S. 43 (1961).
36. Jacobellis v. Ohio, 378 U.S. 184 (1964) and Freedman v. Maryland, 380 U.S. 51 (1965).
37. Interstate Circuit, Inc. v. Dallas, 390 U.S. 676 (1968).
38. *Kingsley,* note 34 *supra*, at 690.
39. *Mishkin,* note 16 *supra*, at 516.
40. "Mr. Justice Black and the Bill of Rights." An interview first broadcast by CBS television, Dec. 3, 1968.
41. Note 11 *supra*, at 511.
42. Note 34 *supra*, at 690.
43. Note 36 *supra*, at 196.
44. Note 16 *supra*, at 517.
45. Note 24 *supra*, at 655.
46. Note 27 *supra*, at 380.
47. CLOR, HARRY, OBSCENITY AND PUBLIC MORALITY, Chicago: University of Chicago Press (1969), 93.
48. Note 3 *supra*, at 160.
49. Note 17 *supra*, at 482.
50. Note 9 *supra*, at 855.
51. Note 3 *supra*, at 160.
52. Note 21 *supra*, at 446.
53. Note 5 *supra*, at 559.
54. Note 34 *supra*, at 691.
55. Note 17 *supra*, at 480.
56. Note 27 *supra*, at 380.
57. Note 40 *supra*.
58. *Mishkin,* note 16 *supra*, at 516.
59. United States v. Dellapia, 433 F. 2d 1252, 1259 (2d Cir. 1970).
60. Decker, R. G., *Justice Hugo L. Black: The Balancer of Absolutes,* 59 CALIF. L. REV. 1335, 1336 (1971).
61. Note 40 *supra*.
62. Durr, Clifford J., *Hugo L. Black: A Personal Appraisal,* 6 GEORGIA L. REV. 1, 16 (1971).
63. Lewis, Anthony, "Justice Black at 75: Still the Dissenter," N.Y. Times Magazine, 26 Feb. 1961, at 74.

Chapter 9

1. CORPUS JURIS SECUNDUM, Contempt, § 1.
2. GOLDFARB, RONALD L. THE CONTEMPT POWER, New York: Anchor books (1971), xxii. The preface was written in 1970; the study itself was originally published in 1963.
3. Sheppard v. Maxwell, 384 U.S. 333 (1966).
4. Estes v. Texas, 381 U.S. 532 (1965).
5. Irvin v. Dowd, 366 U.S. 717 (1961). See also Rideau v. Louisiana, 373 U.S. 723 (1963).
6. Bridges v. California, Times-Mirror Co. v. Superior Court, 314 U.S. 252 (1941).
7. Pennekamp v. Florida, 328 U.S. 331 (1946).
8. Craig v. Harney, 331 U.S. 367 (1947).

9. Advisory Committee on gnair Trial and Free Press, American Bar Association Project for Minimum Standards for Criminal Justice, *Fair Trial and Free Press*, approved draft, March, 1968.

10. *Id.* at Section 4.1 (a) (i) and 4.1 (b). Section 4.1 (a) (i) recommends that contempt power be used "against a person who, knowing that a criminal trial by jury is in progress or that a jury is being selected for such a trial: disseminates by any means of public communication an extrajudicial statement relating to the defendant or to the issues in the case that goes beyond the public record of the court in the case, that is willfully designed by that person to affect the outcome of the trial, and that seriously threatens to have such an effect." Section 4.1 (b) recommends contempt proceedings "against a person who knowingly violates a valid judicial order not to disseminate, until completion of the trial or disposition without trial, specified information referred to in the course of a closed judicial hearing. . . ."

11. See, *e.g.*, *In re* Look Magazine, 164 A. 2d 95 (N.J., 1970); *In re* Matzner, 283 A. 2d 737 (N.J., 1971).

12. Bridges v. California, 314 U.S. 252, 269 (1941).

13. See, *e.g.*, Branzburg v. Hayes, 461 S.W. 2d 345 (Ky., 1970), affirmed 408 U.S. 665 (1972); Lightman v. State, 274 A. 2d 149 (Md., 1972); *In re* Bridge, 295 A. 2d 3 (N.J., 1972); Farr v. Superior Court for Los Angeles County, 99 CAL. RPTR. 342, 22 Cal. App. 3d 60 (1971).

14. See State v. Knops, 183 N.W. 2d 93 (Wis., 1971); *In re* Pappas, 266 N.E. 2d 297 (Mass., 1971); Buchanan v. Oregon, 436 P. 2d 729 (Ore., 1968) cert. den., 392 U.S. 905 (1968).

15. 408 U.S. 665 (1972).

16. 17 CORPUS JURIS SECUNDUM, Contempt, § 62 (2).

17. GOLDFARB, note 2 *supra*, and *passim*, Chapter 1.

18. Wilm. 243 (1765).

19. GOLDFARB, note 2 *supra*, at 15. (Since the opinion was never officially reported, scholars have had to rely on notes of Justice Wilmot which were published later by his son.)

20. *Ibid.*

21. *Id.* at 14.

22. 4 BLACKSTONE, COMMENTARIES 284.

23. 4 BLACKSTONE, COMMENTARIES 285.

24. 4 Stat. 487.

25. Toledo Newspaper Co. v. United States, 247 U.S. 402 (1918).

26. CORPUS JURIS SECUNDUM, Contempt, § 3.

27. *Id.* at § 4.

28. Toledo Newspaper Co. v. United States, 247 U.S. 402 (1918); Patterson v. Colorado, 205 U.S. 454 (1907).

29. 314 U.S. 252 (1941).

30. *Id.* at 264.

31. *Id.* at 266.

32. *Id.* at 264.

33. *Id.* at 269.

34. Shortly before the *Bridges* decision, the Supreme Court had ruled that an 1831 federal statute (4 Stat. 487) restricted the right of *federal* judges to issue indirect contempt citations against the news media: Nye v. United States, 313 U.S. 33 (1941).

35. 328 U.S. 331 (1946).

36. 331 U.S. 367 (1947).

37. 370 U.S. 375 (1962).

38. 326 U.S. 224 (1945).

39. *Id.* at 227.

40. *In re* Murchison *et al.*, 349 U.S. 133 (1955).

41. *Id.* at 137.

42. *Id.* at 138.

43. 370 U.S. 230 (1962).

44. 382 U.S. 162 (1965).

45. 17 CORPUS JURIS SECUNDUM, Contempt § 4, 5.

46. *Id.* at Section 6.

47. For discussion see NELSON, HAROLD L., and TEETER, DWIGHT L., JR., LAW OF MASS COMMUNICATIONS, Mineola, N.Y.: Foundation Press (1969), 287–92.

48. Article III provides that in federal courts, "The Trial of all Crimes, except in Cases of Impeachment, shall be by Jury."

49. Sacher *et al.* v. United States, 343 U.S. 1 (1952).

50. *Id.* at 20.

51. *Id.* at 22.

52. *Id.* at 23.
53. 356 U.S. 165 (1958).
54. *Id.* at 198.
55. *Id.* at 216.
56. *Id.* at 195.
57. *Id.* at 193.
58. *Id.* at 203.
59. *Id.* at 198.
60. 362 U.S. 610 (1960).
61. *Id.* at 622.
62. Black dissented, joined by Douglas; Justice Arthur Goldberg wrote a separate dissent, joined by Warren and Douglas.
63. United States v. Barnett, 376 U.S. 681 (1964), reh. den., 377 U.S. 973 (1964).
64. *Id.* at 726–27.
65. *Id.* at 727.
66. 384 U.S. 373 (1965).
67. *Id.* at 387, 392.
68. 391 U.S. 194 (1968).
69. *Id.* at 201.
70. 395 U.S. 147 (1969), reh. den., 396 U.S. 869 (1969).
71. *Id.* at 160.
72. 400 U.S. 455 (1971).

Chapter 10

1. See, *e.g.*, his dissent in United States v. Thirty-Seven Photographs, 402 U.S. 363, 379 (1971), or his opinion for the majority in Bridges v. California, 314 U.S. 252 (1941).
2. New York Times v. United States, 403 U.S. 713, 717 (1971).
3. Yates v. United States, 354 U.S. 298, 344 (1957).
4. *Access to the Press—A New First Amendment Right,* 80 HARV. L. REV. 1641 (1967).
5. *Id.* at 1655–56.
6. *Id.* at 1642.
7. BLACK, HUGO L., A CONSTITUTIONAL FAITH, New York: Alfred A. Knopf (1969), 57–58.
8. 383 U.S. 131, 151 (1966).
9. 393 U.S. 503, 515 (1969).
10. Associated Press v. United States, 326 U.S. 1 (1945).
11. *Id.* at 20.
12. Printing plants are said to be "captive plants" when they are owned and operated by business firms not primarily engaged in printing. Captive plants are usually specialty plants designed to provide the owner firm with a certain kind of printing service faster, cheaper, or with greater security than is available in the trade.
13. It should be noted that although advertising does serve an information function for the reader, and in that respect advertising department employees perform journalistic functions, newspaper management decision-making does not operate on those principles. Advertising is the major revenue source for daily newspapers and management seeks to maximize this aspect of the business while seeking to hold down costs in the editorial department, which, because of the inequities of the joint-pricing structure of the industry, is seen as "not paying its way."
14. 342 U.S. 143 (1951).
15. 334 U.S. 100 (1948).
16. *Id.* at 105.
17. United States v. Aluminum Co. of America, 148 F. 2d 416, 429 (2d Cir. 1945).
18. American Tobacco Co. v. United States, 328 U.S. 781, 809 (1946).
19. International Salt Co. v. United States, 332 U.S. 392, 396 (1947).
20. Griffith, note 15 *supra,* at 107.
21. Standard Oil Co. of California and Standard Stations v. United States, 337 U.S. 293 (1949).
22. Brown Shoe Co. v. United States, 370 U.S. 294, 332 (1962).
23. Citizen Publishing Co. v. United States, 394 U.S. 131 (1969). See also United States v. Times-Mirror Co., 390 U.S. 712 (1968). For *per curiam* ruling upholding lower decision, see 274 F. Supp. 606 (C.D. Calif. 1967).

24. 344 U.S. 392, 395 (1953).
25. Note 10 *supra,* at 7.
26. *Id.* at 13–14.

Chapter 11

1. 408 U.S. 665 (1972).
2. See, *e.g.,* Neubauer, Mark, *The Newsman's Privilege after "Branzburg": The Case for a Federal Shield Law,* 24 U.C.L.A. L. REV. 160–93 (1976), and sources cited there; Kirtz, Bill, *Libel Loser Urges More Named Sources,* EDITOR & PUBLISHER, Jan. 24, 1976, at 15, and *National Shield Legislation Divides Reporters' Groups,* FOI DIGEST, May/June, 1975, at 4.
3. See WIGMORE, JOHN HENRY, EVIDENCE IN TRIALS AT COMMON LAW, 4th ed., revised by MCNAUGHTON, JOHN T., Boston: Little, Brown & Co. (1961), Vol. 8, especially § 2192, at 70.
4. See 408 U.S. 665, at 725–752 for Justice Stewart's dissent, and at 711–25 for Justice Douglas's dissent.
5. 314 U.S. 252 (1941).
6. *Id.* at 265.
7. See Lewis, Anthony, *"Justice Black at 75: Still the Dissenter,"* N.Y. Times Magazine, 26 Feb. 1961, reprinted in LEVY, LEONARD, ed., THE SUPREME COURT UNDER EARL WARREN, New York: Quadrangle Books (1972), 130–31. Lewis contrasted the Black and Frankfurter positions, with the latter looking first to governmental needs, a position Justice Black saw as lacking in protection for the individual.
8. New York Times Co. v. United States and United States v. Washington Post Co., 403 U.S. 713, 719 (1971). *Compare* the balancing formula offered in *Branzburg* by Justice Powell, 408 U.S. 665, 710.
9. *Id.* New York Times Co. at 719–20, quoting from De Jonge v. Oregon, 299 U.S. 353, 365 (1937).
10. See, *e.g.,* McCartney, James, *The Washington Post and Watergate: How Two Davids Slew Goliath,* COL. JOURN. REV., July/August, 1973, pp. 8–22.
11. See, *e.g.,* Blasi, Vince, *The Justice and the Journalist,* THE NATION, Sept. 18, 1971, pp. 198–99. For evidence on the *number* of stories which have their basis in confidentiality, see Guest, James A., and Stanzler, Alan L., *The Constitutional Argument for Newsmen Concealing Their Sources,* 64 NORTHWESTERN U. L. REV. 18, at 43–44, and Appendix at 57–61 (1969). See also Blasi, Vince, *Press Subpoenas: An Empirical and Legal Analysis,* Reporters Committee for Freedom of the Press, Study Report, Washington, D.C. (1972), especially at 20–29. In regard to the increasing use of confidential sources, see also House of Representatives, Committee on Government Operations, Foreign Operations and Government Information Subcommittee, *Government News from Anonymous Sources* (1972), 1; and Miller, Merle, *Washington, the World, and Joseph Alsop,* HARPER'S, June, 1968, n., p. 43.
12. Mills v. Alabama, 384 U.S. 214, 219 (1966). Italics added.
13. Black, Hugo L., *The Bill of Rights,* 35 N.Y.U.L. REV. 865, 881 (1960).
14. Nugent v. Beale, 18 Fed. Cas. 471, Case No. 10, 375 (C.C.D.C., 1848).
15. Burdick v. United States, 236 U.S. 79 (1915).
16. The unreported cases, most of which were located in searches through EDITOR & PUBLISHER and N.Y. TIMES INDEX, are documented in Gordon, A. David, "The Protection of News Sources: The History and Legal Status of the Newsman's Privilege," unpublished Ph.D. dissertation, University of Wisconsin, 1971, pp. 431–728, *passim.*
17. The (Louisville) Courier-Journal, 5 March 1934, p. 4. The complete text of the letter was also printed in EDITOR & PUBLISHER, March 17, 1934, p. 6, but with several variations in style from the original, as well as with several typographical errors.
18. Details of this incident are recounted in The Courier-Journal, 5–16 March 1934, *passim,* and in EDITOR & PUBLISHER, March 17, 1934, pp. 5–6, and March 24, 1934, p. 4.
19. Details of this incident are reported in The Courier-Journal, 19 July to 4 Aug. 1934, *passim,* and in EDITOR & PUBLISHER, July 28, 1934, pp. 6 and 22; Aug. 4, 1934, pp. 3–4 and 20; and Aug. 11, 1934, pp. 26 and 36. For details of these two cases, see also Gordon, David, "The 1934 Kentucky Newsman's Privilege Cases," paper delivered at annual convention, Association for Education in Journalism, Columbia, S.C., 1971.
20. See, *e.g.,* N.Y. Times, 29 June 1966, p. 23, and 1 July 1966, p. 14, in regard to the Annette Buchanan case (State v. Buchanan, 250 Ore. 244, 436 P. 2d 729, 1968). In fairness, it should be noted that cases have been dropped because the term of the in-

vestigating grand jury had expired. But, of course, the issue could have been renewed with subsequent grand juries, if the prosecutor had been so inclined.

21. Letter to the author from Curtis Miller, the editor involved in the case, July 1, 1971.
22. Case No. 111,567, District Court of St. Louis County, Minnesota: Canadian Brotherhood of Railway, Transport and General Workers, *et. al.* v. Seafarers' International Union of North America, Canadian District *et al.*, request for temporary injunction, July 24, 1961, and subsequent dates.
23. Interview with former Judge Sidney Kaner, Duluth, Minn., June 15, 1971.
24. 259 F. 2d 545, 548 (2d Cir., 1958), cert. den., 358 U.S. 910 (1958). Emphasis added.
25. *Id.* at 550.
26. See, *e.g.*, Arnold, Edmund C., *Editors Protect "Legal" Rights*, PUBLISHERS AUXILIARY, May 23, 1959, p. 4.
27. EDITOR & PUBLISHER, Feb. 14, 1959, p. 6.
28. Perhaps the most striking example of this failure to distinguish the circumstances of subsequent cases came in Appeal of Goodfader, 45 Haw. 317, 367 P. 2d 472 (1961), which involved a municipal government reporter's story of the firing of the city-county personnel director. There was some question in this case about the centrality of the information sought from the reporter and of its possible availability from other sources. See text at note 99 *infra*.
29. Justice Douglas dissented from the refusal to grant certiorari in *Torre* and in Murphy v. Colorado, cert. den., 365 U.S. 843 (1960). There were no recorded dissents from the Court's action denying certiorari in State v. Buchanan, 250 Ore. 244, 436 P. 2d 729, cert. den., 392 U.S. 905 (1968).
30. Law review articles by and about Justice Black over the past 15 or so years (up until 1976, at least) did not mention the subject of journalist's privilege, nor was it discussed in a CBS television interview with him, broadcast Dec. 3, 1969. A search of THE READERS GUIDE TO PERIODICAL LITERATURE and of VITAL SPEECHES yielded no articles or speeches by Justice Black. And there was no mention of journalist's privilege in newspaper accounts of the Carpentier Lectures delivered at Columbia University by Justice Black in March, 1968. See N.Y. Times, 21 March 1968, p. 43; 22 March 1968, p. 41; and 24 March 1968, p. 38. For an example of a ringing defense of First Amendment protection in libel that contrasts sharply with his silence on the privilege issue, see Justice Black's dissent to the Supreme Court's refusal to grant certiorari in Ginzburg v. Goldwater, 396 U.S. 1049 (1970), in which Justice Douglas joined. By contrast, Justice Black was silent when the Supreme Court refused to review the three privilege cases. See note 29 *supra*.
31. 402 U.S. 942 (1971).
32. *Bridges,* note 5 *supra,* and see the following text *supra*.
33. See Marsh v. Alabama, 326 U.S. 501 (1946); Jamison v. Texas, 318 U.S. 413 (1943); Martin v. Struthers, 319 U.S. 141 (1943); and Winters v. State of New York, 333 U.S. 507 (1948). Justice Black wrote the majority opinions in *Marsh, Jamison,* and *Martin.*
34. *Marsh, id.* at 509.
35. NAACP v. Alabama *ex rel.* Patterson, 357 U.S. 449 (1958). See also Bates v. Little Rock, 361 U.S. 516 (1960), to the same effect.
36. 362 U.S. 60 (1960).
37. *Id.* at 64.
38. *Ibid.*
39. *Id.* at 65. The parallel was drawn to *NAACP* and *Bates,* both note 35 *supra.*
40. People *ex rel.* Phelps v. Fancher, 2 Hun (N.Y.) 226, 4 Thomp. & C. 467 (S. Ct. N.Y., 1st Dept., 1874); and Pledger v. State, 77 Ga. 242, 3 S.E. 320 (Ga., 1887). The *Fancher* case was subsequently used as precedent in Plunkett v. Hamilton, 136 Ga. 72, 70 S.E. 781 (Ga., 1911) and in People *ex rel.* Mooney v. Sheriff of New York County, 269 N.Y. 291, 199 N.E. 415 (Ct. of Appeals, N.Y., 1936) as well as in a third case of lesser importance. The *Pledger* case was subsequently used as precedent in the *Plunkett* decision, along with one other less important case. The *Plunkett* decision, which relied for precedent on *Fancher, Pledger,* and one other case, was also used as precedent (along with *Fancher* and four other cases) in the *Mooney* decision. *Mooney* was the leading journalist's privilege case from 1936 until *Torre* (note 24 *supra*) in 1958; and was still being cited in the early 1970s. *Torre,* itself the leading privilege case from 1958 to 1972, cited only five privilege cases as precedent, including both *Mooney* and *Plunkett.* Thus, the influence of the two anonymous publication cases has, indeed, been strong in the subsequent development of precedent involving confidential sources and information.
41. 376 U.S. 254 (1964).
42. 418 U.S. 323 (1974).

43. Note 41 *supra,* at 281, quoting Coleman v. MacLennan, 78 Kan. 711, 723, 98 Pac. 281 (1908).
44. *Id.* at 279–80.
45. *Id.* at 296–97.
46. 385 U.S. 374 (1967).
47. Guest and Stanzler, note 11 *supra,* at 35–36.
48. Note 46 *supra,* at 398.
49. *Id.* at 401.
50. *Id.* at 399. Justice Black wrote that he concurred in what he viewed as a watered-down statement of First Amendment rights only to allow the Court to reach a decision that in fact would extend the *Sullivan* doctrine a little bit; Justice Black, however, wanted it extended much further than the Court was willing to go. He also warned of the dangers of creating a right of privacy which would be equal, or superior, to the right of free press. See 385 U.S. 374 at 400.
51. 403 U.S. 29 (1971).
52. See Rosenblatt v. Baer, 383 U.S. 75 (1966). See Justice Douglas's concurrence, in which he argued that freedom of discussion " 'must embrace all issues about which information is needed or appropriate to enable the members of society to cope with the exigencies of their period,' " at 89–90 — quoting Thornhill v. Alabama, 310 U.S. 88, at 101–2 (1946). See also *Rosenblatt,* at 91, where Justice Douglas said "the question is whether a public *issue,* not a public official, is involved."
53. Note 51 *supra,* at 57, quoting from the plurality opinion by Justice Brennan, at 44.
54. Pickering v. Board of Education, 391 U.S. 563, especially 571–74 (1968). For the application of this doctrine to other areas of public employment, in situations where the statements are not injurious to morale and don't interfere with the performance of duties, see *inter alia* Muller v. Conlisk, 429 F. 2d 901 (1970); Burkett v. United States, 402 F. 2d 1002 (1968); and Meehan v. Macy, 392 F. 2d 822 (1968) reargued 425 F. 2d 472 (1968) petition for reconsideration granted 425 F. 2d 469 (1968), a decision which was reconsidered and its scope enlarged following the *Pickering* decision.
55. 361 U.S. 516, 528 (1960), citing United States v. Rumely, 345 U.S. 41, 56 (1953).
56. Yates v. United States, 354 U.S. 298, 344 (1957). Justice Black dissented in part in *Yates* because the Court failed to direct the acquittal of all 14 "second-string" communists charged under the Smith Act. The leading case to the contrary, prior to *Yates,* was Dennis v. United States, 341 U.S. 494 (1951), in which Justices Black and Douglas were the only dissenters.
57. Brandenburg v. Ohio 395 U.S. 444 (1969).
58. Roviaro v. United States, 353 U.S. 53 (1957).
59. DiNardo, John A., *Constitutional Law—Evidence—Compulsory Disclosure of Newsman's Informant is Not Violative of First Amendment or Any Testimonial Privilege,* 34 NOTRE DAME LAWYER 259, 263 (1959). This article argues for a limited and flexible privilege in the wake of the *Torre* decision. Note that as of January, 1976, shield laws of varying types had been passed by 26 states and one county. For an excellent, concise overview of the varying provisions of state shield legislation as of 1973, see *Shield Laws,* Lexington, Ky.: The Council of State Governments (1973), 10–19.
60. Transcript of "Justice Black and the Bill of Rights," as broadcast over CBS television, Dec. 3, 1968, pp. 11–12.
61. 408 U.S. 665, 681 (1972).
62. See, *e.g.,* Garland v. Torre, 259 F. 2d 545, 548, n. 4, for the contention that "a journalist's professional status does not entitle him to sources of news inaccessible to others." The footnote cited United Press Associations v. Valente, 308 N.Y. 71, 123 N.E. 2d 777 (1954); and Tribune Review Publishing Co. v. Thomas, 254 F. 2d 883 (3rd Cir., 1958). See also Appeal of Goodfader, 45 Haw. 317, 367 P. 2d 472, 479 (1961).
63. 408 U.S. 665, 708.
64. *Id.* at 683.
65. *Id.* at 697, quoting from 326 U.S. 1, 20 (1945), and noting that Justice Black's words were cited to the contrary by the Court of Appeals in Caldwell v. United States, 434 F. 2d 1081, 1085 (1970).
66. 408 U.S. 665, 697, 700 (1972).
67. *Id.* at 709–10.
68. *Id.* at 710. Note Justice Powell's reference at 710 to the choice between "fair balancing" of interests and "subordinated" interest in law enforcement.
69. Petition for a Writ of Certiorari to the Court of Appeals of Maryland, in the Supreme Court of the United States, October Term, 1972, Lightman v. State, 6–8, especially at 8, where "the questionable behavior of the State's Attorney" is cited as evidence that "the Grand Jury

was used to punish and intimidate a critical press rather than to develop necessary information about criminal activities." This position is supported by newspaper accounts of Lightman's eventual testimony, which quoted the state's attorney as saying, "I don't know why these damned newspapermen think they are above God," St. Louis Post-Dispatch, 13 June 1973, p. 5A.

70. St. Louis Post-Dispatch, *ibid*. For the denial of certiorari in this case, see 411 U.S. 951 (1973).

71. 408 U.S. 665, 710 (1972).

72. *Id*. at 743, n. 33, which notes that *Torre* "recognized a newsman's First Amendment right to a confidential relationship with his source."

73. *Id*. at 738.

74. *Id*. at 725-26, 736. For Justice Douglas's dissent, see *id*. at 711 ff., and the discussion below.

75. *Id*. at 726, citing *inter alia*, at 727, Mills v. Alabama in 1966 (see note 12 *supra*); and a reference, at 726, n. 3, to the First Amendment theories of Alexander Meiklejohn, *infra*. See also Justice Stewart's reference, at 727, to Justice Black's opinions in Marsh v. Alabama, 326 U.S. 501 (1946) and in Martin v. City of Struthers, 319 U.S. 141 (1943), in reference to the right to distribute information (which he equated with the right to gather it) without prior governmental approval.

76. *Branzburg*, 408 U.S. 665, 730, 734, 735, respectively. The quote is given at 730, n. 6.

77. *Id*. at 743.

78. 354 U.S. 234, 245 (1957) quoted by Justice Stewart at 408 U.S. 665, 739. Other sources for the Stewart formula included Gibson v. Florida Legislative Investigating Committee, 372 U.S. 539 (1963), in which Justice Stewart dissented, and particularly in the Goldberg plurality opinion at 372 U.S. 546: "it is an essential prerequisite to the validity of an [legislative] investigation which intrudes into the area of constitutionally protected rights of speech, press, association and petition that the State convincingly show a substantial relation between the information sought and a subject of overriding and compelling state interest"; and a case decided on due process grounds, Watkins v. United States, 354 U.S. 178 (1957).

79. 408 U.S. 665, 745-46. For Justice Powell's position regarding a case-by-case approach, see *id*. at 710.

80. *Id*. at 713 (United States v. Caldwell, dissenting opinion).

81. *Ibid*.

82. *Id*. at 716, n. 5.

83. *Id*. at 721. Justice Douglas earlier quoted Meiklejohn, Alexander, *The First Amendment is an Absolute*, 1961 SUPREME COURT REVIEW 245, 254. See 408 U.S. 665, 713-14.

84. 403 U.S. 713, 717 (1971), quoted at 408 U.S. 665, 721 (1972). See the text at notes 8 and 9 *supra*, for other emphases in Justice Black's Pentagon Papers opinion.

85. *Branzburg*, at 726, n. 3.

86. 376 U.S. 254, 297, citing MEIKLEJOHN, ALEXANDER, FREE SPEECH AND ITS RELATION TO SELF-GOVERNMENT, New York: Harper (1948). The quote is repeated in Justice Black's concurring and dissenting opinion (in which Justice Douglas joined) in Rosenblatt v. Baer, 383 U.S. 75, 95. Note also Justice Black's comment in Cahn, Edmond, *Justice Black and First Amendment "Absolutes": A Public Interview*, 37 N.Y.U.L. REV. 549, 559 (1962) that "[t]here is strong argument for the position taken by a man whom I admire very greatly, Dr. Meiklejohn, that the First Amendment really was intended to protect *political* speech, and I do think that was the basic purpose."

87. MEIKLEJOHN, ALEXANDER, POLITICAL FREEDOM: THE CONSTITUTIONAL POWERS OF THE PEOPLE, 1st ed., New York: Harper and Brothers (1960), 75.

88. *Id*. at 60. *Compare* the similar comment by Meiklejohn in 1961, note 83 *supra*, at 255, that "[s]elf government can exist only insofar as the voters acquire the intelligence, integrity, sensitivity, and generous devotion to the general welfare that, in theory, casting a ballot is assumed to express." Quoted by Justice Douglas in his *Branzburg/Caldwell* dissent, 408 U.S. 665, 714. *Compare* also CHAFEE, ZECHARIAH, JR., FREE SPEECH IN THE UNITED STATES, Cambridge, Mass.: Harvard University Press (1954), 559: "We must do more than remove the discouragements to open discussion. We must exert outselves to supply active encouragements."

89. MEIKLEJOHN, POLITICAL FREEDOM, note 87 *supra*, at 8.

90. *Id*. at 29-31, 33. See also 75-76. *Compare* CHAFEE, note 88 *supra*, at 33-35, which noted both *social* and *individual* interests in free speech, but concluded that both could be abridged under certain circumstances.

91. MEIKLEJOHN, POLITICAL FREEDOM, *id*. at 76. See also 36-37, where Meiklejohn based his interpretation of two concepts of speech on the argument that the Supreme Court—

regardless of the original meaning of the word "liberty" in the Fifth Amendment — has construed that term to include "the liberty of speech." In the Fifth Amendment, he wrote, this liberty is grouped with the private rights of "life" and "property."

92. *Id.* at 42.
93. *Id.* at 37. Meiklejohn contrasted this type of unconditionally protected speech with the individual "wish to speak" on private matters given limited protection by the Fifth Amendment.
94. Meiklejohn, *The First Amendment is an Absolute,* note 83 *supra,* at 254.
95. Meiklejohn, Alexander, *What Does the First Amendment Mean?* 20 U. CHI. L. REV. 461, 479 (1953).
96. Cahn, note 86 *supra,* at 555.
97. Lieberman, J. Ben, *Restating the Concept of Freedom of the Press,* 30 JOURNALISM QUARTERLY, 131-38 (1953), especially at 133-34.
98. *Id.* at 134.
99. See Appeal of Goodfader, 45 Haw. 317, 367 P. 2d 472 (1961), especially at 482. See discussion, note 28 *supra.* There is some danger in following this kind of a dichotomy in regard to journalist's privilege situations, since it would effectively set up judges as the arbiters of what kind of material is "important" enough to the public to warrant First Amendment protection.
100. Baker v. F & F Investment, 339 F. Supp. 942 (D. N.Y., 1972), 470 F. 2d 778 (2d Cir., 1972), cert. den., 411 U.S. 966 (1973).
101. *Id.* at 470 F 2d at 782, 785. The "limited principle" reference is at 779-80.
102. See, *e.g.:* Brown v. Commonwealth, 214 Va. 775, 204 S.E. 2d 429 (1974); State v. St. Peter, 315 A. 2d 254 (Vt., 1974); Bursey v. United States, 466 F. 2d 1059 (1972), reversing *In re* Grand Jury Witnesses, 322 F. Supp. 573 (1970); People v. Marahan, 81 Misc. 2d 637, 368 N.Y.S. 2d 685 (1975); People v. Monroe, 82 Misc. 2d 850 (1975); Morgan v. State, 337 So. 2d 951 (Fla., 1976), United States v. Pretzinger, 542 F. 2d 517 (1976).
103. Democratic National Committee v. McCord, et al., 356 F. Supp. 1394, 1397 (1973). See also Gilbert v. Allied Chemical Corp., 411 F. Supp. 505 (1976); and Loadkholtz v. Fields, 389 F. Supp. 1299 (1975), which involved confidential information rather than confidential sources, and which quoted heavily from Baker v. F&F Investment, *supra* notes 100, 101, to establish the principle that although " '. . . a journalist's right to protect confidential sources may not take precedence over that rare overriding and compelling interest, *we are of the view that there are circumstances, at the very least in civil cases, in which the public interest in non-disclosure of a journalist's confidential sources outweighs the public and private interest in compelled testimony.* The case before us is one where the First Amendment protection does not yield.' " 470 F. 2d at 782-83, quoted (and emphasis added) at 389 F. Supp. 1301-2. See also the text at note 47 *supra.*
104. *Compare* Cervantes v. Time, Inc., 330 F. Supp. 936, 464 F. 2d 986, cert. den. 409 U.S. 1125 (1972), with Carey v. Hume, 492 F. 2d 631 (CA D.C. Cir., 1974), cert. den. 417 U.S. 938. For a discussion of these differing results, which compares common factors in the two decisions, see Watkins, John J., *The Status of Confidential Privilege for Newsmen in Civil Libel Actions,* 52 JOURNALISM QUARTERLY, 505-14 (1975). See also Caldero v. Tribune Publishing Co., 562 P. 2d 791 (1977), in which the Idaho Supreme Court held, in a 3-2 decision, that a libel defendant has neither absolute nor qualified First Amendment protection for confidential sources, even if it has not been established that the identity is crucial to the case or that alternative means of learning it have been exhausted.
105. See, among other cases, Lightman v. State, 294 A 2d 149, cert. den. 411 U.S. 951 (1973); People by Fischer v. Dan, 41 A.D. 2d 687, 342 N.Y.S. 2d 731, appeal dismissed 32 N.Y. 2d 764, 344 N.Y.S. 2d 955 (1973); United States v. Liddy, 354 F. Supp. 208, 478 F. 2d 586 (D.C. Cir., 1972); Dow Jones & Co. v. Superior Court, 303 N.E. 2d 847 (Mass., 1973); *In re* Lewis, 501 F. 2d 418 (1974), cert. den. 420 U.S. 913 (1975); *In re* Dan v. Simonetti, 80 Misc. 2d 399, 363 N.Y.S. 2d 493 (1975); and Rosato v. Superior Court, 51 Cal. App. 3d 190, 124 CAL. RPTR. 427 (1975), cert. den., 427 U.S. 912, 96 S. Ct. 3200 (1976), discussed in more detail at note 109, *infra.* For two 1970s cases involving subpoenas issued to newsmen by federal administrative agencies, see Mark Neubauer, *op. cit.,* note 2, where the author concludes that First Amendment protection in this area is still largely untested.
106. See *In re Bridge,* 120 N.J. Super. 460, 295 A. 2d 3, affirmed 62 N.J. 80, 299 A 2d 78 (1972), cert. den. 410 U.S. 991 (1973); and, among the various actions involving Farr, see Farr v. Superior Court, 99 CAL. RPTR. 342, 22 Cal. App. 3rd 60 (1971, as modified on denial of rehearing, 1972), cert. den. 409 U.S. 1011 (1972), with Justice Douglas dissenting; Farr v. Pitchess, 409 U.S. 1243 (1973), opinion by Justice Douglas in chambers, as Circuit Justice for the Ninth Circuit; *In re Farr,* 111 CAL. RPTR. 649 (1974) and Farr v. Pitch-

ess, 522 F. 2d 464 (9th Cir., 1975), cert. den. 427 U.S. 912, 96 S. Ct. 3200 (1976). For a critique of the somewhat questionable ethics involved in publication of the stories involved in both the *Farr* and *Bridge* cases, see *Who's Hobbling the Press?* THE NEW REPUBLIC, Dec. 16, 1972, pp. 5-7.

107. 408 U.S. 665, 706.

108. For details of the case, see Branzburg v. Pound, 461 S.W. 2d 345 (1970).

109. Farr v. Superior Court, *in re Farr* and Farr v. Pitchess; and Rosato v. Superior Court, all *supra* note 106; and Ammerman v. Hubbard Broadcasting, Inc., 551 P. 2d 1354 (1976), invalidating most of Section 20-1-12.1, New Mexico Statutes Annotated. Although *Rosato* stressed the impact of the separation of powers doctrine on the state shield law (see especially 124 CAL. RPTR. 427 at 446-47), this case was not mentioned in the *Ammerman* decision. Note that in the *Farr* proceedings, the California appellate court chose not to confront the issue of whether ex-reporters were covered by the state shield statute. See 99 CAL. RPTR. 342 at 347-48. Note also that Farr, Bridge, and Rosato and his colleagues went to jail in states with shield laws, and Lightman revealed some of his confidential material so that he would avoid a jail sentence — also in a state with a shield law. Caldwell and Branzburg also faced the threat of a jail term for contempt despite the fact that their cases arose in states with shield statutes. But see, Jenoff v. Hearst Corp., 3 Media L. RPTR. 1911 (1978).

110. Curtis Publishing Co. v. Butts and Associated Press v. Walker, 388 U.S. 130, 172 (1967).

111. Lewis, note 7 *supra,* at 133. Lewis wrote that Justice Black believed that the storm of criticism which broke after his appointment to the Court was occasioned more by dislike of his radical economic views than of his brief membership in the Ku Klux Klan.

112. *Compare* the comment of Chief Justice Burger in his majority opinion in Miami Herald Publishing Co. v. Tornillo, 418 U.S. 241 at 256 (1974): "A responsible press is an undoubtedly desirable goal, but press responsibility is not mandated by the Constitution and like many other virtues it cannot be legislated."

113. This distinction was also suggested in a dissent in Appeal of Goodfader, 45 Haw. 317, 367 P. 2d 472, at 496-97 (1961). The contrast was drawn to the "private" news in the *Torre* case. See notes 28, 99 *supra.*

114. Two decisions in New Jersey and one each in Louisiana and Texas have been decided in this manner since 1956. See Brogan v. Passaic Daily News, 22 N.J. 139, 123 A. 2d 473 (1956); Beecroft v. Point Pleasant Printing & Publishing Co., 22 N.J. Super. 269, 197 A. 2d 416 (1964); Miller, Smith and Champagne v. Capital City Press, 142 So. 2d 462 (La., 1962); and Adams v. Associated Press, 46 F. R. D. 439 (U.S.D.C., S.D., Tex., 1969). See also the libel cases cited in note 104 *supra.*

115. *Compare* also the fact situation in State v. Knops, 49 Wis. 2d 647, 183 N.W. 2d 93 (1971).

116. "Stifling Subpoena," *ANPA General Bulletin,* No. 16, April 23, 1970, p. 83 (reprint of a speech to the Chicago Headline Club, 26 Feb. 1970).

117. *Ibid.*

118. See, *e.g.,* Justice Black's opinion for the Court in Adderley v. Florida, 385 U.S. 39 (1966), especially at 48: "people who want to propagandize protests or views [do not] have a constitutional right to do so whenever and however and wherever they please." See also his dissent in Tinker v. Des Moines School District, 393 U.S. 503 at 515 (1969). Note also his failure to join Justice Douglas in dissent, in United States v. O'Brien, 391 U.S. 367 (1968).

119. See State v. Buchanan, 436 P. 2d 729 at 732 (Ore., 1968), citing Near v. Minnesota, 283 U.S. 697, 721 (1931).

120. See Branzburg v. Pound, 461 S.W. 2d 345 (1970). *Compare* State v. Donovan, 129 N.J. Law 478, 30 A. 2d 421 (1943).

121. See State v. Owens, No. 677 Misc., Cir. Court, Carroll County, Md., May 11, 1925, as reported in N.Y. Times, 12 May 1925, p. 23; the case citation is given in 35 PENN. BAR ASSOC. Q. 197, 198, n. 4 (1964).

122. In the contempt area, see, *e.g.:* Bridges v. California, note 5 *supra;* Pennekamp v. Florida, 328 U.S. 331 (1946); and In re Jameson, 340 F. 2d 423 (1959). In regard to "gag" orders and the contempt citations that can follow their violation, see, in general, Gillmor, Donald M., "Judicial Restraints on the Press," *Freedom of Information Foundation Series,* No. 2, March, 1974, and cases cited there. See also the leading Supreme Court decision on this topic, Nebraska Press Association v. Stuart, 427 U.S. 539 (1976). On the government-informer privilege question, see Roviaro v. United States, note 58 *supra,* and the multitude of cases which have followed it — for example, those discussed in connection with the Federal Rules of Criminal Procedure at 18 U.S. Code Annotated 412, Rule 26, n. 385.

123. Several of these affidavits, along with material from other journalists arguing in favor of confidentiality, are printed in WHALEN, CHARLES W., JR., YOUR RIGHT TO KNOW, New York: Vintage Books (1973), 116-18, 124. See also the statement from William Small of

CBS News, reprinted *Ibid.*, pp. 131-32, regarding the importance of journalist's privilege to broadcasters. This book, as a whole, provides a very full compendium of the journalist's privilege controversy as of 1973.

124. This approach would be entirely consistent with the four state decisions listed in note 114 *supra;* and with Caldero v. Tribune Pub. Co., note 104 *supra.*

125. 259 F. 2d 545, 550.

126. N.Y. Times, 29 June 1966, p. 23.

127. Murphy v. State of Colorado, cert. den., 365 U.S. 843 (1960). See also Guest and Stanzler, note 11 *supra,* at 22.

128. See notes 17-19 *supra* and accompanying text.

129. See Gordon, David, "Newsman's Privilege and the Law," *Freedom of Information Foundation Series,* No. 4, August, 1974, pp. 25-43.

130. Justices Douglas and Black both referred frequently to "chilling effects" on the exercise of First Amendment rights. See in particular Justice Black's concurring opinion in Time, Inc. v. Hill, 385 U.S. 374, 400, where he argued that similar decisions "can frighten and punish the press so much that publishers will cease trying to report news in a lively and readable fashion." In his concurrence in the same case, 385 U.S. 374, 401, Justice Douglas referred specifically to "the 'chilling effect' on freedom of expression." He quoted from the opinion by Justice Brennan in Dombrowski v. Pfister, 380 U.S. 479, 487 (1965), in regard to the ". . . chilling effect upon the exercise of First Amendment rights." For a thorough discussion on the "chilling effect" question, see Murasky, Donna, *The Journalist's Privilege: Branzburg and Its Aftermath,* 52 TEXAS L. REV. 829, 851-66 (1974), and the cases cited there.

131. Douglas, William O., *Mr. Justice Black,* THE PROGRESSIVE, November, 1971, p. 23.

132. MENDELSON, WALLACE, JUSTICES BLACK AND FRANKFURTER: CONFLICT IN THE COURT, Chicago: University of Chicago Press (1961), 52.

133. CHAFEE, ZECHARIAH, JR., GOVERNMENT AND MASS COMMUNICATIONS: A REPORT FROM THE COMMISSION ON FREEDOM OF THE PRESS, Vol. II, Chicago: University of Chicago Press (1947) 794.

134. Commission on Freedom of the Press, A FREE AND RESPONSIBLE PRESS, Chicago: University of Chicago Press (1947), especially at p. 113: the purpose of free expression ". . . is that *the level of social conflict shall be lifted from the plane of violence to the plane of discussion.*"

135. See Roe v. Wade, 410 U.S. 113 (1973), especially at 153, 156, 163; and Doe v. Bolton, 410 U.S. 179, especially at 192, 196-97. Although physician-patient confidentiality is not explicitly discussed here, the opinion repeatedly stresses the importance of the general relationship between doctor and patient (which inherently includes confidentiality) and of the consultations between them (which would be crippled without such legally sanctioned confidentiality).

136. Desmond, Thomas C., *The Newsman's Privilege Bill,* 13 ALBANY L. REV. 1, at 9-10 (1949).

137. Justice Black frequently noted the dangers of balancing away First Amendment rights to strengthen other societal values. See, *e.g.,* note 50 *supra.* See also his dissent in Scales v. United States, 367 U.S. 203 at 262 (1961), warning against a dilution of First Amendment protections in order to strengthen internal security. The balancing test, he wrote, could abridge First Amendment freedoms any time a Supreme Court majority agreed on a government interest important enough to warrant such an incursion.

138. N.Y. Times, 17 Oct. 1957, p. 30. See also TORRE, MARIE, DON'T QUOTE ME, Garden City, N.Y.: Doubleday and Co. (1965), 12. See also N.Y. Times, 13 Nov. 1957, p. 30, where the presiding judge noted on the record that Torre's demeanor was "entirely respectful to the court."

139. *Bridges,* note 6 *supra.* Emphasis added in State v. Knops, 183 N.W. 2d 93, 98.

140. Knops, *ibid.*

141. American Bar Association Section of Criminal Law, *Bar Leadership and Civil Disorders,* Chicago: American Bar Center (n.d.), p. 20.

Chapter 12

1. *Justice Black Dissents—Turning Conservative?* U.S. NEWS AND WORLD REPORT, March 21, 1966, at 26. *Justice Black: Recent Opinions Hint at a More Conservative Philosophy,* Wall

Street Journal, 2 Nov. 1965, p. 18. Also: Lazarus, Simon, *End of the Warren Court: The New Jurisprudence of Justice Black*, THE NEW LEADER, Jan. 15, 1967.

2. *Reflections on Justice Black and Freedom of Speech*, 6 VALPARAISO U.L. REV., 317, 331 (1972). However, Black's conservative colleague Associate Justice John M. Harlan disagreed: "Those who have purported to discern in some of Mr. Justice Black's recent opinions a shift from 'liberalism' to 'conservatism' have, it seems to me, missed the true essence of his judicial philosophy." See Harlan, John M., *Mr. Justice Black—Remarks by a Colleague*, 81 HARV. L. REV. 1, 2 (1967).

3. BLACK, HUGO L., A CONSTITUTIONAL FAITH, New York: Alfred A. Knopf (1969), xiv.

4. Dennis v. United States, 341 U.S. 494, 581 (1951).

5. Dilliard, Irving, *The Individual and the Bill of Absolute Rights*, in STRICKLAND, STEPHEN P., ed., HUGO BLACK AND THE SUPREME COURT: A SYMPOSIUM, Indianapolis: Bobbs-Merrill (1967).

6. Decker, Raymond C., *Justice Hugo L. Black: The Balancer of Absolutes*, 59 CALIF. L. REV. 1335, 1340 (1971).

7. BLACK, note 3 *supra*, at xvi.

8. 383 U.S. 131, 166 (1966).

9. Note 3 *supra*, at 50.

10. *Id.* at 55.

11. *Id.* at 53.

12. EMERSON, THOMAS I., THE SYSTEM OF FREEDOM OF EXPRESSION, New York: Vintage Books (1970), 294–95. For an expanded theoretical analysis of the speech-conduct distinction, see Hines, Jay L., *Of Shadows and Substance: Freedom of Speech, Expression and Action*, 1971 WISC. L. REV. 1209.

13. BLACK, note 3 *supra*, at 60.

14. 383 U.S. 502, 518 (1966).

15. 391 U.S. 308, 332–33 (1968).

16. Note 3 *supra*, at 58.

17. 312 U.S. 287, 292 (1941).

18. *Id.* at 317.

19. *Id.* at 314.

20. Note 15 *supra*, at 332.

21. 336 U.S. 490, 498 (1949).

22. Note 8 *supra*, at 142.

23. Note 8 *supra*, at 157.

24. Ash, Michael, *Growth of Justice Black's Philosophy of Freedom of Speech: 1962–1966*, 1967 WISC. L. REV. 840, 844.

25. Adderley v. Florida, 385 U.S. 39, 47 (1966).

26. Cox v. Louisiana, No. 24, 379 U.S. 536, 578 (1965).

27. *Id.* at 579.

28. *Id.* at 583.

29. Coates v. Cincinnati, 402 U.S. 611, 617 (1971). This decision is consistent with an earlier analysis, which indicates, "He [Justice Black] insisted that when reviewing courts were confronted with intertwined speech/conduct, they must decide the constitutionality of the questioned exercise of power by balancing the undesirability of the conduct against the effect on expression of forbidding it." See Ash, note 24 *supra*, at 861–62.

30. EMERSON, note 12 *supra*, at 79–80.

31. *Notes—Symbolic Conduct*, 68 COLUMBIA L. REV. 1091, 1117 (1968).

32. Cohen v. California, 403 U.S. 15, 18 (1971).

33. *Id.* at 27.

34. Tinker v. Des Moines School District, 393 U.S. 503, 508 (1969).

35. *Id.* at 517.

36. *Id.* at 518.

37. *Id.* at 521–22.

38. Street v. New York, 394 U.S. 576, 581 (1969).

39. *Id.* at 610.

40. Agreeing with this view is Charles E. Rice, Fordham law professor, who suggests that Black was really saying "that the rights of expression and protest, however worthy the cause in which they are asserted, are bounded at their outer limits by the dictates of an orderly society under the constitutional rule of law." See *Justice Black, the Demonstrators and a Constitutional Rule of Law*, 14 U.C.L.A. L. REV. 454, 466 (1967).

41. Ulmer, S. Sidney, *The Longitudinal Behavior of Hugo Lafayette Black: Parabolic Support*

for Civil Liberties, 1937–1971, 1 FLA. STATE U. L. REV. 131, 133 (1973). Although this paper was completed before the authors became aware of Professor Ulmer's useful study, we believe that in large part it supports our basic contention and we commend it to those interested in a broader view of Justice Black's civil liberties decisions.

42. Cahn, Edmond, *Justice Black and First Amendment "Absolutes": A Public Interview,* 37 N.Y.U.L. REV. 549, 558–59 (1962).

43. Note 41 *supra,* at 152.

44. 403 U.S. 713 (1971).

Index of Cases

[*See also* Notes, pp. 173-94]

Index